797,885 Books
are available to read at

Forgotten Books

www.ForgottenBooks.com

Forgotten Books' App
Available for mobile, tablet & eReader

ISBN 978-1-330-45038-3
PIBN 10063979

This book is a reproduction of an important historical work. Forgotten Books uses state-of-the-art technology to digitally reconstruct the work, preserving the original format whilst repairing imperfections present in the aged copy. In rare cases, an imperfection in the original, such as a blemish or missing page, may be replicated in our edition. We do, however, repair the vast majority of imperfections successfully; any imperfections that remain are intentionally left to preserve the state of such historical works.

Forgotten Books is a registered trademark of FB &c Ltd.
Copyright © 2015 FB &c Ltd.
FB &c Ltd, Dalton House, 60 Windsor Avenue, London, SW19 2RR.
Company number 08720141. Registered in England and Wales.

For support please visit www.forgottenbooks.com

1 MONTH OF FREE READING

at

www.ForgottenBooks.com

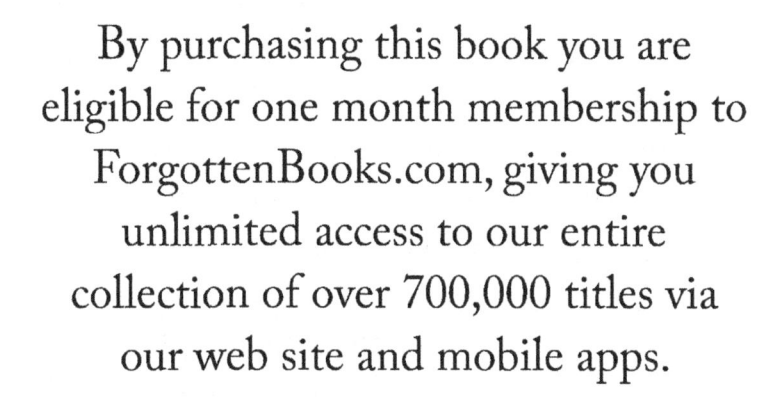

By purchasing this book you are eligible for one month membership to ForgottenBooks.com, giving you unlimited access to our entire collection of over 700,000 titles via our web site and mobile apps.

To claim your free month visit: www.forgottenbooks.com/free63979

* Offer is valid for 45 days from date of purchase. Terms and conditions apply.

English
Français
Deutsche
Italiano
Español
Português

www.forgottenbooks.com

Mythology Photography **Fiction** Fishing Christianity **Art** Cooking Essays Buddhism Freemasonry Medicine **Biology** Music **Ancient Egypt** Evolution Carpentry Physics Dance Geology **Mathematics** Fitness Shakespeare **Folklore** Yoga Marketing **Confidence** Immortality Biographies Poetry **Psychology** Witchcraft Electronics Chemistry History **Law** Accounting **Philosophy** Anthropology Alchemy Drama Quantum Mechanics Atheism Sexual Health **Ancient History** **Entrepreneurship** Languages Sport Paleontology Needlework Islam **Metaphysics** Investment Archaeology Parenting Statistics Criminology **Motivational**

MANUAL OF HEBREW GRAMMAR

(REVISED AND IMPROVED EDITION)

BY

REV. (J. D.) WIJNKOOP
Litt. Hum. Cand. in the University of Leyden,
Rabbi of the Jewish Congregation in
Amsterdam.

TRANSLATED FROM THE DUTCH

BY

REV. DR. C. VAN DEN BIESEN
Prof. of Hebrew at St. Joseph's Foreign Missionary College,
Mill-Hill.

LONDON:
LUZAC & Co.
PUBLISHERS TO THE INDIA OFFICE.
46, GREAT RUSSELL STREET.
1898.

PRINTED BY E. J. BRILL, AT LEYDEN.

AUTHOR'S PREFACE.

As in many respects this grammar differs from other grammars, the plan which has been adopted requires a few explanations. Although modern works on Hebrew Grammar have been consulted by me, I did not think it advisable blindly to follow them. Experience has taught me that this would be far from prudent. The greatest scholars sometimes venture to create rules which have no sufficient basis and even to quote examples which only exist in their imagination. Most curious instances of this could be given. But for what purpose? In spite of a few inaccuracies they remain men who by reason of their learning and hard work are entitled to our respect. — I merely wish, therefore, to point out in few words in what particulars this manual follows a more or less independent course, and the motives which have induced me to do so.

In the first place I thought it necessary to draw a sharp line between the שְׁוָא נָע and שְׁוָא נָח, which really have nothing in common but their form. Whilst the one serves to form an "*anlaut*", which in our western languages is considered a *separate syllable*, e. g. the first syllable of *begin*, *because* — as it frequently occurs in later Hebrew poetry — the latter on the contrary is never to be sounded, and merely serves as a *sign* denoting that a letter stands without a vowel. They ought therefore in my opinion to be treated in two separate paragraphs.

Further, experience has shewn me that even amongst those who have applied themselves seriously to the study of Hebrew Grammar, a deplorable confusion exists concerning the דָּגֵשׁ and מֶתֶג. The reason no doubt is that they find these signs occur where according to existing rules they are least of all to be expected. For the purpose of helping to remove this difficulty, I thought it advisable to call to memory, and prominently to set forward, the fundamental principle of ancient scholars, that every point in a letter is *not* a דָּגֵשׁ קַל or דָּגֵשׁ חָזָק, and that every perpendicular little line on the left of a sound is *not* a *half-tone*. — It was a pleasant surprise for me to learn that such a veteran Hebrew scholar as Dr. Graetz had treated the subject of the דָּגֵשׁ on the same principle in the *October-* and *Novemberheft* of his "*Monatschrift für Geschichte und Wissenschaft des Judenthums*" Krotoschin 1887.

Every student of Hebrew, moreover, is aware how difficult it is to distinguish the forms of the נֶחִי ע׳ from those of the כפולים and of many other stems. Even after the conjugation of these verbs has been thoroughly learnt by heart, difficulties innumerable appear in all directions. Let me state a few of them.

AUTHOR'S PREFACE.   VII

1) With the כְּפוּלִים one meets a great many forms which simply follow the regular conjugation of the triliteral stems.
2) It is taught that the ע״י נָחִי and the כְּפוּלִים can be recognised by their distinctive vowel sounds. Yet we find בַּוּ from בוז Zech. 4,10; טַח from טוח Isa. 44,18; יְגוּדֶנּוּ from גדד Gen. 49,19; יְגוּרֵם from גרר Prov. 21,7; בְּחוּקוֹ from חקק Prov. 8,27; יְחִיתַן from חתת Hab. 2,17; תָּמוּד from מדד Ez. 45,3; יָמֵר from מור Ez. 48,14; יָמוּךְ from מכך Lev. 25,25; and many other forms of the same kind.
3) In the first two conjugations of the ע״י נָחִי the student becomes accustomed to the use of *two* stem-letters, whilst in the פָּעַל, פִּעֵל and הִתְפַּעֵל he is suddenly transferred into the sphere of the כְּפוּלִים.
4) In the conjugation of the ע״י נָחִי the *stem-letter* ו or י disappears, an omission which it is almost impossible to account for.

Now there exists a simple theory, which although old is not obsolete[1]), which goes a long way to remove all confusion and contradiction. Is it right to reject or to ignore such a theory when it facilitates and promotes the study of Hebrew, simply because it is not generally in vogue? — I have therefore in this manual ventured to adopt the older system of admitting *biliteral stems* in addition to the *triliteral*. I have however applied this

---

1) That this theory is not obsolete appears from the testimonies of scholars who during the last thirty years have advocated it.

system only to the נָחֵי ע׳ and כְּפוּלִים. I could have extended it also to many other stems, like several Jewish grammarians have done, but this would have caused too great a revolution in Hebrew grammar, whilst I only aimed at simplifying it by combining two kinds of stems, which are of the same nature and origin, into one kind.

I am quite aware that against the theory of *biliteral* stems certain objections may be raised. Indeed chiefly from comparison with cognate languages, and also from derived substantives which undeniably contain a ו or י in the stem, arguments against it may be brought forward. Yet these objections are not at present held to be of sufficient strength completely to rule this theory out of court. Against them moreover remains the fact that there are several stems with ו or י as second stem-letter which they never lose; e. g. חיה, היה, צוה which very often occur, and many others which are less frequently found such as לוה, שוע, קוה, עות.

The main reason however which has led me to adopt biliteral verbal stems is this. When we speak of the נָחֵי ע׳ and the כְּפוּלִים, the two stem-letters which regularly appear, are (on the principle that they are triliteral verbs) the 1st and 3d stem-letters. Yet when we compare their conjugation with that of the other triliteral verbs, with which they indeed have many points in common (cf. §§ 37—42), it is evident that the so called 1st and 3d stem-letters of the נָחֵי ע׳ and כְּפוּלִים are the main factors in the conjugation, and that they have the same functions as two *successive* stem-letters of an ordinary triliteral verb. What theory therefore is more simple than to adopt that these two letters (i. e. the 1st and 3d of the נָחֵי ע׳ and the כְּפוּלִים) are the two *only* stem-letters of a biliteral verb. (Cf. my article on this subject in the April number, 1898, of the Jewish Quarterly Review).

To render the learning of the conjugation of the verb easier, *stem-forms* have been adopted in this manual, from which the other forms may be derived according to general rules.

As regards both the nomina and verba, attention has been drawn to the *alteration of vowels* and the causes by which it is occasioned.

No one I hope will find fault with me that, whilst using the Hebrew terms, I have not omitted the Latin ones. The latter more than once promote conciseness without injuring the cause of clearness.

It is perhaps not superfluous to remark here that by Hebrew is meant the language in which the 24 books of the Bible are written. (תּוֹרָה נְבִיאִים כְּתוּבִים by abbreviation called תָּנַ״ךְ); except the Chaldee portions of Daniel and Ezra, and a few Chaldee expressions in the other books.

Finally, it should be borne in mind that many observations in the course of this manual are destined only for more advanced students, and it is left to the teacher's discretion to take care that the beginner is made acquainted only with what is suitable for him. That this manual may help to animate and promote the study of the sacred language is the most ardent wish of the

AMSTERDAM. *Author.*

DIRECTIONS FOR STUDENTS NOT HAVING THE ASSISTANCE OF A TEACHER.

I. ORDER OF STUDYING THE GRAMMAR.

Spelling §§ 1; 2; 3 A; 4—6 (without Remarks); 7,4.
The verb §§ 11; 12; 13 till n°. 8; 14 till n°. 8; 15—25. (Without Rem.).
The noun §§ 52—54; 57; 58; 60 till A; 65. (Without Rem.).
The adjective §§ 66; 68. (Without Rem.).
Pronouns §§ 70, 1 (not 2); 71—74. (Without Rem.).
Suffixes §§ 46; 62; 69. (Without Rem.).
Adverbs §§ 80; 81. (Without Rem.).
Prepositions §§ 82—84. (Without Rem.).
Conjunctions §§ 85; 86. (Without Rem.).
Numerals §§ 75; 76, 1—4; 77.
Irregular verbs §§ 26—34. (Without Rem.).
Biliteral verbs §§ 35—43. (Without Rem.).
Alterations of the verb §§ 47—49. (Without Rem.).
Alterations of the noun §§ 59—61; 63; 64. (Without Rem.).

Derivation of the noun and adjective §§ 56; 67. (Without Rem.).

All remaining portions.

The accents §§ 87—90.

II. ORDER OF READING THE SCRIPTURES.

A. Genesis ch. 1—48; Exodus 1—20; Deut. 1—32; 34; Joshua; Judges 1—4; 6—21; Ruth.

B. Jerem. 18—29; 32—45; Jonah; Esther; Haggai; Obadiah; remaining books of the Pentateuch; Samuel; Kings; Ezra; Nehemiah; Chronicles; Malachi; Psalms 1—10; 18—57; 69—75; 78—86; 89—150.

C. Lam.; Cant.; Eccl.; Judges 5; Zephaniah; Joel; Amos; Isaiah; remaining portions of Jerem.; Ezechiel; remaining Psalms; Proverbs; Job; Hosea; Micah; Daniel; Zechariah, Nahum; Habakkuk.

N.B. The value of the letters and vowel-points (page 5 and Appendix V) has been given according to the Italian pronunciation of the vowels.

CONTENTS.

PART I. Spelling.

CHAPTER I. *Spelling in general.*

§ 1. The signs of the Hebrew language.................... 1

CHAPTER II. *The letters.*

§ 2. The names of letters............................. 1
§ 3. Division of the letters........................... 3

CHAPTER III. *The vowel-signs.*

§ 4. The vowels and half-vowels....................... 5
§ 5. The מַפִּיק, פַּתַח גְּנוּבָה, נַח נִרְאֶה, נַח נִסְתָּר, הֲבָרוֹת 8

CHAPTER IV. *The remaining signs.*

§ 6. The דָּגֵשׁ... 11
§ 7. The מקף, נגינות or טְעָמִים...................... 13
§ 8. The נָסוֹג אָחוֹר................................. 14
§ 9. The מתג or גַעְיָא............................... 15

PART II. Etymology.

CHAPTER I.

§ 10. The meaning of etymology...................... 17
§ 11. The division of the words...................... 17

CONTENTS.

CHAPTER II. *The verb in general.*

	Page.
§ 12. Division of the verbs.	18
§ 13. The בנינים	20
§ 14. The meaning of the conjugations.	22
§ 15. The conjugation of the verb in general.	23
§ 16. The stem-forms of the conjugation.	24
§ 17. The preformatives and afformatives.	25
§ 18. General rules concerning the preformatives and afformatives.	26

CHAPTER III. *The regular conjugation of the triliteral verbs.*

§ 19. The קַל	28
§ 20. The נִפְעַל	29
§ 21. The פִּעֵל	30
§ 22. The פֻּעַל	31
§ 23. The הִפְעִיל	32
§ 24. The הָפְעַל	33
§ 25. The הִתְפַּעֵל	34

CHAPTER IV. *The deviations from the regular conjugation because of one or more gutturals being in the stem.*

§ 26. The verba primae gutturalis.	35
§ 27. The verba mediae gutturalis.	37
§ 28. The verba tertiae gutturalis.	38

CHAPTER V. *The* חסרים.

§ 29. The חסרי פ"נ.	40
§ 30. The חסרי ל"נ and the חסרי ל"ת.	41

CHAPTER VI. *The* נָחִים.

§ 31. The נָחֵי פ"א.	42
§ 32. The נָחֵי פ"י.	45
§ 33. The נָחֵי ל"א.	49
§ 34. The נחי ל"ה.	53

CONTENTS.

CHAPTER VII. *The Biliteral stems.*

Page.

§ 35. The different kinds of conjugation.................... 59
§ 36. The biliteral stems with duplication of the second stem-letter. 59
§ 37. The biliteral stems restricted to two stem-letters........ 60
§ 38. The קַל.. 62
§ 39. The נִפְעַל..................................... 65
§ 40. The הִפְעִיל.................................... 67
§ 41. The הֻפְעַל..................................... 71
§ 42. The מְעֵל, פֵּעֵל and הִתְפַּעֵל of the biliteral stems....... 73
§ 43. The deviations from the regular conjugation of the biliteral stems..................................... 74

CHAPTER VIII. *Alterations of the verbal forms.*

§ 44. The various kinds of alterations..................... 76
§ 45. The shorter, longer, or modified forms of the עָתִיד and the דֶּרֶךְ הַצִּוּוּי........................... 76
§ 46. The pronominal suffixes of the verbal forms........... 78
§ 47. Alterations of the regular triliteral verbs in consequence of the appending of suffixes........................ 79
§ 48. Alterations of the irregular verbs through the appending of suffixes..................................... 83
§ 49. The biliteral stems with suffixes..................... 84

CHAPTER IX. *The nomina.*

§ 50. The different kinds of nomina....................... 87
§ 51. The alterations of the nomina....................... 87

CHAPTER X. *The noun.*

§ 52. Division of the nouns.............................. 88
§ 53. Proper names.................................... 89
§ 54. The gender of the nouns........................... 89
§ 55. Primitive nouns................................... 90
§ 56. Derivatives...................................... 91
§ 57. Compound nouns................................. 96

CONTENTS.

		Page.
§ 58.	The number of the noun	97
§ 59.	Alterations of the noun before it receives its plural ending.	99
§ 60.	Status Constructus	102
§ 61.	The 'ה locative	106
§ 62.	The pronominal suffixes of the noun	107
§ 63.	Alterations of the singular nouns before they are connected with pronominal suffixes	108
§ 64.	Alterations of the dual and plural nouns before they are connected with pronominal suffixes	111
§ 65.	The nouns with the literae praefixae	111

CHAPTER XI. *The adjective.*

§ 66.	The gender of the adjectives	112
§ 67.	The derivation of the adjectives	113
§ 68.	The number of the adjectives	115
§ 69.	Other causes through which the adjectives undergo alteration.	116

CHAPTER XII. *The pronouns.*

§ 70.	Division of the pronouns	117
§ 71.	The personal pronoun	118
§ 72.	The demonstrative pronoun	119
§ 73.	The relative pronoun	119
§ 74.	The interrogative pronoun	120

CHAPTER XIII. *The numerals.*

§ 75.	Division of the numerals	120
§ 76.	The cardinal numbers	121
§ 77.	The ordinal numbers	124
§ 78.	Manner of expressing the other numbers	125

CHAPTER XIV. *The particles.*

§ 79.	Division of the particles	125
§ 80.	The adverb	126
§ 81.	The adverb with suffixes	127
§ 82.	The prepositions	127
§ 83.	The vowels of the letter prepositions	128

CONTENTS.

	Page.
§ 84. The prepositions with pronominal suffixes	129
§ 85. The conjunctions	131
§ 86. The interjections	133

CHAPTER XV. *The place of the accent.*

§ 87. The general rules	134
§ 88. The particular rules	135
§ 89. (מַאֲמָר) הֶפְסֵק The alteration of the vowels and the shifting of the tone because of the distinctive accents	137
§ 90. Alteration of vowels in consequence of the מַקֵּף	139
I. Appendix. Names and tokens of the accents	140
II. Appendix. Forms of the נָחִי פּ״י	144
III. Appendix. List of verbal forms with pronominal suffixes	146
IV. Appendix. List of certain nouns in the *st. constr.* and with pronominal suffixes	152
V. Appendix. The names of the letters and vowel tokens in Latin characters	157

PART I.

SPELLING (Orthography).

CHAPTER I.

§ 1. Spelling teaches us the various tokens for pronouncing and writing the words of a language and the manner in which such tokens are joined together.

These tokens are:

1) letter-tokens or letters (אוֹתִיוֹת *consonantes*),
2) vowel-tokens or vowels (תנועות *vocales*),
3) other tokens for securing the true pronunciation.

CHAPTER II.

The Letters.

§ 2. The Hebrew language uses 22 letters.

Token.	Name.	Pronunciation.			
א	אָלֶף		See	*Remark*	1
ב	בֵּית	v or b	„	„	2
ג	גִּימֶל	g			2

Token.	Name.	Pronunciation.			
ד	דָּלֶת	d	See	*Remark*	2
ה	הֵא	h	″	″	3
ו	וָו	w			4
ז	זַיִן	z			
ח	חֵית	ch	″	″	5
ט	טֵית	t or th			6
י	יוֹד, or יוּד	y			
כ	כַּף	ch or k			2
ל	לָמֶד	l			
מ	מֵם	m			
נ	נוּן	n			
ס	סָמֶךְ	s			
ע	עַיִן	ng			7
פ	פֵּא	f	″	″	2
צ	צָדִי	tz			
ק	קוֹף or קוּף	k			
ר	רֵישׁ	r			
שׁ	שִׁין	sh and s			8
ת	תָּו	s, th or t	″	″	2 and 6.

Rem. 1. א without a vowel is not sounded at all. When it has a vowel it merely reproduces the sound of that vowel, e. g. אָ ă אֱ ĕ.

Rem. 2. As to the pronunciation of the letters בגדכפת with or without a point in them see § 6 footnote 1.

Rem. 3. ה without a vowel is generally not sounded. When however it terminates a syllable and is to be sounded (a difficult matter for western nations) a point is usually placed in it. See § 5, 4.

Rem. 4. ו is a softly, scarcely audible pronounced *w*, which sound is produced by a quick opening of the lips (See § 4 Rem. 4 and conf. § 85 B 1*a*).

THE LETTERS.

Rem. 5. By the western nations ח is pronounced *ch*, as in German *doch*. It really is an *h* with a yet deeper guttural sound than the ה, and in this way it is pronounced by orientals at the present time.

Rem. 6. Whether ט corresponds to *t* or *th* cannot with certainty be decided. The same remark applies to ת.

Rem. 7. The ע is by many pronounced as *ng* in the word *song*. This pronunciation is certainly not correct. No one doubts that the ע is a guttural. When pronounced by orientals, it has a still harder guttural sound than the ח.

Rem. 8. שׁ is sometimes to be pronounced as *sh* sometimes as *s*. To distinguish the pronunciation a point stands over the right shoulder (שׁ) when it is *sh*, and on the left (שׂ) when it is *s*.

2) Five of the 22 letters כמנפצ have a different form when placed at the end of a word; viz. [מַנְצְפַּךְ רְסוּףְץ]¹). These are called *final letters*.

3) א when followed by ל is sometimes contracted with it, and is then written ﭏ.

Division of the Letters.

§ 3. A. According to the organs (מוֹצָאוֹת) with which they are pronounced.

1) In this respect they are divided into·

(a) *Gutturals* (אוֹתִיוֹת הַגָּרוֹן) [אַהֲחַע] אהחע,

(b) *Palatals* (אוֹתִיוֹת הַחֵךְ) [גִּיכַק] גיכק,

(c) *Linguals* (אוֹתִיוֹת הַלָּשׁוֹן) [דַטְלְנַת] דטלנת,

(d) *Dentals* (אוֹתִיוֹת הַשִּׁנַּיִם) [וַסְשַׁץ] זסצש,

(e) *Labials* (אוֹתִיוֹת הַשְּׂפָתַיִם) [בּוּמַףְ] בומפ.

---

1) By this mnemonic word (*vox memorialis*) they are indicated in the Talmud and by Jewish grammarians. Throughout this work the voces memoriales will be placed between parentheses [ ].

2) The ר belongs both to the *gutturals* and to the *linguals*, whilst מ and נ when taken together may be said to form a separate class of *nasal letters*.

> Rem. 1. The *dentals* are also known by the name of *sibilants* because of the sound which they produce.

3) A separate class moreover is formed by the letters אהוי [אֱהֶוִי] because they have the peculiarity that they are sometimes written although not pronounced. (See § 5, 4).

4) The letters of one and the same class are sometimes interchanged; e. g. גָּאַל in the sense of גָּעַל *to abhor*, סָגַר = סָכַר *to close*, נִצְטַדָּק instead of נִצְתַדָּק *we shall justify ourselves*, יִשְׂחָק instead of יִצְחָק *Isaac*, בְזַר instead of פְזַר *to scatter*, אַלְמְנֹתָיו in the sense of אַרְמְנֹתָיו *his palaces*, תּוֹסְפוֹן = תֹּאסְפוּן *you will add*, פָּדְיוֹם instead of פִּדְיוֹן *price of redemption*.

B. According to their function.

1) *Root-* or *stem-letters* (שָׁרָשִׁיּוֹת), letters which form the stem of a word. Of this function all the letters are capable.

2) *Servile letters* (שִׁמּוּשִׁיּוֹת), i. e. letters which are placed before, between, or after the stem-letters for forming the derivations and inflections of words. The *servile letters* are eleven viz. אבהויכלמנשת משה וְכָלֵב [אֵיתָן מֹשֶׁה וְכָלֵב]. Four of these אבלש [אֶלְבַּשׁ] can only serve as preformatives, the remaining seven הויכמנת [תָּכֵן הַיּוֹם] both as preformatives and afformatives, whilst ו and י may stand also between the stem-letters.

> Rem. 2. The ר is sometimes added to or placed between the stem-

letters to alter the meaning of the word, e. g. שרבים from שבט, רְטַפַּשׁ from טָפַשׁ.

3) *Additional letters* (נוֹסָפוֹת) which now and then are placed before, between or after the stemletters without changing the meaning of the word. They are the letters הם אהוין [אֱהֵוִין]; e. g. קָאם = קָם *he rose up*, הם = הֵמָה *they*, תְבִיאָמוֹ = תְבִיאָם *thou bringest them*, עֲוֹנְכִי = עֲוֹנֵךְ *thy sins*, יִצְרֶנְהוּ = יִצְרֵהוּ *he protects him*.

Rem. 3. The same letters may sometimes be omitted without causing a change of meaning; e. g. מָצָאתִי = מָצָתִי *I have found*, נְשָׂא = שָׂא *bear, carry*.

CHAPTER III.

Vowels and Half-vowels.

§ 4. 1) In order to pronounce the letters vowels are used in the first place.

Grammarians distinguish 10 different vowels and divide them into 5 long vowels (תְּנוּעוֹת גְדוֹלוֹת or אָבוֹת *vocales longae*) and into 5 corresponding short vowels (תְּנוּעוֹת קְטַנוֹת or תּוֹלָדוֹת *vocales breves*).

2) The five long vowels are: ָ (ā) קָמֵץ; ֵ (ē) צֵירֶה; מְלֹאפוּם or שׁוּרֶק (ū) וּ; חוֹלָם (ō) וֹ or ֹ; חִירֶק גָדוֹל (ī) יִ.
The five short vowels are: (ă) פַּתַח; ֶ (ĕ) סֶגוֹל; שׁוּרֶק קָטָן or קִבּוּץ (ŭ) ֻ; קָמֵץ חָטוּף (ŏ) ָ; חִירֶק קָטָן (ĭ) ִ.

Rem. 1. The pronunciation of the 1st 2d and 4th long vowel is not the same amongst all Israelites. The so called אַשְׁכְּנַזִים (Ashchenazie Jews) pronounce them as *o* in *rode*, *i* in *white*, *ou* in *loud*, whilst with the others they sound *ā*, *ē* and *ō*.

Rem. 2. The short vowel is more easily pronounced when the following letter is נַח נִרְאָה (see § 5, 3—7). When this letter however is followed by a vowel or half-vowel, a point is placed in it to denote that the preceding vowel is short in pronunciation. Hence a long vowel is seldom followed by a letter with a point in it. Where this occurs it is a token, either drawing attention to something peculiar, e. g. in the ה of בָּתִּים perhaps to call attention to the irregular plur. form of בַּיִת; or denoting that a letter is missing, e. g. the נ in הַאֻזְנָה Gen. 4, 23; Jes. 32, 9.

Rem. 3. The ָ is קָמֵץ חָטוּף

a. When it is derived from a חוֹלָם, e. g. עָזִי from עֹז *strength*.

b. When it appears in a closed syllable which has not the accent, e. g. the first ָ in קָרְבָּן.

Otherwise ָ is קָמֵץ.

3) Besides the vowels the Hebrew language employs a half-vowel ְ (שְׁוָא נָע or חֲטָף). The ְ is found also connected with ַ, ֶ and ָ, viz. as ֲ חֲטָף פַּתַח, ֱ חֲטָף סְגוֹל, and ֳ חֲטָף קָמֵץ.

These three forms of the half-vowel (ֲ, ֱ, ֳ) are generally used only with the gutturals [1]).

---

[1]) In certain manuscripts, and in imitation of them in some printed editions, the ֳ is found where a ָ would have been expected, to denote that the ָ arose out of חוֹלָם and that it is קָמֵץ חָטוּף, e. g. שִׁבֳּלִים from שִׁבֹּלֶת. ֳ also occurs sometimes instead of שְׁוָא נָע just as ֱ and ֲ, in order to secure the proper pronunciation of the letter under which it stands, e. g. הַבְּרָכָה Gen. 27, 38, לְקֻחָה Gen. 2, 23.

VOWELS AND HALF-VOWELS.

Rem. 4. All the vowels and half-vowels stand under the letter with which they are pronounced, except the two last long vowels. The חוֹלָם is a point placed over the right shoulder of the following letter (the וֹ therefore of וֹ is an inperceptibly quiescent letter following חוֹלָם See § 5, 4). When the letter with חוֹלָם is a שׁ or the subsequent letter a שׁ the point of חוֹלָם coalesces with that of the שׁ, e. g. מֹשֶׁה, שֹׂבַע.

The שׁוּרֵק or מְלֹאפוּם is a point which properly should be placed in the letter with which it is pronounced. As this however would cause confusion with the point of דָּגֵשׁ (see § 6) the שׁוּרֵק is placed in the וּ which is similar in pronunciation and consequently inperceptibly quiescent. (See § 5, 4).

Rem. 5. The gutturals are generally preceded by a *long* vowel when they themselves have a vowel, and by פַּתַח or סֶגוֹל when they themselves are without any vowel. Their own vowel is by preference סֶגוֹל or פַּתַח.

4) When the half-vowel for some reason or other is to be changed into a vowel, the short vowels and by preference פַּתַח, סֶגוֹל or חִירֶק קָטָן are used. Such a short vowel we shall call an *auxiliary vowel*.

Rem. 6. The vowels are sometimes interchanged with one another, chiefly the long vowels with the corresponding short vowels, e. g. אָסִיר = אַסִּיר *prisoner*, כֶּעָפָר = כְּעָפָר *as the dust* Jes. 41, 2. Yet

---

All this shows an over anxious desire to obtain correctness of pronunciation, in which the scribes have by no means been consistent as to their method. The same inconsistency appears as regards מֶתֶג, דָּגֵשׁ and other signs. (See § 6 note 2, § 9 note 2, and 1st appendix note 2). These inconsistencies have given rise to various rules which however have no sufficient grammatical basis.

8   HEBREW GRAMMAR.

long and short vowels are also interchanged mutually, when they are in any way affiliated, as חוֹלָם with שׁוּרְק e. g. טוֹב and טוּב *good;* קָמֶץ חָטוּף with קִבּוּץ e. g. הָשְׁלַךְ and הֻשְׁלַךְ *to be thrown;* שֶׁקַמְתִּי = שַׁקַּמְתִּי *that I arose* Judges 5,7 (conf. §§ 63; 66,4; 67,2—6; 69,3).

The Syllables (הַבָּרוֹת).- שְׁוָא נָח, נָח נִרְאֶה, נָח נִסְתָּר, פתח גנובה, מַפִּיק.

§ 5. 1) One or more letters connected with one of the 10 vowels and pronounced at the same moment are called a syllable.

Rem. 1. The number, therefore, of the syllables of a word is determined by the number of its vowels.

2) A syllable may be either *closed* or *open*. A syllable is *open* (הֲבָרָה פְּשׁוּטָה) when after the vowel no letter is sounded, e. g. בָּרָא, כֹּה, בִּי. It is *closed* (הֲבָרָה מֻרְכֶּבֶת) when after the vowel one or more letters are sounded, e. g. כָּל, קֹשְׁטְ *certainty*, the first syllable of חָכְמָה.

3) The letter which follows a vowel and belongs to the same syllable, is called *quiescent* (נָח).

If this letter is sounded, it is called *perceptibly quiescent* (נָח נִרְאֶה), e. g. the ל in כָּל, the שׁ and ט in קֹשְׁטְ; but if it is not sounded, it is called *inperceptibly quiescent* (נָח נִסְתָּר), e. g. the י in בִּי, the ה in כֹּה, the א in בָּרָא.

The four letters אהוי [אֶהֱוִי] alone can be נָח נִסְתָּר.

4) The א is never נָח נִרְאֶה.

The ה without vowel or half-vowel is נָח נִסְתָּר, except when it belongs to the stem of a word (see §§ 26; 27;

THE SYLLABLES.   9

28), or when it is the fem. suffix (see § 46, 2; 62, 3), for in these cases it is נַח נִרְאֶה.

When the ה as נַח נִרְאֶה occurs at the end of a word it is marked with a point called מַפִּיק, e. g. גָּבַהּ, לָהּ.

The ו is נַח נִסְתָּר after חוֹלָם and שׁוּרְק (see § 4 Rem. 4); after the other vowels it is נַח נִרְאֶה, except in the word הוּא = הִוא.

The י is נַח נִסְתָּר after צֵירה, חִירְק and סֶגוֹל; after other vowels it is נַח נִרְאֶה except in the endng ־ָיו (see § 62, 5) = ־ָו.

<blockquote>
Rem. 2. Every vowel at the end of a word must be followed by a letter whether it be נַח נִסְתָּר or נַח נִרְאֶה, except קָמַץ, which occurs at the end of a word without any נַח. e. g. קָרָאתָ, שָׂמֶךָ.

The י is always נַח נִסְתָּר after חִירְק גָּדוֹל and the ו after חוֹלָם and שׁוּרְק.
</blockquote>

5) It is often difficult to make the ה and also the ח and ע audible, when they stand without vowel at the end of a word. This difficulty chiefly occurs after צֵירה, חִירְק, חוֹלָם and שׁוּרְק. For this reason a פַּתַח, similar to the sound which the pronunciation produces, is placed under the ה, ח or ע, e. g. שׁוֹמֵעַ, בְּרִיחַ, אֱלוֹהַּ, רוּחַ. This פַּתַח, called פַּתַח גְּנוּבָה (*pathach furtivum*) is not considered to be a vowel, nor does it form a syllable.

6) When a letter is נַח נִרְאֶה in the middle of a word, a שְׁוָא (ְ) is placed under it, e. g. יִנְבַּל. This שְׁוָא, called שְׁוָא נַח, is not audible, and is to be carefully distinguished from the שְׁוָא נָע spoken of in § 4. The שְׁוָא נַח only denotes that the letter, under which it stands, closes a syllable. When therefore it is not written, we know that the

letter under which it is omitted is *not* to be pronounced, e. g. the 2^d שׁ in יִשָּׂשכָר.

7) At the end of a word the שְׁוָא נַח is not placed except:

(*a*) when the word ends with ךְ, e. g. בְּךָ;

(*b*) when the word ends with two letters, both being נַח נִרְאֶה, e. g. קֹשְׁטְ;

(*c*). with the word אַתְּ, and under the fem. personal ending תְּ (see § 17, 2) e. g. שָׁמַעַתְּ *thou hast heard*[1]).

8) In most cases the שְׁוָא נָע can easily be distinguished from the שְׁוָא נַח. The שְׁוָא at the end of a word is always שְׁוָא נַח, and at the beginning always שְׁוָא נָע.

For distinguishing the שְׁוָא in the middle of a word the following rules may be laid down:

1. When two שְׁוָאִים follow one another the second always is שְׁוָא נָע, e. g. תִּחְקְעוּ.
2. Under a letter with דָּגֵשׁ (see § 6) the שְׁוָא is שְׁוָא נָע, e. g. נִדְּלוּ.
3. The שְׁוָא under the first of two letters which are the same generally is שְׁוָא נָע, e. g. הַלְלִי.
4. The שְׁוָא after the מֶתֶג or after an accent which takes its place (see § 9 Rem. and n° 4), is שְׁוָא נָע, e. g. הַמְשָׁרְתִים, הָיְתָה.

---

1) In certain editions also under the ending תְ־, e. g. וְשָׁתִית, וְצָמִת Ruth 2, 9.

CHAPTER IV.

Remainging Signs.

§ 6. The דָּגֵשׁ (*Dagesh*).

1) For the same reason as with the ה (see § 5, 4), viz. to promote the true pronunciation, a point is placed in the letters, בגדכפת [וּבְגַדְכְּפַת]. This point is called דָּגֵשׁ קַל (*Dagesh lene*) 1).

2) The letters בגדכפת have a דָּגֵשׁ קַל at the beginning of a word.

(a) When the preceding word has a disjunctive accent (see § 7, 2), e. g. אַחֲרֵי דֶרֶךְ, and consequently also at the beginning of a sentence, e. g. בְּרֵאשִׁית Gen. 1, 1.

(b) When the preceding word terminates with a closed syllable, e. g. בְּצָרָה תָשִׂים, מִשּׁוֹר פָּר, אֶת כֹּל.

(c) When בּ with שְׁוָא נָע is immediately followed by ב or פ; or כ with שְׁוָא נָע by another כ, e. g. וַיְהִי הֲלֹא כְכַרְכְּמִישׁ ; וָאֶכְבְּדָה בְּפַרְעֹה Ex. 15, 17; בְּבוֹאָם 1 Sam. 16, 6; Jes. 10, 9.

---

1) With some of these letters the difference of pronunciation still exists. By a part of the Israëlites ב is pronounced as *v* and בּ as *b*, כ as *ch* and כּ as *k*, פ as *f* and פּ as *p*, ת as *s* and תּ as *t*. By others this difference is only observed with כ and פּ, whilst ג is by them pronounced as *g* and גּ as the French *gu*. Between ד and דּ all difference in sound seems now to have been lost.

3) The same letters frequently have דָּגֵשׁ קַל in the middle of a word, but only after the שְׁוָא נַח, e. g. יִגְדַּל.

Rem. 1. With nomina however in the *status constructus* (see § 60) this דָּגֵשׁ is generally omitted when one of the letters בגדכפת is the third stem-letter of the word e. g. כִּתְפוֹת, עַבְדֵי. The כ also of the suffix (see § 46 seq. § 62 seq.) usually stands without דָּגֵשׁ קל e. g. יְרִכֶם, וְקִבֶּצְךָ, בִּנְךָ.

4) The דָּגֵשׁ further serves to indicate that the preceding letter has fallen out. This דָּגֵשׁ, called דָּגֵשׁ חָזָק (*Dagesh forte*), doubles the pronunciation of the letter in which it stands (*assimilation*), e. g. יִטֹּר (read יִטְטֹר) instead of יִנְטֹר; שִׁחֲתָם (read שִׁחְתְּהֶם) instead of שִׁחַתְתֶּם. This דָּגֵשׁ may be placed in all the letters except אהחער.

5) All the letters moreover, אהחער again excepted, usually are marked with דָּגֵשׁ when followed by a vowel or half-vowel and immediately preceded by a short vowel. דָּגֵשׁ אַחַר תְּנוּעָה קְטַנָּה (see § 4 Rem. 2), e. g. לַפִּיד, הַמְּרוּקָה, בִּכּוּרִים.

Rem. 2. When, however, they are followed by an *auxiliary* vowel, as in the segolate forms (§ 56,2) דָּגֵשׁ is not inserted, e. g. בֶּגֶד, זַיִת.

6) When the letters אהחער are followed by a vowel or half-vowel they are usually preceded by a long vowel (§ 4 Rem. 5) which may serve also to supplement the absence of דָּגֵשׁ חָזָק, e. g. בְּאֵר, הִתְבָּרֵךְ (conf. § 26, 3; 27, 4).

7) Conclusion.
The letters בגדכפת can have a דָּגֵשׁ of every kind.
The letters אהחער can have no דָּגֵשׁ at all.

THE ACCENTS.

The remaining 11 letters can have every דָּגֵשׁ with the exception of דָּגֵשׁ קַל ²).

The Signs of Interpunction, Tone and Melody
(נְגִינוֹת or טְעָמִים *accent*s), and the מַקֵּף.

§ 7. 1) The signs of interpunction serve to indicate the mutual relation or connection of words ¹).

They are placed either over or under the words except the פָּסִיק which stands at the side of a word.

2) They are divided into:

(*a*) Disjunctive signs (מַפְסִיקִים or מְלָכִים *distinctivi*) which denote that the word which is marked by them, is to be separated from the following.

(*b*) Conjunctive signs (מְעַטְפִים or מְשָׁרְתִים *conjunctivi*) which denote that the word so marked is connected with the following ²).

---

2) A point is sometimes placed in a letter for other reasons also; e. g. in the ס of וַיֶּאֱסֹר to indicate that the א has not חֲטַף סֶגוֹל as in Gen. 42, 24; or in the first letter of a word when the previous word terminates with the same letter, as לָהֶם מִיָּגוֹן, בֶּן־נוּן, for which purpose however the sign פָּסִיק (l) is also used, as הַגּוֹיִם׀וּמְנָחָה (See § 4 Rem. 2 and App. 1 note 2). In a short work like the present this subject cannot be fully treated. A consistent plan, moreover, has not been followed by the scribes, and the remark made § 4 note 2 also applies to the present case.

1) From this it would seem that they properly belong to the syntax. Yet as signs of tone their place is the Grammar, and we shall therefore explain them as far as is necessary.

2) Their names and further particulars are given in App. I.

3) Every word in the Bible has generally one or more of these signs. A word which is without them is most closely connected with the following and this connection is indicated by the sign (־) מַקָּף, placed between the two words, e. g. עַל־פְּנֵי.

4) The signs of tone show which syllable is to be accented. They are placed either on the last syllable, and called מִלְרַע, or on the last but one, and called מִלְעֵיל; e. g. סֵפֶר, אָמַר.

> Rem. 1. Before gutturals the accent sometimes stands *apparently* on the syllable preceding the penultimate, e. g. נֶעֶרְמוּ Ex. 15,8. נֶעֶרְמוּ however really is equivalent to נֶעְרְמוּ, so that the vowel of the guttural in this respect does not count as a vowel. See § 26,2.
>
> Rem. 2. The rules for placing the accents will be given later § 87 seq.

5) The same signs also serve as guides in the recital of the words to a certain melody, and as such they are called נְגִינוֹת *musical signs*.

The Shifting of the Accent (נָסוֹג אָחוֹר).

§ 8. 1) Two successive syllables in one word cannot have an accent each. The same thing is to be avoided with two words connected together, i. e. of which the first word has a conjunctive accent. The accent in this case, provided the connection is not affected by it, is moved forward, when it should have stood on the last syllable and the following word has its accent on the first syllable, e. g. וְהָיְתָה לּוֹ, קָרָא לָיְלָה.

> Rem. The half-vowel at the beginning of the second word is in this

respect generally considered as a vowel, e. g. וַיִּיטַב לְךָ and יִיטַב לָךְ (Conf. § 9 Rem.).

2) When however the first word ends in תם (see § 88 I, 1) or in a closed syllable with a long vowel (see § 87, 1) this shifting of the accent but rarely occurs, e. g. יוּבַל הוּא ׳וַהֲבֵאתָם שָׁמָּה.

3) The shifting also rarely occurs when a closed syllable with a short vowel precedes, e. g. וְנִסְלַח לוֹ ׳וְנִרְצָה לוֹ.

The Half-tone (מֶתֶג or נַעְיָא).

§ 9. 1) The מֶתֶג or נַעְיָא is a small perpendicular line placed on the left of a vowel. It has the value of half an accent, and serves to render the pronunciation more correct [1]).

2) The מֶתֶג stands by an open syllable which is the second before the accent, when it has a long vowel, or a short vowel followed by a guttural or שְׁוָא נָע, e. g. בְּרָכָה ׳בֶּעָפָר ׳הַעִידֹתִי ׳הָאַחֶרֶת ׳יַעֲשֶׂה.

If however the vowel is short, and is not followed by a guttural or שְׁוָא נָע, the מֶתֶג if possible is shifted to the preceding syllable, e. g. מַחֲרַצַּנִּים ׳הָרִמּוֹנִים.

Rem. Here also the half-vowel which immediately precedes the ac-

---

1) In mss. the מתג is used also for other purposes, sometimes even to modify the meaning of the words.

In old editions and mss. other signs were also in use to secure correctness of pronunciation. As however in later editions these have become obsolete, we need not mention them.

centuated syllable, is counted as a vowel and forms a syllable, e. g. בְּגָדְהָ (Conf. § 8 Rem.).

3) The second syllable before the מֶתֶג, if it is capable, likewise receives the מֶתֶג e. g. הָעֻזִּיאֵלִי.

4) A closed syllable only has the מֶתֶג in long words, e. g. וּמֶמְשַׁלְתְּךָ, or in a word which by מַקֵּף is joined to the following word, e. g. וַיִּתֶּן־לְךָ, unless an open syllable precedes, e. g. הָעִיר־הַהִוא.

5) When a word has 4 or more syllables the מֶתֶג is sometimes exchanged for a conjunctive accent, e. g. עֲרִיסֹתֵיכֶם.

PART II.

ETYMOLOGY.

CHAPTER I.

§ 10. The etymology of a language teaches us the various forms or inflections of the words or stem-words with respect to the difference of signification obtained by them.

The Division of the Words.

§ 11. All the words of the Hebrew language belong to one of the three following groups:

(a) *Verbs* (פְּעָלִים *verba*) [1];

(b) *Nouns* and *adjectives* (שֵׁמוֹת *nomina*), names of living beings, of inanimate things, of ideas, of quantities and qualities.

(c) *Particles* (מִלּוֹת *particulae*), words which denote the

---

1) As the stems of the Hebrew words more clearly appear in the verbs, from which the words of the other two groups for the greater part are derived, we shall treat of the verbs first.

relation between words and sentences, or which determine a quality or operation.

CHAPTER II.

The Verb (פֹּעַל) in general.

§ 12. *The division of the verbs.*

A. According to their signification.

1) *Transitive verbs* (פֹּעַל יוֹצֵא) i. e. verbs which govern a passive object which is connected with the verb without any particle or servile letter, e. g. גִּלַּח *to shave.*

2) *Reflexive verbs* (פֹּעַל חוֹזֵר), verbs of which the form indicates that the agent is the passive object, e. g. הִתְגַּלַּח *to shave oneself,* נִדְבַּר *to speak with one another.*

3) *Passive verbs* (פֹּעַל מְקַבֵּל) verbs expressing the action which the passive object undergoes, גֻּלַּח *to be shaven,* דֻּבַּר *to be spoken of.*

4) *Intransitive verbs* (פֹּעַל עוֹמֵד), verbs which cannot govern an object which is not connected with the verb by a particle or servile letter, e. g. חָיָה *to live,* גָּדַל *to be great.*

B. According to the number of their stem-letters.
1) Verbs with a *triliteral* stem.
2) Verbs with a *biliteral* stem.

DIVISION OF THE VERBS.

C. According to the nature of their stems.

1) *Primitive verbs*, of which the original stem expresses an action.

2) *Denominative verbs*, verbs derived from a nomen, e. g. לָבַן *to make bricks* from לְבֵנָה *brick*, הֶאֱזִין *to listen* from אֹזֶן *ear*.

D. According to their conjugation.

1) *Regular verbs*, which are conjugated according to the more general principles, and in which all the stem-letters remain visible and audible, e. g. פָּקַד *to visit, to take notice*, גָּדַל *to be great* [1]).

2) *Irregular verbs* which more or less deviate from the regular conjugation.

They are subdivided into:

(*a*) verbs which have one or more *gutturals* in the stem, e. g. שָׁמַע *to hear*, אָמַר *to say*.

(*b*) verbs of which the first or last stem-letter may be *wanting* (חֲסֵרִים) e. g. נָגַע *to touch*, כָּרַת *to cut*.

(*c*) verbs of which the first or last stem-letter may be *inperceptibly quiescent* (נָח נִסְתָּר) the נָחִים. This according to § 5, 3 can only take place with the letters אהוי, e. g. יָלַד *to bear childern*, רָפָא *to heal*.

Rem. Hebrew grammarians are accustomed to take the stem פָּעַל as the standard for all other stems. Hence the first stem-letter is called פ׳ הפעל or פ׳, the second ע׳ הפעל or ע׳, the third ל׳ הפעל or ל׳. The different conjugations of the verb (§ 13) borrow their names from this stem.

---

1) By שְׁלֵמִים verbs are meant which fulfil only the second condition.

The various Conjugations (בִּנְיָנִים *conjugationes*).

§ 13. The stem (שֹׁרֶשׁ) of a verb undergoes much alteration by the change of vowels and by the addition of letters before, after, or between the stem-letters.

The Hebrew language possesses a great many conjugations (בִּנְיָנִים) of which some are more frequent with some verbs and others with other verbs. The more common conjugations are the seven following [1]).

(1) פָּעַל (usually called קַל) in which the stem-letters form the basis of the inflection without addition of other letters; e. g. חָל, פָּקַד.

(2) נִפְעַל the stem-letters with נ prefixed to them; e. g. נָחַל, נִפְקַד.

(3) פִּעֵל the stem-letters without additional letters, e. g. חִלֵּל, פִּקֵּד.

(4) פֻּעַל similarly the stem-letters without additional letters; e. g. חֻלַּל, פֻּקַּד.

(5) הִפְעִיל the stem-letters with ה prefixed to them; e. g. הֵחֵל, הִפְקִיד.

(6) הָפְעַל similarly the stem-letters with ה prefixed to them; e. g. הוּחַל, הָפְקַד.

(7) הִתְפַּעֵל the stem-letters with הת prefixed to them; e. g. הִתְחַלֵּל, הִתְפַּקֵּד.

---

1) Their names express the 3ᵈ pers. masc. sing. of the עָבַר, and hence they already acquaint us with the difference of vowels.

Less common are:

(8) פּוֹעֵל, (9) פּוֹעַל, and (10) הִתְפּוֹעֵל, generally used with the biliteral stems instead of פִּעֵל, פֻּעַל, and הִתְפַּעֵל; e. g. חוֹלֵל, חוֹלַל, and הִתְחוֹלֵל.

Still less common:

(11) פִּלְפֵּל, (12) פָּלְפַּל, and (13) הִתְפַּלְפֵּל with duplication of the two stem-letters, in use with the biliteral stems instead of פִּעֵל, פֻּעַל, and הִתְפַּעֵל; e. g. כִּלְכֵּל, כָּלְכַּל or הִתְכַּלְכַּל, כִּלְכַּל.

Exceedingly rare:

(14) הָתְפָּעַל differing from the הִתְפַּעֵל only in the vowels; e. g. הָתְפָּקַד.

(15) פִּעֲלֵל with duplication of the last stem-letter of the triliteral stems; e. g. שַׁאֲנַן.

(16) פְּעֲלַל with duplication of the last stem-letter; e. g. אֻמְלַל.

(17) פְּעַלְעַל with duplication of the last two stem-letters of the triliteral stems; e. g. סְחַרְחַר.

(18) Finally forms such as תִּרְגַּלְתִּי Hos. 11,3; תִּתְחָרֶה Jer. 12,5 and shortened תִּתְחַר Ps. 37,1; שְׁקַעֲרוּרוֹת Lev 14,37; מְחֻסְפָּס Ex. 16,14; וְנְכַפֵּר Deut. 21,8; נְגֹאֲלוּ Jes 59,3; Lam. 4,14; וְנִוָּסְרוּ Ez. 23,48, and others, belong to yet different conjugations, which do not occur and which therefore should be considered as modifications of the conjugations enumerated.

The Meaning of the different Conjugations.

§ 14. 1) קַל is *active* both with the transitive and intransitive verbs; e. g. פָּקַד *to visit*, חָל *to tremble*.

2) נִפְעַל both *active* and *passive*, sometimes also *reflexive*; e. g. נִשְׁמַר *to guard oneself*, נִלְחַם *to fight with one another*.

3) פִּעֵל generally is *transitive*, chiefly with verbs which in the קַל are *intransitive*, as קָדַשׁ *to be holy* קִדֵּשׁ *to sanctify*. Yet פִּעֵל sometimes is *intransitive*, as פַּחֵד *to fear*, and with verbs which in the קַל are transitive, not uncommonly *frequentative* קָבַר *to bury* קִבֵּר *to bury often*.

4) פֻּעַל is only *passive*, generally the passive of פִּעֵל; e. g. קֻדַּשׁ *to be sanctified*.

5) הִפְעִיל sometimes *intransitive*, as הֶאֱזִין *to listen*, but with verbs which in the קַל are intransitive, generally *transitive*, as הִקְדִּישׁ *to declare holy*.

6) הָפְעַל *passive*; generally the passive of הִפְעִיל, as הָקְדַּשׁ *to be declared holy*.

7) הִתְפַּעֵל often *reflexive*, sometimes also *passive* or *intransitive*, as הִתְקַדֵּשׁ *to make oneself ready*; הִתְרָאָה *to look at one another*; התכפר *to be propitiated*; הִתְהַלֵּךְ *to walk*.

8) As for the other בִּנְיָנִים the פּוֹעֵל and פִּלְפֵּל have the same meaning as פִּעֵל; פּוֹעַל and פֻּלְפַּל the same as פֻּעַל; התפועל and הִתְפַּלְפֵּל the same as הִתְפַּעֵל· הָתְפָּעַל *is passive*; פְּעַלֵל and פִּעֲלַל are both *transitive* and *intransitive*; and פְּעַלְעַל has the same meaning as קַל.

urFther particulars are to be learned from exercise.

The Conjugation of the Verb in general.

§ 15. 1) The conjugation of a verb sets forth the different forms in which a verb occurs.

These forms are twofold *verbal forms* and *nominal forms*.

2) The verbal forms comprise two *moods* (דְּרָכִים *modi*), two *actions*, usually called *tenses* (זְמַנִּים *tempora*), three *persons* (גּוּפִים *personae*), two *genders* (מִינִים *genera*), and two *numbers* (מִסְפָּרִים *numeri*).

3) The two moods are the *indicative* (דֶּרֶךְ הַמַּגְבִּיל) and the *imperative* (דֶּרֶךְ הַצִּוּוּי).

Rem. 1. The פָּעַל and הָפְעַל have no דֶּרֶךְ הַצִּוּוּי. A very rare instance of this in the הָפְעַל is given § 41 *a* Rem. 2.

Rem. 2. Concerning the Jussive and Cohortative see § 45.

The two tenses are the *perfect* (עָבַר) and the *not-perfect* (עָתִיד).[1]

The three persons are the *first pers.* (מְדַבֵּר בְּעַדוֹ), *second pers.* (נֹכַח or נמצא), and the *third pers.* (נִסְתָּר).

The two genders are the *masculine* (זָכָר) and the *feminine* (נְקֵבָה).

The two numbers are the *singular* (יָחִיד) and the *plural* (רַבִּים).

4) The nominal forms are:

The *infinitive* (דֶּרֶךְ הַמָּקוֹר) also called שֵׁם הפעל (*substantivum verbale*), and the *participles* (בֵּינוֹנִים).

The infinitive has the two genders, and the participle the two genders and the two numbers.

---

1) For brevity's sake we shall call these two tenses always עָבַר and עָתִיד.

The Stem-forms of the Conjugation.

§ 16. A. The verbal forms.

a. For the בִּנְיָנִים which usually have an active meaning *two* stem-forms may be adopted from which the other verbal forms are derived.

These two stem-forms are:

1) The 3ᵈ pers. masc. sing. of the עָבַר. On this stem-form all the other forms are based according to the rules of § 18.

2) The masc. sing. of the imperative on which are based the other forms of the same tense and those of the עָתִיד according to the rules of § 18.

b. With the בִּנְיָנִים which never or very seldom have an active sense, viz. פָּעַל, הָפְעַל and הִתְפָּעֵל, all the verbal forms follow the 3ᵈ pers. masc. sing. of עָבַר.

B. The nominal forms.

a. With the triliteral stems the infinitive usually has its own stem-form, and with active verbs also the 2ᵈ stem-form of the verbal forms. Yet in the הָפְעַל, הִפְעִיל and הִתְפַּעֵל and also in the קַל and נִפְעַל of the biliteral verbs the infinitive has *only* the 2ᵈ stem-form of the verbal forms.

With the נָחִי ל"ה (§ 34) the infinitive has always its own stem-form besides that of the verbal forms.

b. 1) The קַל of the triliteral stems has two participles with different stem-forms agreeing with the stems of the nomina (see § 67, 1 A 1 seq.). With the biliteral stems the participle has the stem-form of the עָבַר (see § 38ᵇ 2).

2) All the other בִּנְיָנִים have only one participle. This has a מ as preformative before the stem-form, viz. of the עָתִיד with the triliteral verbs, and of the עָבַר with the biliteral verbs (see § 67 B 1). The נִפְעַל alone has the stem-form of the עָבַר without preformative.

3. The participles therefore generally have a long final vowel. With the triliteral stems this vowel is even lengthened when it is short in the stem-form. '

The Preformatives and Afformatives.

§ 17. A. The verbal forms.

1) To make the different forms of the conjugations, letters are used which are placed either before or after the stem.

2) In the עָבַר the letters הוימנת [הֵוֵי מָנָת] are used and only as afformatives. In the עָתִיד both the preformatives אינת [אֵיתָן] and the afformatives הוינ [וֹנָה] are used. In the imperative only the afformatives הוינ are employed.

Table of preformatives and afformatives.

עָבַר

	Plur.		Sing.	
	2		2	3
masc.	תֶּם—	—וּ	תָּ—	stem-form.
	—נוּ	תִי—		
fem.	תֶּן—		תְּ—	ה—

עָתִיד

	Plur.			Sing.	
	2			2	3
masc.	תְ–וּ	יְ–וּ	אֲ–	תְ	יְ–
fem.	תְ–נָה	תְ–נָה		תְ–י	תְ–

דֶּרֶךְ הַצִּוּוּי

Plur.		Sing.	
–וּ			stem-form.
–נָה			י

Rem. Of the 2ᵈ and 3ᵈ pers. masc. plur. of עָתִיד we find a collateral form on –וּן.

B. The nominal forms are entirely considered as nomina.

General rules for the Pre- and Afformatives of Triliteral Stems.

§ 18. 1) The preformatives of one letter have the half-vowel, which only through supervening circumstances is changed into a vowel. In the קַל where they are followed by a half vowel, they have חִירֶק. In נִפְעַל, הִפְעִיל, הָפְעַל and הִתְפַּעֵל they are contracted with the ה, the vowel of which they take.

The א has in קַל, נִפְעַל and הִתְפַּעֵל the סְגוֹל.

2) The afformatives which have the accent and form a syllable (תֶם and תֶן) have the effect of changing the קָמַץ of the first syllable of the stem into a half vowel, as עֲשִׂיתֶם, קְרָאתֶם, יְרֵאתֶם, פְּקַדְתֶּם; whilst the *closed* syllable immediately preceding always has פַּתַח, as הִבְדַּלְתֶּם, בְּעַרְתֶּם, very seldom סְגוֹל, as שְׁאֶלְתֶּם 1 Sam. 12, 13 (see below n° 5).

3) The afformatives which have the accent but do not form a syllable, cause the vowel of the second syllable of the stem to change into a half vowel, as פָּקְדָה, יִפְקְדוּ, פָּקְדוּ. In consequence of this the half vowel of the first stem-letter becomes a vowel, as פָּקְדוּ, בַּחֲרוּ.

4) In the הִפְעִיל however the חִירֶק גָּדוֹל always remains before afformatives which do not form a syllable. The חִירֶק moreover seldom loses the accent (see § 88 I 3*b*) e. g. הִבְדִּילָה, יַשְׁמִיעוּ.

Rem. 1. We sometimes find also this חִירֶק changed into a half vowel, viz. וַיַּדְבְּקוּ 1 Sam. 14, 22; וַיַּדְרְכוּ Jer. 9, 2; תַּעֲשְׁרֶנָה Ps. 65, 10.

5) With afformatives which have *not* the accent, only the חוֹלָם of the stem is maintained in the *closed* syllable immediately preceding, as תַּחְגֹּרְנָה, יָגֹרְתִּי. Otherwise this syllable always has פַּתַח, e. g. יָשַׁבְתִּי, בְרַכְתָּ, הִקְצַפְנוּ, תֵּלַדְנָה. The צֵירֶה is but seldom kept before ‎־נָה, as in תִּשְׁתַּפֵּכְנָה, לָכֵן, תְּחַלֶּלְנָה viz. סֶגוֹל and is once found shortened into תְּחַבְּרְנָה Ez. 13, 19.

If the preceding syllable is *open*, it always has סֶגוֹל before ‎־נָה (see §§ 32, 2; 34, 8).

Rem. 2. Concerning the pausa see § 89.

CHAPTER III.

The Conjugation of the Regular Triliteral Verb.

בִּנְיָן קַל

§ 19. 1) The verbal forms.

עָבָר stem-form פָּקַד.

Plur.			Sing.		
2			2	3	
פְּקַדְתֶּם	פָּקְדוּ	פָּקַדְתִּי	פָּקַדְתָּ	פָּקַד	masc.
פְּקַדְתֶּן			פָּקַדְתְּ	פָּקְדָה	fem.

פָּקַדְנוּ

עָתִיד stem-form פקד.

Plur.			Sing.		
2			2		
תִּפְקְדוּ	יִפְקְדוּ	אֶפְקֹד	תִּפְקֹד	יִפְקֹד	masc.
תִּפְקֹדְנָה	תִּפְקֹדְנָה		תִּפְקְדִי	תִּפְקֹד	fem.

נפקד

הַדֶּרֶךְ הַצִּוּוּי

פִּקְדוּ	פְּקֹד m.
פְּקֹדְנָה	פִּקְדִי f.

2) The nominal forms.

פָּקַד, פְּקֹד stem-form דֶּרֶךְ הַמָּקוֹר.

בִּינוֹנִי (participle).

בִּינוֹנִי פָּעוּל (passive)		בינוני פועל (active)	
Plur.	Sing.	Plur.	Sing.
פְּקוּדִים	פָּקוּד	פּוֹקְדִים	פּוֹקֵד
פְּקוּדוֹת	פְּקוּדָה	פּוֹקְדוֹת	פּוֹקְדָה or פּוֹקֶדֶת

Rem. 1. The עָבָר of קַל has besides the stem-form פָּקַד two other stem-forms viz. פָּעֵל and פָּעֹל (*verba mediae e et o*). These two stem-

THE TRILITERAL VERBS.

forms are known by the vowel of the second stem-letter, e. g. שָׁפֵל *to be low* or *humble*, קָטֹן *to be small*.

The צוּרָה however only appears in the 3d pers. masc. sing. and in *pausa* in the forms of which the second stem-letter would other wise have the half-vowel, e. g. קָמְלוּ, יָרֵאָה. The remaining forms are similar to those of the verbs *mediae a*. The חוֹלָם appears whenever the second stem-letter has the accent, e. g. קָטֹנְתִּי.

The בֵּינוֹנִי פּוֹעֵל of the verbs *mediae e* and *o* has the same stem-form as the עָבַר, e. g. יָרֵא *being afraid*, יָכֹל *being able*.

Rem. 2. Also the 2d stem-form of קַל has a collateral form, viz. פָּקַד. This form is generally used with the verbs *mediae e* and *o*, e. g. יִקְטֹן, יִשְׁפַּל; sometimes also with other verbs, as יִלְמַד *he learns*, chiefly with those that are intransitive, as יִשְׁכַּב *he lies*, see § 32 B 2.

With the irregular verbs we now and then find a collateral form with צוּרָה; see § 29 Rem. 2; § 30 Rem. 3; § 31, 2; § 32 A³. The עָתִיד therefore like the עָבַר has three stem-forms with the same distinctive vowels (פָּעַל, פָּעֵל, פָּעֹל).

Rem. 3. The collateral forms of the עָבַר are generally used with the intransitive verbs. Sometimes, however, these forms have a transitive meaning; e. g. חָצֵב *he hewed out* Jes. 5,2.

בִּנְיָן נִפְעַל

§ 20. 1) The verbal forms.

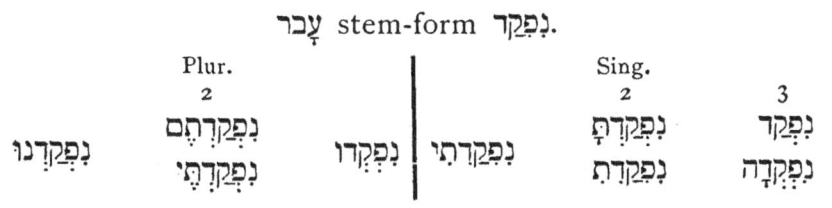

נִפְקַד stem-form עָבַר.

	Plur.			Sing.	
	2			2	3
נִפְקַדְנוּ	נִפְקַדְתֶּם	נִפְקְדוּ	נִפְקַדְתִּי	נִפְקַדְתָּ	נִפְקַד
	נִפְקַדְתֵּי			נִפְקַדְתְּ	נִפְקְדָה

הִפָּקֵד stem-form עָתִיד.

	Plur.			Sing.	
	2	3		2	3
נִפָּקֵד	תִּפָּקְדוּ	יִפָּקְדוּ	אֶפָּקֵד	תִּפָּקֵד	יִפָּקֵד
	תִּפָּקַדְנָה	תִּפָּקַדְנָה		תִּפָּקְדִי	תִּפָּקֵד

דֶּרֶךְ הַצִוּוּי

| הִפָּקְדוּ | הִפָּקֵד |
| הִפָּקַדְנָה | הִפָּקְדִי |

2) The nominal forms.

נִפְקֹד or הִפָּקֵד, הִפָּקֹד stem-form דֶּרֶךְ הַמָּקוֹר

בֵּינוֹנִי

| נִפְקָדִים | נִפְקָד |
| נִפְקָדוֹת | נִפְקָדָה or נִפְקֶדֶת |

Rem. הִפָּקֵד and הִפָּקֹד are contracted forms of הִנְפָּקֵד and הִנְפָּקֹד and therefore the first stem-letter ought to have the דָּגֵשׁ חָזָק. In the עָתִיד the ה coalesces with the preformative which then takes its vowel. The א alone generally keeps its סֶגוֹל. When the infinitive has a prefix the ה does not coalesce with it, e. g. בְּהִכָּבְדִי.

בנין פִּעֵל

§ 21. 1) The verbal forms.

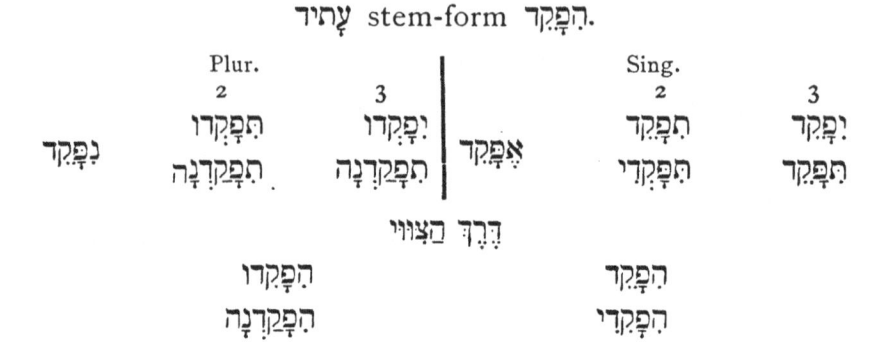

פִּקֵּד stem-form עָבַר.

	Plur.			Sing.	
	2			2	
פִּקַּדְנוּ	פִּקַּדְתֶּם	פִּקְּדוּ	פִּקַּדְתִּי	פִּקַּדְתָּ	פִּקֵּד
	פִּקַּדְתֶּן			פִּקַּדְתְּ	פִּקְּדָה

THE TRILITERAL VERBS.

פָּקֵד stem-form עָתִיד

	Plur.			Sing.	
	2	3		2	
נִפָּקֵד	תִּפָּקְדוּ	יִפָּקְדוּ	אֶפָּקֵד	תִּפָּקֵד	יִפָּקֵד
	תִּפָּקַדְנָה	תִּפָּקַדְנָה		תִּפָּקְדִי	תִּפָּקֵד

דֶּרֶךְ הַצִּוּוּי

פָּקְדוּ	הִפָּקֵד
הִפָּקַדְנָה	הִפָּקְדִי

2) The nominal forms.

פָּקֹד or פָּקֵד stem-form דֶּרֶךְ הַמָּקוֹר.

בֵּינוֹנִי

נִפְקָדִים	נִפְקָד
נִפְקָדוֹת	נִפְקָדָה or נִפְקֶדֶת

Rem. 1. In פָּעֵל and פָּעַל the preformative keeps the half-vowel, because it precedes a letter with a vowel.

Rem. 2. With the participle the preformative is sometimes omitted, e. g. מָאֵן Ex. 7,27.

Rem. 3. The infinitive has sometimes the stem-form of the עָבַר, as נִאֵץ 2 Sam. 12,15.

בִּנְיָן פִּעֵל

§ 22. Stem-form פִּקֵּד.

1) The verbal forms.

עָבַר

	Plur.			Sing.	
	2			2	
פִּקַּדְנוּ	פִּקַּדְתֶּם	פִּקְּדוּ	פִּקַּדְתִּי	פִּקַּדְתָּ	פִּקֵּד
	פִּקַּדְתֶּן			פִּקַּדְתְּ	פִּקְּדָה

עָתִיד

	Plur. 2			Sing. 2	
נִפְקֹד	תִּפְקְדוּ	יִפְקְדוּ	אֶפְקֹד	תִּפְקֹד	יִפְקֹד
	תִּפְקֹדְנָה	תִּפְקֹדְנָה		תִּפְקְדִי	תִּפְקֹד

2) The nominal forms.

פָּקֹד stem-form. דֶּרֶךְ הַמָּקוֹר

בֵּינוֹנִי

מְפַקְּדִים	מְפַקֵּד
מְפַקְּדוֹת	מְפֻקָּדָה or מְפֻקֶּרֶת

Rem. 1. Concerning the preformative see preceding § Rem. 1.

Rem. 2. In the פָּעַל also the preformative of the participle is sometimes omitted, e. g. אֹכֵל Ex. 3,2.

בִּנְיָן הַפְעִיל

§ 23. The verbal forms.

הִפְקִיד stem-form. עָבַר

	Plur. 2			Sing. 2	3
הִפְקַדְנוּ	הִפְקַדְתֶּם	הִפְקִידוּ	הִפְקַדְתִּי	הִפְקַדְתָּ	הִפְקִיד
	הִפְקַדְתֶּן			הִפְקַדְתְּ	הִפְקִידָה

הַפְקֵד and הַפְקִיד stem-form עָתִיד

	2	3	1		
נַפְקִיד	תַּפְקִידוּ	יַפְקִידוּ	אַפְקִיד	תַּפְקִיד	יַפְקִיד
	תַּפְקֵדְנָה	תַּפְקֵדְנָה		תַּפְקִידִי	תַּפְקֵד

דֶּרֶךְ הַצִּוּוּי

הַפְקִידוּ	הַפְקֵד
הַפְקֵדְנָה	הַפְקִידִי

THE TRILITERAL VERBS.

2) The nominal forms.

הִפְקִיד stem-form דֶּרֶךְ הַמָּקוֹר.

בֵּינוֹנִי

| מַפְקִיד | מַפְקִידִים |
| מַפְקִידָה or מַפְקֶדֶת | מַפְקִידוֹת |

Rem. 1. Although the ה coalesces with the preformative it remains in the infinitive after a prefix, e. g. לְהַמְלִיךְ. Sometimes however the ה of the infinitive is omitted after a prefix, e. g. לַצְבּוֹת בֶּטֶן וְלַנְפִּל יָרֵךְ *to make the belly to swell and the thigh to fall away* Num. 5,22; and on the other hand is sometimes written after the preformative, e. g. יְהוֹשִׁיעַ Ps. 116,6.

Rem. 2. The infinitive has but seldom the first stem-form, as הַקְצוֹת Lev. 14,43.

בִּנְיַן הָפְעַל

§ 24. 1) The verbal forms.

Stem-form הָפְקַד.

עָבַר.

3			
הָפְקַד	הָפְקַדְתָּ	הָפְקַדְתִּי הָפְקְדוּ	הָפְקַדְתֶּם הָפְקַדְנוּ
הָפְקְדָה	הָפְקַדְתְּ		הָפְקַדְתֶּן

עָתִיד.

3	I	3	
יָפְקַד	תָּפְקַד	אָפְקַד	יָפְקְדוּ תִּפְקְדוּ נָפְקַד
תָּפְקַד	תָּפְקְדִי		תָּפְקַדְנָה תָּפְקַדְנָה

2) The nominal forms.

הָפְקַד stem-form דֶּרֶךְ הַמָּקוֹר.

בֵּינוֹנִי

| מָפְקָד | מֻפְקָדִים |
| מָפְקָדָה or מָפְקֶדֶת | מָפְקָדוֹת |

Rem. 1. The קָמֵץ חָטוּף of the preformative is sometimes interchanged for שׁוּרֶק קָטָן, e. g. יְשָׁלְכוּ Jes. 34,3; מָשְׁלֶכֶת 1 Kings 13,24.

Rem. 2. The infinitive has sometimes the collateral form הָפְקֵד, e. g. הָחְתֵּל Ez. 16,4.

בנין התפעל

§ 25. The verbal forms.

Stem-form הִתְפַּקֵּד.

עָבָר.

	2			
הִתְפַּקַּדְנוּ	הִתְפַּקַּדְתֶּם / הִתְפַּקַּדְתֶּן	הִתְפַּקְּדוּ	הִתְפַּקַּדְתִּי	הִתְפַּקַּדְתָּ / הִתְפַּקַּדְתְּ	הִתְפַּקֵּד / הִתְפַּקְּדָה

עָתִיד.

	2	3	1	
נִתְפַּקֵּד	תִּתְפַּקְּדוּ / תִּתְפַּקֵּדְנָה	יִתְפַּקְּדוּ / תִּתְפַּקֵּדְנָה	אֶתְפַּקֵּד	תִּתְפַּקֵּד / תִּתְפַּקְּדִי	יִתְפַּקֵּד / תִּתְפַּקֵּד

דֶּרֶךְ הַצִּוּוּי.

| הִתְפַּקְּדוּ | הִתְפַּקֵּד |
| הִתְפַּקֵּדְנָה | הִתְפַּקְּדִי |

2) The nominal forms.

הִתְפַּקֵּד stem-form דֶּרֶךְ הַמָּקוֹר

בֵּינוֹנִי

| מִתְפַּקְּדִים | מִתְפַּקֵּד |
| מִתְפַּקְּדוֹת | מִתְפַּקֶּדֶת or מִתְפַּקְּדָה |

Rem. 1. The ה of the infinitive, like in the preceding conjugations, does not coalesce with the prefix, e. g. לְהִתְגּוֹלֵל.

Rem. 2. If the first stem-letter is a sibilant it changes place with the ה of the pieformative הִת, as הִשְׁתַּפֵּךְ *to be poured out*; הִסְתַּבֵּל

to become heavy, *troublesome*. After the צ the ת is changed into ט, as הִצְטַדָּק *to justify oneself*.

In like manner should the ת after ז be changed into ד, as is the case in the cognate Aramaic, e. g. הִזְדַּמֶּן, but of this no instance is found in the Bible. The ת is entirely omitted when the first stem-letter is ד, ט or ת, e. g. הִדַּכָּא, *to be oppressed* הִטַּהֲרוּ *cleanse yourselves*, הִתַּמְּהוּ *be amazed*, and sometimes also with other stems, as וְתִנַּשֵּׂא Num. 24,7.

EXERCISES.

הִפְעִיל and נִפְעַל in בדל

פָּעַל and פִּעֵל „ בקשׁ

הִפְעִיל and פִּעֵל, פָּעַל, קַל בשׁל

(גָּדַל and גָּדֵל) הִתְפַּעֵל and הִפְעִיל „ „ „ גדל

(דָּבַק and דָּבֵק) הָפְעַל and הִפְעִיל „ „ דבק

(כָּבֵד and כָּבַד) הִפְעִיל and הִתְפַּעֵל, פִּעֵל, נִפְעַל „ כבד

הָפְעַל and הִפְעִיל „ „ כשׁל

CHAPTER IV.

The deviations from the regular verb in consequense of one or more gutturals being in the stem.

§ 26. The verbs of which the first stem-letter is a guttural *(verba primae gutturalis)*.

The deviations only occur in קַל, נִפְעַל, הִפְעִיל and הָפְעַל.

1. When at the beginning of a word the first stem-letter should have the half-vowel, it has here the חֲטֵף, e. g. אָסֹף, אָבַד, עָמֹד, חֲזַק, הֲלֹךְ (see § 4,3).

2. The auxiliary vowel of the preformative is here פַּתַח or סְגוֹל, and the subsequent guttural generally has the corresponding חֲטָף instead of שְׁוָא; e. g. יַחֲבֹשׁ and יַחֲזִיק, הֶחֱזִיק, הַעֲמַדְתָּ, הֶעֱמִיד, יַחֲסֹר and יֶחֱזַק, יֶהְגֶּה, יֶהֱמֶה and יַחֲמֹד, and יֶאֱסֹר ,יַעֲמֹד and יֶאֱסֹר ,הֶחֱסִיר.

This שְׁוָא or חֲטָף sometimes changes into the short vowel of the preformative, when the verb is lengthened at the end by an afformative or otherwise, e. g. נֶעֶרְמוּ *they are heaped up*, נַעַמְדָה *let us stand*, יֶהֶרְסוּ *they press forward*, וְאֶעֶלְצָה *and I shall rejoice*. Concerning the value of this vowel as regards the accent see § 7 Rem. 1.¹).

> Rem. 1. In consequence of what has been said in the previous number it cannot be determined whether the form יַעֲלֶה is קַל or הִפְעִיל; the context alone can decide this.
>
> Rem. 2. Of הָיָה *to be* and חָיָה *to live* the עָתִיד is יִהְיֶה and יִחְיֶה²).

3) When the first stem-letter should have the דָּגֵשׁ חָזָק, for instance in נִפְעַל, the preceding short vowel is changed into a long vowel, e. g. יֵהָרֵם instead of יִהָרֵם (Cf. § 31).

> Rem. 3. The ר in this respect follows the gutturals, e. g. תְּרָגְנוּ instead of תְּרַגְּנוּ.
>
> Rem. 4. Concerning the verbs with א as first stem-letter see § 31.

---

¹) When the guttural has not חֲטָף but שְׁוָא in certain good editions a point is placed in the subsequent letter for the purpose of drawing the attention to it, e. g. אֶעְבֹּד and אֶעְבְּרָה, אֶעְשֶׂה and אֶעְשֶׂה (Conf. § 6 note 2).

²) In certain good editions attention is drawn to this by a מֶתֶג placed at the side of the חִירֶק, as יִהְיֶה and יִחְיֶה (Cf. § 9 note 1).

THE VERBS WITH GUTTURALS.

EXERCISES.

		stem-forms		but	
קל	חמד	stem-forms	חָמַד,	חֲמַד,	יַחְמֹד עָתִיד but
	חזק		חָזַק,	חֲזַק,	" " יֶחֱזַק
	חשב		חָשַׁב,	חֲשֹׁב,	יַחְשֹׁב or יֶחְשַׁב
	הלך		הָלַךְ,	חֲלֹךְ,	" " יֵחֲלֵךְ
	עמד		עָמַד,	עֲמֹד,	" " יַעֲמֹד
נפעל	חשב	"	נֶחְשַׁב,	הֵחָשֵׁב	
	הפך		נֶהְפַּךְ,	הֵהָפֵךְ	
	עזב		נֶעֱזַב,	הֵעָזֵב	
	ערץ		נֶעֱרַץ,	הֵעָרֵץ	
הִפְעִיל	עמד	"	הֶעֱמִיד,	הַעֲמִד or הַעֲמֵד	יַעֲמִיד עָתִיד
הָפְעַל	חרם	"	הָחֳרַם		
	הפך		הָהְפַּךְ		

The verbs of which ע׳הפעל is a guttural.

(verba mediae gutturalis).

§ 27. The deviations occur in all the בִּנְיָנִים, the הִפְעִיל excepted.

1) Instead of the half-vowel the ע׳הפעל has here חֲטָף, and generally חֲטָף פַּתָח, e. g. יִזְעֲקוּ, תִּנְחֲלֶם, יְבַחֲנוּ, יִנְאֲמוּ (cf. § 26, 1).

2) Instead of חִירִק as auxiliary vowel the פ׳הפעל has חֲטָף פַּתָח or סְגוֹל and the ע׳הפעל the corresponding פַּתָח or חֲטָף סְגוֹל; e. g. שָׁאֲלוּ, אָהֲבוּ (cf. 26, 2).

Rem. 1. שְׁחָרוּ Job 6,22 is an exception.

3) The infinitive excepted, the ע׳הפעל changes its חוֹלָם

and sometimes also its צֵירָה into פַּתַח, e. g. יִצְעַק, נָחַל, שָׁאַל; the infin. remains צְחֹק.

Rem. 2. The ך follows the same rule, as קְרַב.

4) In פָּעֵל, פֻּעַל, and הִתְפָּעֵל the short vowel of the פ׳הפעל is changed into a long vowel, viz. חִירָק into צירה, פַּתַח into קָמֶץ, and קִבּוּץ into חוֹלָם (see § 4 Rem. 5); e. g. בֵּאֵר, בָּעֵר, מְגֹאָל, דֹּחוּ.

Rem. 3. Likewise with ר as ע׳הפעל; e. g. בָּרֵךְ.

Rem. 4. On the other hand the ח generally, the ה often, and the ע sometimes retain the preceding short vowel, e. g. נָחַם, נָחַל, יַבְעֵר; and in very few instances even the א, e. g. בַּאֵר.

Rem. 5. Several forms of the verb שָׁאַל in the קַל are conjugated according to the stemform שָׁאַל; e. g. וּשְׁאָלְךָ, שְׁאֵלְתִּיו, שְׁאֵלְתֶם.

EXERCISES.

זעק קַל. נִפְעַל and הִפְעִיל

זרק „ „ and פָּעַל

כחש „ „ נִפְעַל, פָּעַל and הִתְפָּעֵל

נאף, נאץ (נהג, נאץ, נאף) in קַל and פָּעַל (נאץ, נאף, נהג)

נחל in קַל. פָּעַל, הִפְעִיל, הָפְעַל and הִתְפָּעֵל

תעב נִפְעַל, פָּעַל (תָּעֵב, תִּעֵב) and תָּעַב

ברך „ קַל. נִפְעַל, פָּעֵל and הִתְפָּעֵל

The verbs of which the לִ׳הפעל is a guttural.

(verba tertiae gutturalis).

§ 28. The deviations from the regular verb are the following.

THE VERBS WITH GUTTURALS.

(a) Concerning the stems with א as לְהִפָּעֵל see § 33.

(b) The stems with ח or ע as לְהִפָּעֵל change the חוֹלָם or the צֵירָה which precedes this letter into פַּתַח, except in the nominal forms, e. g. שָׁמֵעַ תִּשְׁמַע, שָׁלֵחַ תְּשַׁלַּח.

Rem. The ר sometimes follows the same rule, as עָבַר Job. 21,10.

(c) There are only four verbs which really have ה as לְהִפָּעֵל; they are תמה, נגה, כמה, גבה. Of כמה we only find the form כָּמָה. The other three, in the very few forms which occur, follow rule b), whilst נגה also belongs to the verbs of § 29.

EXERCISES.

בטח (הַבְטֵחַ and הַבְטִיחַ, הִבְטִיחַ) הִפְעִיל and קל in בקע in all the conjugations.

תמה ,, קל and הִתְפַּעֵל

זבח ,, ,, ,, פָּעֵל

שׁבע ,, נִפְעַל and הִפְעִיל

שׁבר ,, קל, נִפְעַל, פָּעֵל, הִפְעִיל and הָפְעַל

Verbs belonging both to §§ 26 and 27 are, e. g. הרג, חרף, ערב, רעץ, חרב.

Verbs belonging both to §§ 26 and 28 are, e. g. הדר, חבר, עזר, רצח, רשע.

Verbs belonging both to §§ 27 and 28 are, e. g. באר, בחר, ברח, בער, גרע, זהר, זרע, כרע.

CHAPTER. V.

Verbs of which one or more stem-letters may in the conjugation be absent. חֲסֵרִים *(verba contracta).*

§ 29. The verbs with נ as פ׳הַפָעַל (חַסְרֵי פ״נ).

1) When the preformative has a vowel (see § 18, 1) the נ falls away, and the second stem-letter is marked with דָּגֵשׁ חָזָק, e. g. יַשֵּׁךְ, הִגִּיעַ. In the infinitive however the נ remains, e. g. לִנְפֹּל, לִנְדֹּחַ.

Rem. 1. No deviations therefore occur in פָּעֵל, פָּעַל and הִתְפַּעֵל.

2) With certain verbs the נ is omitted in the imperative and infinitive of קַל even at the beginning of a word. The infinitive in this case has exclusively the feminine form; e. g. גַּשׁ and גֶּשֶׁת of נגשׁ; of נשׂא, because of the א, שָׂא and שְׂאֵת; of נגע, because of the ע, גַּע and גַּעַת.

Rem. 2. The נ does not fall away when the ע׳הפעל is a guttural, e. g. יִנְעַם, אֶנְעַל, יַנְחֵם, יֶנְהַג. (We find however יחת from נחת Jer. 21,13). In like manner the נ remains in כְּהִנְדֹף תִּנְדֹּף Ps. 68,3; יִנְטֹר Jer. 3,5; יִנְצְרוּ Deut. 33,9; יִנְקֹפוּ Jes. 29,1; הָנְתְקוּ Judges 20,31.

Rem. 3. With the stem לקח the ל often falls away as if the stem were נקח. Thus the imperative is קַח and לְקַח, the infinitive לָקַחַת and קַחַת, the עָתִיד יִקַּח.

Rem. 4. Sometimes also the י when פ׳הפעל falls away. See § 32 Rem. 2.

Exercises.

נגשׁ in קַל, נִפְעַל, הִפְעִיל, הָפְעַל and התפעל

נגשׂ „ „ and „

THE חֲסֵרִים

נפל in קַל, הִפְעִיל and הִתְפַּעֵל
נפץ „ „ פָּעַל and פִּעֵל
נשׁב „ „ and הִפְעִיל

Verbs belonging both to §§ 28 and 29 are נגע, נדר, נטר, נסע, נגה, נטע.

The verbs of which the לְהַפְעַל may fall away (חֲסֵרִי״ל).

§ 30. (*a*) When the לְהַפְעַל is נ, it falls away before the נ of the afformative, which then is marked with the דָּגֵשׁ חָזָק, as הָאֲזָנָה.

Rem. 1. The נ as לְהַפְעַל does not fall away before a suffix, as בְּחָנֵנִי.

Rem. 2. With נתן (belonging to the חֲסֵרִי פ״נ and therefore sometimes called חֲסַר הַקְּצָווֹת) the נ falls away also before ת, e.g. נָתַתִּי. The infinitive of קַל is תֵּת.

Rem. 3. נתן moreover has in the עָתִיד and צִוּוּי of קַל never the stem with חוֹלָם, rarely with פַּתַח, but almost always with צֵירֶה (cf. § 19 Rem. 2), thus תֵּן *give*, יִתֵּן *he gives*.

EXERCISES: מגן, טמן, צפן.

Verbs which belong to § 26 רגן, עשׁן, חתן,
 „ „ „ § 27 מאן, טחן, בחן.

(*b*) When the לְהַפְעַל is ת it falls away before the ת of the afformative, which then is marked with דָּגֵשׁ חָזָק, as שְׁחַתֶּם, כָּרַתִּי.

Rem. 4. This deviation is only found in the עָבַר.

Exercises: שָׁפַת, שָׁבַת, צָמַת.

Verbs belonging to § 26 עָשַׁת, עוּת, עָבַת.
    „   „   „ § 27 שָׁרַת, שָׁחַת, כָּרַת, בָּעַת,
Verb   „   „ § 29 נָשַׁת,
    „   „ §§ 27 and 29 נָחַת.

CHAPTER VI.

Verbs of which one or more stem-letters in the conjugation frequently are נַח נִסְתָּר (נָחִים) *verba quiescentia*).

§ 31. Verbs of which the פֹּהִפְעַל is א (נָחִי פ״א).

In addition to the deviations, already mentioned in § 26, we have here the following.

1) With 6 verbs the half vowel of the preformative is in the קַל changed into חוֹלָם. They are אָבַד *to perish*, אָבָה *to will*, אָחַז *to take hold of*, אָכַל *to eat*, אָמַר *to say*, אָפָה *to bake*; e. g. יֹאבַד. After the א of the preformative the א of the stem falls away, as אֹמַר. Yet we find here also forms such as תֶּאֱחֹז.

  Rem. 1. This חֹלָם of the preformative is sometimes found also in the נִפְעַל, as נֶאֱחֲזוּ Num. 32,30. Now and then this חֹלָם also occurs with other verbs, e. g. אֹהַב *I shall love* along with the form אהב.

  Rem. 2. The א of the stem is sometimes omitted also in other forms, as תֹּסֶף *thou takest away*; יַאֲהֵל = יַהֵל *he shall pitch his tent* Jes. 13,20 (See also Rem. 3).

THE נָחִים.

2) The עָתִיד has here often the stem-form with צֵירֶה, e. g. יַאטְם, תֹּאכֵל, יֹאחֵז (Cf. Rem. 3 and § 30 Rem. 3).

Rem. 3. Instead of לֵאמֹר we always find לֵאמֹר; and in a similar manner we find the צֵירֶה in וְאָחַר Gen. 32,5; אָהַב Prov. 8,17; מֵזִין Prov. 17,4; אֶתָיו Jes. 21,12; תֵּאתֶה Mich. 4,8; וַיֵּתֵא Deut. 33,21.

Rem. 4. In the הִפְעִיל the אַ— is sometimes changed into אָ— or —ָ, e. g. אַאֲזִין = אָזִין *I shall listen* Job. 32,11; וַיַּאֲצֶל from יָאֲצַל or יָאֲצִיל *he separated* Num. 11,25; וַיֶּרֶב from יַאֲרֵב or יַאֲרִיב *he set an ambush* 1 Sam. 15,5.

Rem. 5. The verbs פ״א נָחִי sometimes take their forms from the פ״י (see § 32), as וַיּוֹסֶף *and he collected* 2 Sam. 6,1; וַיִּוָּתֵר *and he remained behind* 2 Sam. 20,5.

EXAMPLE OF CONJUGATION.

קַל

אָסַף עָבַר etc.

אסף stem-form עָתִיד.

נאסף	תַּאַסְפוּ תֶּאֱסֹפְנָה	יַאַסְפוּ תֶּאֱסֹפְנָה	אֶאֱסֹף	תֶּאֱסֹף תַּאַסְפִי	יֶאֱסֹף תֶּאֱסֹף

דֶּרֶךְ הַצִּוּוּי

	אספו אספנה		אסף אספי

נִפְעַל

עָבַר

נֶאֱסַפְנוּ	נֶאֶסַפְתֶּם נֶאֶסַפְתֶּן	נֶאֶסְפוּ	נֶאֱסַפְתִּי	נֶאֱסַפְתָּ נֶאֱסַפְתְּ	נֶאֱסַף נֶאֶסְפָה

HEBREW GRAMMAR.

עָתִיד

נֵאָסֵף	תֵּאָסְפוּ תֵּאָסַפְנָה	יֵאָסְפוּ תֵּאָסַפְנָה	אֵאָסֵף	תֵּאָסֵף תֵּאָסְפִי	אָסֵף. תֵּאָסֵף

דֶּרֶךְ הַצִּוּוּי

	הֵאָסְפוּ הֵאָסַפְנָה	הֵאָסֵף הֵאָסְפִי

הִפְעִיל

עָבַר

הֶאֱבַדְנוּ	הֶאֱבַדְתֶּם הֶאֱבַדְתֶּן	הֶאֱבִידוּ הֶאֱבַדְתִּי	הֶאֱבַדְתְּ הֶאֱבַדְתָּ	הֶאֱבִיד הֶאֱבִידָה

עָתִיד

נַאֲבִיד	תַּאֲבִידוּ תַּאֲבֵדְנָה	יַאֲבִידוּ תַּאֲבֵדְנָה	אַאֲבִיד	תַּאֲבִיד תַּאֲבִידִי	יַאֲבִיד תַּאֲבִיד

דֶּרֶךְ הַצִּוּוּי

הַאֲבִידוּ הַאֲבֵדְנָה	הַאֲבֵד הַאֲבִידִי

The הָפְעַל form we find of אחז in 2 Chr. 9.18.

EXERCISES.

הִתְפַּעֵל and פִּעֵל, קַל in אמץ

הִפְעִיל and פָּעַל, פִּעֵל, נִפְעַל " אכל

הִתְפַּעֵל and הִפְעִיל and קַל in אדם and אבל

Verbs belonging to § 27 אהל, אהב, אחז.
" - " § 28 אמר, אזר, אסר.
Verb " §§ 27 and 28 אחר.
Verbs " § 30 אמן, אזן.

THE נָחִים.

Verbs of which פ׳הפעל is י (נָחִוּ פּ״י).

§ 32. There are two different classes of these stems.

A. Verbs of which the פ׳הַפעל really is ו, but which chiefly at the beginning of a word is changed into י

These verbs deviate from the regular conjugation in the following points.

1) In the stem-forms with a preformative of one letter the vowel of this preformative is contracted with the ו into חוֹלָם or שׁוּרְק; e. g. from ולד is formed נוֹלַד, הוֹלִיד, הוֹלַד; and not נְוֹלַד, הַוְלִיד, הָוְלַד.

2) The remaining stem-forms change the ו into י; e. g. הִתְיַלֵּד, יֻלַּד, יְלֵד, וַיֵּלֶד, יָלַד. There are however three exceptions. — a) The second stem-form of the קַל, in which the ו falls away, as לֵד, and in consequence the vowel of the preformative of the עָתִיד becomes long, e. g. יֵלֵד (cf. § 37, 2); — b) the עָתִיד of the נפעל in which the ו remains, e. g. הִוָּלֵד; — c) the הִתְפַּעֵל in which both the ו and the י appear; e. g. הִתְוַדַּע, הִתְיַלֵּד.

3) The stem-form of the עָתִיד and צִוּוּי has here the צֵירֵה, as שֵׁב, לֵד, but the gutturals have by preference פַּתַח, as דַּע.

B. The verbs of which the פ׳הַפֹּעַל really is י deviate in the following points.

1) The שְׁוָא נַח does not occur under the פ׳הפעל, because it is a י; e. g. יִישַׁר not יְיִשַׁר (cf. § 5, 6). For the

46 HEBREW GRAMMAR.

same reason the vowel of the preformative in the הִפְעִיל is צִירֶה, as הֵיטִיב.

2) In the קַל, the form פָּעַל as second stem-form is the more common, as ירש (cf. § 19 Rem. 2).

Rem. 1. These two classes of the פ״י נָחִי are however not always so clearly distinguished as one would expect, as the one class not unfrequently takes its forms from the other class. (See appendix 2).

Rem. 2. Of יצת, יצע, יצג, יצב it is usually said that the פ׳הפעל in the conjugation is missing, as הִצִּיג, וַיִּצֶת, and consequently a class of פ״י חַסְרֵי has been admitted. Yet we find the ו absent also in הֹלֶדֶת from יָלַד Gen. 40,20; וְאֶסְרֵם from יסר Hos. 10,10; אָצַק and אצק from יצק Jes. 44,3; אֲצוּרְךָ from יצר Jer. 1,5; וַיְשַׁרְנָה from ישר 1 Sam. 6,12, although these forms are classified under the פ״י נָחִי. The forms moreover of יצב in which the פ׳הפעל is missing, may be explained by admitting the stem נצב which seems to appear in the noun נְצִיב. A similar collateral stem is possible also with the other verbs, the more so as we have no sufficient probability for admitting a stem with ו and י as פ׳הפעל for the verbs יצג and יצת. In this manner the forms וַיְבֹשְׁהוּ Nah. 1,4; וַיַּגֶּה and וִידֹן Lam. 3,33.53 could perhaps be traced back to a collateral stem of the פ״נ חַסְרֵי.

Rem. 3. Irregular forms are:
a. יִירַע Ps. 138,6; ייטיב Job. 24,21; וֵילִיל Jes. 15,2.
b. וַתִּתְיַצֵּב = וַתֵּחַצַב Ex. 2,4.
c. יְחַמַּתְנִי = יְחֶמָתְנִי Ps. 51,7.

Rem. 4. The פ״י נָחִי rarely borrow their forms from the פ״א נָחִי, as תַּימִינוּ = תַּאֲמִינוּ or תֵּימִינוּ Jes. 30,21; and vice versa. See § 31 Rem. 5.

THE נָחִים.

EXAMPLE OF CONJUGATION.

קַל

A.   יָלַד stem-form עָבַר

לד stem-form עָתִיד

| נֵלֵד | תֵּלַדְנָה תֵּלְדוּ | אֵלֵד תֵּלַדְנָה יֵלְדוּ | תֵּלֵד תֵּלְדִי | יֵלֵד תֵּלֵד |

דֶּרֶךְ הַצִּוּוּי

| | שְׁבוּ שַׁבְנָה or שְׁבֶנָה | | שֵׁב שְׁבִי |

נִפְעַל

נוֹלַד stem-form עָבַר

הִוָּלֵד stem-form עָתִיד

| נִוָּלֵד | תִּוָּלַדְנָה תִּוָּלְדוּ | אִוָּלֵד תִּוָּלַדְנָה יִוָּלְדוּ | תִּוָּלֵד תִּוָּלְדִי | יִוָּלֵד תִּוָּלֵד |

פַּעֵל stem-forms יַלֵּד and יֻלַּד

פֻּעַל stem-form יֻלַּד

הִפְעִיל

Stem-form הוֹלִיד or הוֹלֵד

עָבַר

| הוֹלַדְנוּ | הוֹלַדְתֶּם הוֹלַדְתֶּן | הוֹלַדְתִּי הוֹלִידוּ | הוֹלַדְתָּ הוֹלַדְתְּ | הוֹלִיד הוֹלִידָה |

עָתִיד

נוֹלִיד | תּוֹלִידוּ יוֹלִידוּ | אוֹלִיד | תּוֹלִיד   יוֹלִיד
         תּוֹלַדְנָה תּוֹלַדְנָה | | תּוֹלִידִי תּוֹלִיד

דֶּרֶךְ הַצִּוּוּי

הוֹלִידוּ   הוֹלֵד
הוֹלַדְנָה   הוֹלִידִי

---

stem-form הוֹלַד הָפְעַל

יוֹלַד עָתִיד   הוֹלַד עָבַר

---

stem-form הִתְיַלֵּד הִתְפַּעֵל

B. קַל stem-forms יָנַק and יָנַק

יָרֵשׁ   דֶּרֶךְ הַצִּוּוּי   ;יִינַק עָתִיד   יָנַק עָבַר

נִפְעַל In the עָבַר no stem-form occurs with י, but always with ו, e. g. נוֹעַץ. In the עָתִיד the only stem-form with י is יִירָה from ירה, otherwise always with ו, as תִּוָּרֵא.

הֵיטֵב or הֵיטִיב stem-form הִפְעִיל

יֵיטִיב עָתִיד   הֵיטִיב עָבַר

דֶּרֶךְ הַצִּוּוּי

הֵיטִיבוּ   הֵיטֵב
הֵיטַבְנָה   הֵיטִיבִי

הָפְעַל like the stem-forms of A.

נָחִי ל"א THE

The verbs of which א (נָחִי ל"א) is לְהִפָעֵל

§ 33. The deviations from the conjugation of the regular verb.

1) When the א is the last letter of the word the פַּתַח or חוֹלָם of the עַהַפַעֵל is in the verbal forms changed into קָמֵץ, as יִקְרָא, נִקְרָא, קָרָא.

2) In the עָבַר of קַל the vowel of the עַהַפַעֵל is the same as that of the stem-form, as קָרָאתָ from קָרָא, יָרֵאתִי from יָרֵא.

3) In the other forms when the א is not in the last syllable of the word the עַהַפַעֵל has צֵירֵה, as נִקְרֵאתָ; except with the afformative ־נָה (cf. § 18, 5); e. g. מְצֶאנָה.

Rem. The נָחִי ל"א not unfrequently take their forms from the נָחִי ל"ה e. g. דָכָא = דָכָה Ps. 143,3; חטא = חטה Eccl. 8,12; רפאתי = מלאת 1 Sam. 10,6; וְהִתְנַבִּאתָ = וְהִתְנַבֵּיתָ 2 Kings 2,21; רפאתי from מָלֵא; בּוֹטֶה = בּוֹטֵא Prov. 12,18; קל inf. of מלא = חלא.

EXAMPLE OF CONJUGATION.

קַל

עָבַר stem-form מָצָא.

מָצָאנוּ	מְצָאתֶם מְצָאתֶן	מָצָאתִי מָצְאוּ	מָצָאתָ מָצָאת	מָצָא מָצְאָה

עָתִיד stem-form מְצֹא.

נִמְצָא	תִּמְצְאוּ תִּמְצֶאנָה	יִמְצְאוּ אֶמְצָא	תִּמְצָא תִּמְצְאִי	יִמְצָא תִּמְצָא

HEBREW GRAMMAR.

דֶּרֶךְ הַצִּוּוּי

מָצָא　　　　　מִצְאוּ
מִצְאִי　　　　מְצֶאנָה

דֶּרֶךְ הַמָּקוֹר　מָצֹא, מְצֹא

מָצוּא　בֵּינוֹנִי פָּעוּל　　מוֹצֵא　בֵּינוֹנִי פּוֹעֵל

נִפְעַל

עָבַר stem-form נִמְצָא.

נִמְצֵאנוּ	נִמְצֵאתֶם　נִמְצֵאתִי	נִמְצְאוּ	נִמְצֵאתָ	נִמְצָא
	נִמְצֵאתֶן		נִמְצֵאת	נִמְצְאָה

עָתִיד stem-form הִמָּצֵא.

נִמָּצֵא	תִּמָּצֶאוּ　אֶמָּצֵא	יִמָּצְאוּ	תִּמָּצֵא	יִמָּצֵא
	תִּמָּצֶאנָה	תִּמָּצֶאנָה	תִּמָּצְאִי	תִּמָּצֵא

דֶּרֶךְ הַצִּוּוּי

הִמָּצֵא　　　　הִמָּצְאוּ
הִמָּצְאִי　　　הִמָּצֶאנָה

פִּעֵל

עָבַר stem-form מִלֵּא.

מִלֵּאנוּ	מִלֵּאתֶם　מִלֵּאתִי	מִלְּאוּ	מִלֵּאתָ	מִלֵּא
	מִלֵּאתֶן		מִלֵּאת	מִלְּאָה

עָתִיד stem-form מַלֵּא.

נְמַלֵּא	תְּמַלְּאוּ　אֲמַלֵּא	יְמַלְּאוּ	תְּמַלֵּא	יְמַלֵּא
	תְּמַלֶּאנָה	תְּמַלֶּאנָה	תְּמַלְּאִי	תְּמַלֵּא

דֶּרֶךְ הַצִּוּוּי

מַלֵּא　　　　מַלְּאוּ
מַלְּאִי　　　מַלֶּאנָה

דֶּרֶךְ הַמָּקוֹר　מַלֵּא, מַלֹּא

THE נֶחִי ל"א

פָּעַל

Stem-form מָלָא.

עָבַר

מָלָאנוּ	מְלָאתֶם מְלָאתֶן	מָלֵאתִי מָלְאוּ	מָלֵאתָ מָלֵאת	מָלֵא מָלְאָה

עָתִיד

נִמְלָא	תִּמְלְאוּ תִּמְלֶאנָה	אֶמְלָא יִמְלְאוּ תִּמְלֶאנָה	תִּמְלָא תִּמְלְאִי	יִמְלָא תִּמְלָא

הִפְעִיל

הִמְצִיא stem-form עָבַר.

הִמְצֵאנוּ	הִמְצֵאתֶם הִמְצֵאתֶן	הִמְצֵאתִי הִמְצִיאוּ	הִמְצֵאתָ הִמְצֵאת	הִמְצִיא הִמְצִיאָה

הַמְצֵא, הַמְצִיא stem-form עָתִיד.

נַמְצִיא	תַּמְצִיאוּ תַּמְצֶאנָה	אַמְצִיא יַמְצִיאוּ תַּמְצֶאנָה	תַּמְצִיא תַּמְצִיאִי	יַמְצִיא תַּמְצִיא

דֶּרֶךְ הַצִּוּוּי

הַמְצִיאוּ הַמְצֶאנָה	הַמְצֵא הַמְצִיאִי

הֻפְעַל

Stem-form הֻמְצָא.

עָבַר

הֻמְצֵאנוּ	הֻמְצֵאתֶם הֻמְצֵאתֶן	הֻמְצֵאתִי הֻמְצְאוּ	הֻמְצֵאתָ הֻמְצֵאת	הֻמְצָא הֻמְצְאָה

HEBREW GRAMMAR.

עָתִיד

| נִמְצָא | תִּמְצֶאוּ
תִּמְצֶאנָה | יִמְצְאוּ
תִּמְצֶאנָה | אֶמְצָא | תִּמְצָא
תִּמְצְאִי | יִמְצָא
תִּמְצָא |

הִתְפַּעֵל

Stem-form הִתְמַלֵּא.

עָבַר

| הִתְמַלֵּאנוּ | הִתְמַלֵּאתֶם
הִתְמַלֵּאתֶן | הִתְמַלֵּאתִי
הִתְמַלְּאוּ | הִתְמַלֵּאתָ
הִתְמַלֵּאת | הִתְמַלֵּא
הִתְמַלְּאָה |

עָתִיד

| נִתְמַלֵּא | תִּתְמַלְּאוּ
תִּתְמַלֶּאנָה | יִתְמַלְּאוּ
תִּתְמַלֶּאנָה | אֶתְמַלֵּא | תִּתְמַלֵּא
תִּתְמַלְּאִי | יִתְמַלֵּא
תִּתְמַלֵּא |

דֶּרֶךְ הַצִּוּוּי

| הִתְמַלְּאוּ
הִתְמַלֶּאנָה | הִתְמַלֵּא
הִתְמַלְּאִי |

EXERCISES.

קַל, נִפְעַל, פִּעֵל, פֻּעַל and הִתְפַּעֵל (הדכא) in דכא

„ „ „ „ „ „ (הַטַמֵא) טמא

רפא, חטא, חבא Verbs belonging also to § 26

קרא, ברא „ „ „ § 27

נשא, נבא „ „ „ § 29 „ „ „

יצא belongs also to § 32

ירא „ „ to §§ 27 and 32.

The verbs נָחִי ל״ה.

§ 34. Verbs which really have ה as לְהַפְעֵל have been already spoken of in § 28 c. Here verbs are meant which in appearance only are נָחִי ל״ה but which in reality have ו or י as לְהַפְעֵל.

The deviations in the conjugation of these verbs are the following.

1) When the ו or י occur at the end of a word they are changed into ה, e. g. וַיַּעַשׂ, צִוָּה, עָנָה. In the בֵּינוֹנִי פָּעוּל of the קַל however, and often also in the fem. form of בֵּינוֹנִי פּוֹעֵל of the קַל the י remains, e. g. עָשׂוּי, פּוּרִיָּה, אוֹתִיּוֹת.

2) Before חִירֶק גָּדוֹל and שׁוּרֶק at the end of a word the ו and י are omitted, e. g. צַו, עָשׂוּ, תְּפַסִּי, עֲשִׂי.

3) In the middle of a word the ו is changed into a י, as עָנִיתִי.

4) The עַ׳הַפְעֵל has in the עָבַר before the י in the *transitive* conjugations the חִירֶק and in the *intransitive* conjugations the צֵירֶה, as צִוִּיתִי *I have commanded* צֻוֵּיתִי *I was commanded.*

Rem. 1. The צֵירֶה however occurs now and then also in the *transitive* forms as הֶעֱלֵיתָ along with הֶעֱלִיתָ; and sometimes, but rarely, vice versa, נִגְלֵינוּ = נִגְלִינוּ *we revealed ourselves.*

5) Before the ה the עַ׳הַפְעֵל has in the עָבַר the קָמֶץ, in the עָתִיד and the בֵּינוֹנִי (except the בֵּינוֹנִי פָּעוּל of the קַל see n° 1) the סֶגוֹל, in the דֶּרֶךְ הַצִּוּוּי the צֵירֶה, in the דֶּרֶךְ הַמָּקוֹר often the חוֹלָם, as בָּנָה, צִוָּה, הֶעֱלָה, צִוָּה, יִבְנֶה, יְצַוֶּה, עָשֹׂה, בְּנֵה, הַעֲלֵה, צַוֵּה, בְּנֹה, יְצַוֹּה, יַעֲלֹה.

Rem. 2. The more usual form of the infinitive is the collateral form ending in וֹת, —ֹ, as בְּנוֹת, צַוֺּת.

7) In the 3ᵈ pers. fem. sing. of the עָבר the לְהִפְעֵל is changed into ת after which the ה may be omitted, as עָשְׂתָה and עָשָׂת.

8) The עֲהִפְעֵל has before נָה always the סֶגוֹל, as גְּלֶינָה, תְּצַוֶּינָה (cf. § 33, 2, and § 18, 5).

9) The forms of the עָתִיד are usually shortened, when the ו *conversive* is prefixed to them (§ 85 B 1*e*); e. g. וַיַּעַשׂ, וַיִּבֶן, וַתֵּצַו, or when they express a wish or command, as יַעַשׂ *may he do it* (cf. § 45, 4. 6). Also in the דרך הצווי the לְהִפְעֵל not unfrequently falls away, as הֶרֶף, צַו.

Rem. 3. The stem-letters ו and י more than once reveal themselves. The י regularly in the instances of n° 1 and sometimes also in the verbal forms, as חָסָיו, יִרְבְּיוּן, and in the nomina derived from them, as הִגָּיוֹן. The ו in certain verbal forms, as שָׁלַוְתִּי *I am quiet* Job 3, 25, in the form *mediae e* as participle, שָׁלֵו Job 16, 12, and in nouns derived from such stem-forms, as שַׁלְוָה.

Rem. 4. The נָחִי לְ״ה sometimes borrow their forms from the נָחִי לְ״א, e. g. יַפְרִיא from פרה *to blossom* Hos. 3, 15; וְרָצָאתִי from רצה *to delight in* Ez. 43, 27. (cf. *vice versa* § 33 Rem.).

EXAMPLE OF CONJUGATION.

קל

עָבר stem-form גָּלָה.

| גָּלִינוּ | גָּלִיתֶם
גְּלִיתֶן | גָּלִיתִי | גָּלוּ | גָּלִיתָ
גָּלִית | גָּלָה
גָּלְתָה |

נָחֵי ל״ה THE

עָתִיד stem-form גָּלָה or גָּלֶה.

נִגְלֶה	תִּגְלוּ	יִגְלוּ	תִּגְלֶה
	תִּגְלֶינָה	אֶגְלֶה | תִּגְלֶינָה	תִּגְלִי

דֶּרֶךְ הַצִּוּוּי

גְּלוּ   גְּלֵה
גְּלֶינָה   גְּלִי

דֶּרֶךְ הַמָּקוֹר   גְּלוֹת, גָּלֹה, גְּלֹה, גְּלוֹ

בֵּינוֹנִי פּוֹעֵל

גּוֹלִים   גּוֹלֶה
גּוֹלוֹת   גּוֹלָה

בֵּינוֹנִי פָּעוּל

גְּלוּיִם   גָּלוּי
גְּלוּיוֹת   גְּלוּיָה

נִפְעַל

עָבַר stem-form נִגְלָה.

נִגְלֵינוּ	נִגְלֵיתֶם	נִגְלֵיתִי | נִגְלוּ	נִגְלֵיתָ | נִגְלָה
	נִגְלֵיתֶן		נִגְלֵית | נִגְלְתָה

עָתִיד stem-form הִגָּלֶה or הִגָּלָה.

נִגָּלֶה	תִּגָּלוּ	יִגָּלוּ	תִּגָּלֶה
	תִּגָּלֶינָה	אֶגָּלֶה | תִּגָּלֶינָה	תִּגָּלִי

דֶּרֶךְ הַצִּוּוּי

הִגָּלוּ   הִגָּלֵה
הִגָּלֶינָה   הִגָּלִי

דֶּרֶךְ הַמָּקוֹר   הִגָּלוֹת, הִגָּלֹה, הִגָּלֵה

HEBREW GRAMMAR.

בֵּינוֹנִי

נִגְלִים	נִגְלֶה
נִגְלוֹת	נִגְלָה

פִּעֵל

עָבַר stem-form גִּלָּה.

גִּלִּינוּ	גִּלִּיתֶם / גִּלִּיתֶן	גִּלִּיתִי / גִּלּוּ	גִּלִּיתָ / גִּלִּית	גִּלָּה / גִּלְּתָה

עָתִיד stem-form גַּלֶּה or נַּלֶּה.

נְגַלֶּה	תְּגַלּוּ / תְּגַלֶּינָה	יְגַלּוּ / אֲגַלֶּה / תְּגַלֶּינָה	תְּגַלֶּה / תְּגַלִּי	יְגַלֶּה / תְּגַלֶּה

דֶּרֶךְ הַצִּוּוּי

גַּלּוּ	גַּלֵּה
גַּלֶּינָה	גַּלִּי

גַּלֵּה, נַלֵּה, גַּלּוֹת דֶּרֶךְ הַמָּקוֹר

בֵּינוֹנִי

מְגַלִּים	מְגַלֶּה
מְגַלּוֹת	מְגֻלָּה

פֻּעַל

עָבַר stem-form גֻּלָּה.

גֻּלִּינוּ	גֻּלֵּיתֶם / גֻּלֵּיתֶן	גֻּלֵּיתִי / גֻּלּוּ	גֻּלֵּיתָ / גֻּלֵּית	גֻּלָּה / גֻּלְּתָה

עָתִיד stem-form גֻּלֶּה.

נְגֻלֶּה	תְּגֻלּוּ / תְּגֻלֶּינָה	יְגֻלּוּ / אֲגֻלֶּה / תְּגֻלֶּינָה	תְּגֻלֶּה / תְּגֻלִּי	יְגֻלֶּה / תְּגֻלֶּה

נָחִי ל״ה THE

גָּלָה, גָּלוֹת דֶּרֶךְ הַמָּקוֹר

בֵּינוֹנִי

מְגֻלִּים	מְגֻלֶּה
מְגֻלּוֹת	מְגֻלָּה

הֻפְעִיל

הִגְלָה stem-form עָבַר

הִגְלִיתֶם	הִגְלִיתִי	הִגְלוּ	הִגְלִיתָ
הִגְלִיתֶן			הִגְלִית

הִגְלִינוּ

הִגְלָה
הִגְלְתָה

יַגְלֶה stem-form and יִגְלֶה עָתִיד

תַּגְלוּ	אַגְלֶה	יַגְלוּ	תַּגְלֶה
תַּגְלֶינָה		תַּגְלֶינָה	תַּגְלִי

נַגְלֶה

יִגְלֶה
לֶה

דֶּרֶךְ הַצִּוּוּי

הַגְלוּ	הַגְלֵה
הַגְלֶינָה	הַגְלִי

הַגְלֵה, הַגְלֵה, הַגְלוֹת דֶּרֶךְ הַמָּקוֹר

בֵּינוֹנִי

מַגְלִים	מַגְלֶה
מַגְלוֹת	מַגְלָה

הָפְעַל

הָגְלָה stem-form עָבַר

הָגְלִיתֶם	הָגְלִיתִי	הָגְלוּ	הָגְלִיתָ
הָגְלִיתֶן			הָגְלִית

הָגְלִינוּ

הָגְלָה
הָגְלְתָה

יָגְלֶה stem-form עָתִיד

תָּגְלוּ	אָגְלֶה	יָגְלוּ	תָּגְלֶה
תָּגְלֶינָה		תָּגְלֶינָה	תָּגְלִי

נָגְלֶה

יָגְלֶה
לֶה

HEBREW GRAMMAR.

בֵּינוֹנִי

| מְגֻלִּים | מְגֻלֶּה |
| מְגֻלּוֹת | מְגֻלָּה |

הִתְפַּעֵל

stem-form הִתְגַּלָּה. עָבַר

| וְ | הִתְגַּלִּיתִי | הִתְגַּלִּיתָ | הִתְגַּלָּה |
| הִ | הִתְגַּלּוּ | הִתְגַּלִּית | הִתְגַּלְּתָה |

stem-form הִתְגַּלֶּה and הִתְגַּלֶּה.

| תְּ | יִתְגַּלּוּ | אֶתְגַּלֶּה | תִּתְגַּלֶּה | יִתְגַּלֶּה |
| תְּ | תִּתְגַּלֶּינָה | | תִּתְגַּלִּי | תִּתְגַּלֶּה |

דֶּרֶךְ הַצִּוּוּי

| הִתְגַּלּוּ | הִתְגַּלֵּה |
| הִתְגַּלֶּינָה | הִתְגַּלִּי |

דֶּרֶךְ הַמָּקוֹר הִתְגַּלּוֹת, הִתְגַּלֹה, הִתְגַּלָּה

בֵּינוֹנִי

| מִתְגַּלִּים | מִתְגַּלֶּה |
| מִתְגַּלּוֹת | מִתְגַּלָּה |

VERBS FOR EXERCISE.

פָּעַל and קַל in כלה, נִפְעַל and פָּעֵל
הִתְפַּעֵל and פָּעֵל, נִפְעַל
הִפְעִיל and „
הָפְעַל and הִפְעִיל, פֻּעַל
§ 26 belonging to הָגָה, הָיָה, חִוָּה, חָלָה, חָצָה, עָוָה
§ 27 זָרָה, דָּחָה

Verbs belonging to §§ 26, 27 ראה, חרה.
" " § 29 נשה, נכה.
" " § 31 אפה, אוה, אבה.
" " § 32 ירה, יפה, ידה

CHAPTER VII.

The biliteral Stems.

§ 35. The biliteral stems have a twofold kind of conjugation.

1) When the second stem-letter is doubled.

2) When the stem is restricted to the two stem-letters.

§ 36. The biliteral stems strengthened by duplication of the second stem-letter.

1) The conjugation of these verbs is similar to that of the triliteral stems, e. g. גָּזַז, לִסְבֹּב, סָבַב, וְשִׁנַּנְתָּ, מְחַצְצִים, וָאֶתְחַנַּן, הַרְנִינוּ, מְחֹקָק, חִצְצוּ.

2) Instead of the פִּעֵל, פָּעַל and הִתְפָּעֵל of these verbs, the פּוֹעֵל, פּוֹעַל and הִתְפּוֹעֵל are often used; e. g. קוֹמֵם, הִתְלוֹצֵץ, וְדוֹמַמְתִּי.

The forms of these בִּנְיָנִים are similar to those in place of which they are used.

Rem. When both forms are found, they usually have a different meaning, as מוֹלֵל *to cut*, מִלֵּל *to speak*, הִתְהוֹלֵל *to rage*, הִתְהַלֵּל *to exalt oneself.*

Example of Conjugation.

פּוֹעֵל stem-form רוֹמֵם.

עָבַר

רוֹמַמְנוּ	רוֹמַמְתֶּם רוֹמַמְתֶּן	רוֹמְמוּ	רוֹמַמְתִּי	רוֹמֵם רוֹמְמָה
			רוֹמַמְתָּ רוֹמַמְתְּ	

עָתִיד

נְרוֹמֵם	תְּרוֹמְמוּ תְּרוֹמַמְנָה	יְרוֹמְמוּ תְּרוֹמַמְנָה	אֲרוֹמֵם	יְרוֹמֵם תְּרוֹמֵם
			תְּרוֹמֵם תְּרוֹמְמִי	

דֶּרֶךְ הַצִּוּוּי

רוֹמְמוּ	רוֹמֵם
רוֹמַמְנָה	רוֹמְמִי

דֶּרֶךְ הַמָּקוֹר   רוֹמֵם

בֵּינוֹנִי

מְרוֹמְמִים	מְרוֹמָם
מְרוֹמְמוֹת	מְרוֹמָמָה or מְרוֹמֶמֶת

פֻּעַל stem-form רוֹמָם. Similar to פּוֹעֵל except that the last syllable is מַם or מָם instead of מֵם.

הִתְפּוֹעֵל stem-form הִתְרוֹמֵם, like פּוֹעֵל with the preformative נִתְ, אֶתְ, תִּתְ, יִתְ, הִתְ, and מִתְ.

---

§ 37. The conjugation of the biliteral stems restricted to the two stem-letters.

1) This conjugation only occurs in the 4 בִּנְיָנִים, קַל, הָפְעַל, הִפְעִיל, נִפְעַל. Its forms are very similar to those

of the חַסְרֵי פּ׳, of which the two last stem-letters alone occur.

2) The preformative here has a vowel (cf. on the contrary § 18, 1). The vowel becomes a half-vowel when the accent is shifted back, e. g. תָּמֻתְנָה = תְּמוּתֶינָה from the stem מוּת; יָגוּדֶנּוּ from גוּד. (cf. § 18, 2).

3) The stem-vowel, because here it is the *only* vowel of the stem, usually is retained even in the 3ᵈ pers. fem. and plur. (cf. on the contrary § 18, 3) e. g. רַבּוּ from רַב *to be much* or *many*; יָחֹגּוּ from חַג *to turn round*; הֵחֵלָּה from הֵחֵל *to begin*. The חוֹלָם however as stem-vowel sometimes becomes a half-vowel (cf. n° 1) e. g. יִקְּדוּ (sing. יִקֹּד) *to bow*; יִתַּמּוּ (sing. יִתֹּם) *to be completed*.

Rem. 1. The same thing now and then occurs with forms which are not like the corresponding forms of the חַסְרֵי פּ׳, as וְנָבְלָה = וְנַבְּלָה *and we will confound*; תְּצֻרִי = תֵּצָרִי *thou wilt be oppressed*.

4) The 1ˢᵗ and 2ᵈ pers. have a prolonged collateral form with חוֹלָם after the second stem-letter, as בִּינוֹתָ – בַּנְתָּ *thou understandest*; הֲנִיפוֹתִי = הֲנַפְתִּי *I wave*.

5) Before the termination ־נָה the preceding open syllable has the סְגוֹל, as תְּמוּתֶינָה (cf. § 18, 5).

6) Frequently a דָּגֵשׁ is found even after a long vowel, as הֵחֵלָּה, יָחֹגּוּ.

Rem. 2. The interchange of affiliated vowels is here very common (cf. § 4 Rem. 6).

בִּנְיָן קַל

§ 38. (*a*) The verbal forms.

1) The stem-forms of the עָבר are like those of the triliteral stems when their first stem-letter is omitted (See § 19 with Rém. 1); e. g. בוֹשׁ, מֵת, תַּם.

In addition to these there are stem-forms with קָמֵץ and חִירק, as קָם *to rise up,* דִיג *to fish.*

2) The conjugation is according to § 37, 3, except that the צירה shows itself only in the 3ᵈ pers., and in the other forms is changed into פַתח (cf. § 19 Rem. 1); e. g. מֵת, מֵתָה, מַתְנוּ.

Rem. 1. The stem-forms with חִירק are very rare. They only occur in וְדִיגוּם *and they shall fish* Jer. 16, 16; וּפְשַׁתֶּם *and ye shall spread yourselves* Mal. 3, 20; רִיבוֹתִי *thou strivest* Job. 33, 13; בִינוֹתִי *I understood* Dan. 9, 2.

Rem. 2. The קָמֵץ is sometimes lengthened by a subsequent א; e. g. קָם = קָאם Hos. 10, 14; שָׁט = שָׁאט Ez. 28, 24.

3) The stem-form of the עָתיד and צווי has חוֹלָם or פַתח (See § 19 with Rem. 2). But we find also many stem-forms with חִירק and שׁוּרק; e. g. סֹב *to turn,* קַל *to be light,* קוּם, רִיב.

The stem-form with פַתח is naturally the more common with the guttural verbs; e. g. חַם *to be hot;* מַר *to be bitter,* רַע *to be bad.*

4) The vowel of the preformative is צירה, קָמֵץ or חִירק; viz. קָמֵץ with all the stem-forms, חִירק when the stem-

form has חוֹלָם, and צירה when it has פַּתַח; e. g. יָסֹב, יָלֻן *to pass the night*, יָסֹב = יסב, יָקוּם, יָרִיב, יֵקַל:

Rem. 3. We very seldom find קָמֵץ before a stem with פַּתַח. Before the same stem we also occasionally find a preformative with הִירֶק, as יִסַּג *he draws back*, which before a guttural is sometimes changed into פַּתַח, e. g. יַחַד *he sharpens*, תַּחַשׁ *thou makest haste*. The צירה is found before בוֹשׁ, therefore יֵבוֹשׁ.

Rem. 4. The long vowel of the 2^d stem-form is shortened when the וּ֯הַמְהַפֵּךְ (§ 85 B 1 c en d) is prefixed to it; e. g. וַיָּסָב from יָסֹב; וַיָּקָם from יָקוּם, וַיָּרֶב from יָרִיב, וַיָּרֶם from יָרָם, וַיָּצַץ. Num. 17, 23 however makes an exception. When one of the two stem-letters is a guttural the vowel generally is פַּתַח; e. g. וַיָּסַר from יָסוּר, וַיָּנַע from יָנוּעַ. Yet we find וַיָּעָז, וַתָּחָס, וַיִּחַם from תָּעֹז, יָעוּף, תָּחוֹם, יָחֹם. In וְיָבוֹא the long vowel remains, which in consequence retains the accent.

Rem. 5. The חוֹלָם and שׁוּרֶק here are frequently interchanged, as שׁוֹב = שׁוּב.

(*b*) The nominal forms.

1) The infinitive has the stem-form of the עָתִיד (cf. § 16 B*a*), as שִׂים = שׂוֹם = שֹׂם, רֹד.

2) The קַל of these stems has only one participle and this has the stem-form of the עָבַר, as מָד *measuring*, רָשׁ *being poor*, לֵץ *scoffing*, בָּס *treading*. In addition to this the participle has in a few instances the stem-form שׁוּרֶק, as סוּר *departing*, occasionally with a passive meaning like the בינוני פָעוּל of the triliteral stems, e. g. סוּג *being hedged in*, חוּשׁ *being armed*.

EXAMPLE OF CONJUGATION.

עָבַר

Stem-form סַב.

| סַבּוֹנוּ | סַבּוֹתֶם
סַבּוֹתֶן | סַבּוֹתִי סַבּוּ | סַבּוֹתָ
סַבּוֹת | סַב
סַבָּה |

Stem-form מֵת.

| מַתְנוּ | מַתֶּם
מַתֶּן | מַתִּי מֵתוּ | מַתָּ
מַתְּ | מֵת
מֵתָה |

Stem-form בֹּשׁ.

| בֹּשְׁנוּ | בָּשְׁתֶּם
בָּשְׁתֶּן | בָּשְׁתִּי בֹּשׁוּ | בָּשְׁתָּ
בָּשְׁתְּ | בֹּשׁ
בֹּשָׁה |

Stem-form קָם.

| קַמְנוּ | קַמְתֶּם
קַמְתֶּן | קַמְתִּי קָמוּ | קַמְתָּ
קַמְתְּ | קָם
קָמָה |

עָתִיד

Stem-form חוֹלֶם.

| נָסֹב | תָּסֹבּוּ
תְּסֻבְנָה or תְּסֻבֶּינָה or תסבינה | יָסֹבּוּ אָסֹב | יָסֹב תָּסֹב
תָּסֹבִּי תָּסֹב |

Stem-form פַּתַח.

| נֵחַת | תֵּחַתּוּ
תֶּחֱתַנָה or תֵּחַתְנָה or תְּחִתֶּינָה | יֵחַתּוּ אֵחַת | יֵחַת תֵּחַת
תֵּחַתִּי תֵּחַת |

Stem-form חִירֶק.

| נָשִׂים | תָּשִׂימוּ
תְּשִׂימֶינָה | יָשִׂימוּ אָשִׂים | תָּשִׂים יָשִׂים
תָּשִׂימִי תָּשִׂים |

THE BILITERAL STEMS.

Stem-form שׁוּרֻק.

נָקוּם	תָּקוּמוּ	יָקוּמוּ	אָקוּם	יָקוּם · תָּקוּם
	תָּקֹמְנָה or תְּקוּמֶינָה	תָּקֹמְנָה or תְּקוּמֶינָה		תָּקוּם · תָּקוּמִי

דֶּרֶךְ הַצִּוּוּי

	stem-form שִׂים	stem-form קוּם	stem-form סֹב
	שִׂים	קוּם	סֹב
שִׂימוּ	קוּמוּ	סֹבּוּ
does not occur	שִׂימוּ	קוּמִי	סֹבִּי
	קֹמְנָה	סֻבְנָה

The דֶּרֶךְ הַצִּוּוּי with the stem-form פַּתַח is not found.

דֶּרֶךְ הַמָּקוֹר

רֹד, שִׂים, קוּם, סֹב

בֵּינוֹנִי

מֵתִים	מֵת	קָמִים	קָם	סַבִּים	סַב
מֵתוֹת	מֵתָה	קָמוֹת	קָמָה	סַבּוֹת	סַבָּה
רִיבִים	רָב	סוֹרִים	סוֹר	בּוֹשִׁים	בּוֹשׁ
רִיבוֹת	רִיבָה	סוֹרוֹת	סוֹרָה	בּוֹשׁוֹת	בּוֹשָׁה

בִּנְיָן נִפְעַל

§ 39. (*a*) The verbal forms.

1) The stem-form of the עָבַר is like that of a triliteral verb in the קַל after נ has been prefixed to the stem (cf. § 19 with Rem. 1). The conjugation is according to § 37, 3 and 6; e. g. נָמַק *to perish*, נָגֹל *to be rolled*, נָמֵס *to melt*; נָמַסָה, נָגֹלָה, נָמַקָה.

Rem. 1. The preformative sometimes has חִירֶק, as נחל *to be defiled*, which before a guttural is changed into צֵרָה, e. g. נֵאַר *to be cursed*, נהם *to be disturbed*; rarely חוֹלֶם, as נוֹעַז *to become powerful*.

Rem. 2. The stem-form with צֵירָה is the least common.

2) The stem-form of עָתִיד and צִוּוּי is formed by prefixing the preformative הִנ with the omission of the נ (cf. § 20). The stem has חוֹלָם or פַּתַח like the triliteral verbs in the קַל, rarely צִירֶה, as הָמַק, הִגוֹל, הָמֵס.

The חִירֶק of the preformative becomes צִירה before a guttural; as הֵאוֹר *to be made light*, הֵרָם *to be raised, to be taken away*.

(*b*) The nominal forms.

1) The infinitive has the stem-form of the עָתִיד (cf. § 16 B*a*), as הִבּוֹק *to be emptied*, הֵחַל and הֵחֵל · הָמֵם.

2) The participle has the stem-form of the עָבַר (cf. § 16 B*b* 2), e. g. נָכוֹן *being established*; נָקֵל and נֵקַל *light*.

The vowel of the preformative becomes a half-vowel, as is the case with the other nomina, when the first stem-letter loses its accent, (cf. § 59 A *c* 1 and § 88 II 3); e. g. נְמַגִּים, נְשַׁמּוֹת, נְבֹכִים.

Rem. 3. The use of the נִפְעַל is on the whole very limited, for many biliteral stems are intransitive in the קַל. When the נִפְעַל occurs it is either the passive of הִפְעִיל, as נָמַר *to be changed* from הֵמִיר, or it differs in meaning but little from the קַל, as נֵקַל from קַל *to be light*, נָפוֹץ *to be dispersed* from פּוּץ. (cf. תִּשָּׁאֶה and שְׂאוּ Jes. 6,11).

If the קַל is transitive the נפעל naturally is passive, as נָבֹק *to be emptied* from בָּק.

THE BILITERAL STEMS.

EXAMPLE OF CONJUGATION.

עָבַר

Stem-form נָסַב.

| נְסַבּוֹנוּ | נְסַבּוֹתֶם
נְסַבּוֹתֶן | נָסַבּוּ | נְסַבּוֹתִי | נְסַבּוֹתָ
נְסַבּוֹת | נָסַב
נָסַבָּה |

Stem-form נָמֹג.

| נְמֹגְנוּ | נְמֹגְתֶם
נְמֹגְתֶן | נָמֹגוּ | נְמֹגְתִי | נְמֹגוֹתָ
נְמֹגוֹת | נָמֹג
נָמֹגָה |

עָתִיד

Stem-form הֵסַב.

| נָסֵב | תָּסֵבּוּ
תְּסַבְנָה | יָסֵבּוּ
תְּסַבְנָה | אָסֵב | תָּסֵב
תְּסַבִּי | יָסֵב
תָּסֵב |

Stem-form הָמֹג.

| נָמֹג | תָּמֹגוּ
תְּמֹגְנָה | יָמֹגוּ
תְּמֹגְנָה | אָמֹג | תָּמֹג
תָּמֹגִי | יָמֹג
תָּמֹג |

דֶּרֶךְ הַצִּוּוּי

הָמֹגוּ   הָמֹג
הָמֹגְנָה   הָמֹגִי

הִמֵּס הָמֹג   דֶּרֶךְ הַמָּקוֹר

בֵּינוֹנִי

| נמגים | נָמֹג | נְסַבִּים | נָסַב |
| נמגות | נָמֹגָה | נְסַבּוֹת | נְסַבָּה |

בִּנְיָן הִפְעִיל

§ 40. (*a*) The verbal forms.

1) The stem-form of the עָבַר is formed by prefixing

ה to the stem. The stem has חִירֶק (cf. § 23) צֵירֶה and chiefly with gutturals הֵפִיר, הֵפֵר, הָפֵר; פַּתַח to break.

The conjugation is like that of the triliteral stems (cf. § 23). In the forms however which are lengthened, the first stem-letter always has חִירֶק or צֵירֶה, as הֲנִיפוֹתָ from הֵנִיף to wave; הֲקִלּוֹת from הֵקַל to make light; הֲרִמוֹתָ and הֲרִימוֹת to raise.

2) When the accent is shifted (cf. § 37, 2) the half-vowel of the preformative frequently becomes before a guttural, פַּתַח, as הַחִלּוֹתָ thou hast begun; הַעִידֹתִי I testified.

Rem. 1. The preformative of בֹּשׁ frequently has חוֹלֶם, as הוֹבִישׁ, הוֹבַשְׁתָּ, but the prolonged forms are like those of the other stems, as הֲבִישׁוֹתָ thou makest ashamed.

3) The stem-form of the עָתִיד and צִוּוּי has חִירֶק or צֵירֶה (cf. § 23), and with the gutturals sometimes פַּתַח; whilst the preformative is הָ; e. g. הָצֵר, הָפֵר, הָפִיר.

The preformative also sometimes has פַּתַח, as הַסִית and הָסִית to incite (cf. § 37, 1) occasionally with difference of meaning; e. g. הָחֵל to begin, הַחֵל to profane.

Rem. 2. Certain stems have in עָבַר a collateral form resembling that of the פ' חסרי, and generally with difference of meaning, as הֵנִיחַ to give rest, הִנִּיחַ to let loose; with other stems this form is the only stem-form found, as הִנִּיר to make to flow. These verbs are conjugated like the פ' חסרי in the הִפְעִיל; and sometimes lose their stem-vowel (cf. § 18 Rem. 1), as וַיִּכְתוּ and they crushed.

Rem. 3. The חִירֶק and צֵירֶה are here often interchanged (§ 37 Rem. 2), as יָנֵר and יַנִּיר, הֶעֱרָתָ and הָעִידוֹת.

THE BILITERAL STEMS.

4) The forms of the עָתִיד with וְהַמְהַפֵּךְ shorten the stem-vowel at the end of the word into סֶגוֹל, and with gutturals generally into פַּתַח, as וַיָּמָת, וַיַּעַד.

(*b*) The nominal forms.

1) The infinitive (cf. § 16 B*a*) of verbs with a guttural or ר, sometimes has פַּתַח, as לְהָבַר *in order to cleanse* Jer. 4,11.

Rem. 4. A strange feminine form is הֲנָפָה *to sift* Jes. 30,28.

2) The participle (§ 16 B*b* 2) of the verbs which in the conjugation resemble the חסרי פ' is like that of these verbs; as מֵסִית, מָלִין *murmuring*.

EXAMPLE OF CONJUGATION.

עבר

Stem-form הֵרִים.

	הרמתם		הֲרִמֹתָ		הֵרִים
	הֲרִימוֹתֶם		הֲרִימוֹתָ		
הֲרִמְנוּ	הֲרִימֹתֶם		הֲרִמוֹתָ		
הֲרִימוֹנוּ	הֲרִמְתֶּן	הֵרִימוּ	הֲרִימוֹתִי	הֵרִימָה
הֲרִמוֹנוּ	הֲרִימֹתֶן		הֲרִימוֹתִי	הרימות	
	הֲרִמְתֶּן			הרמות	

Stem-form הֵשַׁם.

	השמתם		הֲשִׁמְתָ		הֵשַׁם
הֲשִׁמְנוּ	הֲשִׁמוֹתֶם		הֲשִׁמוֹתָ		
הֲשִׁמוֹנוּ	הֲשַׁמְתֶּן	הֵשַׁמּוּ	הֲשִׁמוֹתִי	הֵשַׁמָּה
	הֲשַׁמוֹתֶן			הֲשִׁמוֹת	

HEBREW GRAMMAR.

Stem-form הֵחֵל.

הֶחֱלַֽנוּ	הֶחֱלֹתֶם		הֶחֱלֹתִי	הֶחֱלַתָּ	הֵחֵל
הֶחֱלֹונוּ	הֶחֱלֹתֶן	הֵחֵלּוּ	הֶחֱלֹותִי	הֶחֱלֹותָ	
				הֶחֱלַתְּ	הֵחֵלָה
				הֶחֱלֹות	

Stem-form הֵנִים.

הֲנַחְנוּ	הֲנַחְתֶּם	הֱנִיחוּ	הֲנִחֹתִי	הֲנַחְתָּ	הֵנִים
	הֲנַחְתֶּן			הֲנַחְתְּ	הֵנִיחָה

Stem-form הֵרִים.

עָתִיד

נָרִים	תָּרִימוּ		יָרִימוּ	אָרִים	תָּרִים	יָרִים
	תָּרִימְנָה (תְּרִימֶנָה)		תָּרִימְנָה (תְּרִימֶנָה)		תָּרִימִי	תָּרִים

Stem-form הָחֵל.

נָחֵל	תָּחֵלּוּ		יָחֵלּוּ	אָחֵל	תָּחֵל	יָחֵל
	תְּחַלֶּינָה		תְּחַלֶּינָה		תָּחֵלִּי	תָּחֵל

Stem-form הֻנִּים.

נֻנִּים	תֻּנִּיחוּ		יֻנִּיחוּ	אֻנִּים	תֻּנִּים	יֻנִּים
	תֻּנַּחְנָה or תֻּנִּחְנָה		תֻּנַּחְנָה or תֻּנִּחְנָה		תֻּנִּיחִי	תֻּנִּים

Stem-form הֻתַּם.

נֻתַּם (עֻתַּם)	תֻּתַּמּוּ		יֻתַּמּוּ	אֻתַּם (אָתֳּם)	תֻּתַּם	יֻתַּם
	תֻּתַּמֶּינָה		תֻּתַּמֶּינָה		תֻּתַּמִּי	תֻּתַּם

דֶּרֶךְ הַצִּוּוּי

הָקִימוּ	הָקֵם		הָפִירוּ	הָפֵר
הָקֵמְנָה or הָקִימְנָה	הָקִימִי		הָפֵרְנָה	הָפֵרִי

	הַנִּיחוּ	הַנַּח or הָנִיחַ
	הַנַּחְנָה	הָנִיחִי

THE BILITERAL STEMS.

הָבַר, הַנִּיחַ, הָפַר, הָקִים הֶרֶךְ הַמָּקוֹר

בֵּינוֹנִי

מָאוֹר	מְאִירִים	מֵרַע	מְרֵעִים
מְאִירָה	מְאִירוֹת	מְרֵעָה	מְרֵעוֹת
מֵסֵב	מְסִבִּים	מֵלִין	מְלִינִים
מְסִבָּה	מְסִבּוֹת	מְלִינָה	מְלִינוֹת

בִּנְיַן הָפְעַל

§ 41. A. The verbal forms.

The conjugation is entirely like that of the חֲסָרֵי פ׳, except that the קִבּוּץ is often interchanged for the שׁוּרֶק, e. g. הָבַן and הוּבַן *to be made ready*.

Rem. 1. The stem-vowel is sometimes retained in the conjugation, e. g. יֻכַּתּוּ *they will be crushed* Jer. 46,5.

Rem. 2. The stem נח has in the 3ᵈ person a collateral form with חִירֶק, as הֻנִּיחַ *to be laid down* Zech. 5,11.

B. The nominal forms.

1) The infinitive only occurs in הָשַּׁמָּה *to be devastated* Lev. 26,34 et seq.

2) The final vowel of the participle is sometimes prolonged (cf. § 19 B*ᵇ* 3), e. g. מֻנָד *to be moved*, מוּשָׁב *to be brought back*.

Rem. 3. The forms of the הָפְעַל are on the whole very rare with the biliteral stems.

HEBREW GRAMMAR.

EXEMPLE OF CONJUGATION.

עָבַר

Stem-form הוּשַׁב.

| הוּשַׁבְנוּ | הוּשַׁבְתֶּם
הוּשַׁבְתֶּן | הוּשְׁבוּ | הוּשַׁבְתִּי | הוּשַׁבְתָּ
הוּשַׁבְתְּ | הוּשַׁב
הוּשְׁבָה |

Stem-form הֻכַּת (belongs also to § 30 *b*).

| הֻכַּתְנוּ | הֻכַּתֶּם
הֻכַּתֶּן | הֻכּוּ | הֻכֵּתִי | הֻכַּתָּ
הֻכַּתְּ | הֻכַּת
הֻכְּתָה |

עָתִיד

Stem-form הוּשַׁב.

| נוּשַׁב | תּוּשְׁבוּ
תּוּשַׁבְנָה | יוּשְׁבוּ
תּוּשַׁבְנָה | אוּשַׁב | תּוּשַׁב
תּוּשְׁבִי | יוּשַׁב
תּוּשַׁב |

Stem-form הֻכַּת.

| נֻכַּה | תֻּכּוּ
תֻּכַּתְנָה | יֻכּוּ
תֻּכַּתְנָה | אֻכַּת | תֻּכַּת
תֻכִּתִי | יֻכַּת
תֻּכַּת |

הַשֵּׁם (הֻכַּת הוּשַׁב)   דֶּרֶךְ הַמָּקוֹר

בֵּינוֹנִי

| מוּסַבִּים
מוּסַבּוֹת | מוּסָב
מוּסַבָּה | מוּשָׁבִים
מוּשָׁבוֹת | מוּשָׁב
מוּשָׁבָה |

VERBS FOR EXERCISE.

כל נִפְעַל and קַל in כף ;הִפְעִיל and קַל in
מס „ קַל, נפעל and הפעיל
מד „ קַל, נִפְעַל, פּוֹעֵל and הִתְפּוֹעֵל
מל „ קַל, נִפְעַל, פּוֹעֵל and הִפְעִיל and הִתְפּוֹעֵל
נר „ קַל, פּוֹעֵל, הִפְעִיל and התפועל

THE BILITERAL STEMS.

§ 42. The פָּעֵל, פִּעֵל and הִתְפַּעֵל of the biliteral stems.

1) In order to give to a biliteral verb the meaning of the פִּעֵל, פָּעֵל and הִתְפַּעֵל, the conjugations mentioned in § 36 are used. In addition to these, there are other conjugations serving the same purpose, which are obtained by doubling both stem-letters, e. g. כִּלְכֵּל, שִׁעֲשַׁע, הִתְמַהְמַהּ.

2) They are conjugated in the same manner as the פִּעֵל, פָּעֵל and הִתְפַּעֵל of the triliteral stems, with this difference that here the vowel of the first stem-letter is followed by a נַח נִרְאֶה (cf. § 4 Rem. 2) and that in the פִּעֵל the קִבּוּץ is often interchanged for the קָמַץ חָטוּף (cf. § 4 Rem. 6).

EXAMPLE OF CONJUGATION.

כלכל stem (פִּלְפֵּל) פִּעֵל
עָבַר כִּלְכֵּל, כִּלְכְּלָה, כִּלְכַּלְתָּ etc.
עָתִיד יְכַלְכֵּל, תְּכַלְכֵּל etc.

כלכל stem (פָּלְפַּל, פָּלְפֵּל) פָּעֵל
כָּלְכַּל, כָּלְכְּלָה, כָּלְכַּלְתָּ etc.

התכלכל stem (הִתְפַּלְפֵּל) הִתְפַּעֵל
הִתְכַּלְכֵּל, הִתְכַּלְכְּלָה, הִתְכַּלְכַּלְתָּ etc.

Rem. 1. Also with the triliteral stems one or more letters are occasionally doubled.

If the לְ הַפֹּעַל alone is doubled (פִּעֲלֵל and פָּעֲלַל § 13 n⁰ 15 and 16) the verb is conjugated, as if the two first stem-letters were but one letter, e. g. אָמְלְלוּ, שַׁאֲנַנּוּ. If the two last stem-letters are doubled, (פִּעֲלְעַל § 13 n⁰ 17), they are simply placed between the פ' and ע'הַפֹּעַל, e. g. חֲמַרְמָרוּ.

Rem. 2. There are moreover forms which could be referred to a quadriliteral stem, but in which the regular triliteral stem may easily be discovered. They are the following פִּרְשֵׁז Job 26,9; יְכַרְסְמֶנָּה Ps. 80,14; מְכֻרְבָּל 1 Chr. 15,27; רָטֲפַשׁ Job 33,25; וְאַשְׂמְאִילָה Gen. 13,9.

§ 43. Deviations from the regular conjugation of the biliteral stems.

1) The same reasons which cause certain deviations with the triliteral stems, also occur here, and generally with the same consequences; e. g. מְסַתּוֹלֵל Ex. 9,17; תְּתַמָּם Ps. 18,26; אָרוֹמָם Jes. 33,10; יִשְׁתַּקְשְׁקוּן Nah. 2,5; הִשְׁתָּרֵר Num. 16,13 from רם, תם, שק, סל and שר (according to § 25 Rem. 2); נְאָרִים Mal. 3,9; יֵרַד (§ 26 Rem. 3); מַתַי (§ 30a); תָּרֹנָּה (§ 28 Rem. § 38,9); יָמַר, הֵפַר הֲבֵאתִי, בָּאתָ (§ 30b); (§ 33,2).

2) If, however, the 1st stem-letter is א, י or נ, either the verb is conjugated with three letters, as ילל, or else the 1st stem-letter does *not* follow the rules of §§ 31, 32 and 29, because it here serves as consonant and cannot be missed, e. g. נָוֹד, וַיָּאִיצוּ.

THE BILITERAL STEMS.

VERBS FOR EXERCISE.

Verbs belonging to § 26.

הל in קַל, נִפְעַל, פֻּעַל, הִפְעִיל, הִתְפַּעֵל and הִתְפּוֹעֵל
חם „ „ and נִפְעַל;
חל „ all the בנינים.
רם „ קל נִפְעַל, פֻּעַל, הִפְעִיל, הָפְעַל and הִתְפּוֹעֵל

Verbs belonging to § 28.

נח „ „ הָפְעַל and נִפְעַל.
נע „ „ „ „ הִפְעִיל.
שח „ „ „ „ הִתְפּוֹעֵל.

Verbs belonging to §§ 26 and 28.

אר „ „ הָפְעַל and הִפְעִיל, פֻּעֵל, נִפְעַל.
ער „ „ הִתְפּוֹעֵל and הִפְעִיל.
רע „ „ הִתְפּוֹעֵל and הפעיל, פועל.

Verbs belonging to § 30.

בן „ „ הָפְעַל and הִפְעִיל, פּוֹעֵל, נִפְעַל.
בן „ „ הִתְפּוֹעֵל and הִפְעִיל, פּוֹעֵל, נִפְעַל.
כת „ „ הָפְעַל and הִפְעִיל, פֻּעַל.
מת „ „ הָפְעַל and הִפְעִיל, פּוֹעֵל.

Verbs belonging to §§ 26 and 30.

חן „ „ הִתְפַעֵל and הָפְעַל, פּוֹעֵל, פֻּעַל, נִפְעַל.
רן „ „ הִתְפּוֹעֵל and הִפְעִיל, פֻּעַל, פֻּעֵל.

Verbs belonging to § 33.

בא „ „ הָפְעַל and הִפְעִיל.
קא „ „ and הִפְעִיל.

CHAPTER VIII.

The alterations which the verbal forms undergo.

§ 44. 1) The verbal forms undergo a threefold kind of alteration.

a. to modify their signification;
b. to connect them with suffixes;
c. when ו *conversive* is prefixed to them.

2) *a* only occurs with the עָתִיד and דֶרֶךְ הַצִּוּוּי; *b* with all the verbal forms of a transitive verb; *c* only with the עָבַר and the עָתִיד.

3) The alterations of *b* and *c* are restricted to the change of vowels.

Rem. *c* is treated of later on see § 85 B 1.

§ 45. The longer, shorter or modified forms of the עָתִיד and דרך הצווי.

1) The forms of the עָתִיד are sometimes lengthened through the addition of ־ָה with the accent, for the purpose of strengthening their meaning *modus adhortativus*. With the triliteral stems the rule given in § 18, 3.4 is to be here applied, e. g. אֶזְכְּרָה from אזכר *I will remember*, in הִפְעִיל אַזְכִּירָה from אַזְכִּיר.

Rem. 1. The prolonged form almost exclusively occurs with the 1st pers. sing. and plur., rarely with the other persons, as וְתָבוֹאָה *and let it come* Jes. 5,19.

Rem. 2. The prolongation is sometimes made by ־ֶה, e. g. יְרַשְּׁנֶה Ps. 20,4; and when fem. by תָה, e. g. תְבוֹאָתָה Deut. 33,16.

ALTERATIONS OF THE VERBAL FORMS. 77

2) The imperative masc. sing. also is sometimes prolonged under the rule set out in § 18,3; e. g. שָׁמְרָה, אֶסְפָה, שִׁכְבָה. The influence of a guttural or ר as ע׳ or ל׳ הַפְעַל now and then effects the lengthening of the vowel of the penultimate stem-letter, in consequence of which the half-vowel of the פ׳ הַפְעַל remains, e. g. יִרְשָׁה, שִׁמְעָה from יָרַשׁ, שְׁמַע.

Rem. 3. Here also the termination ־ָה occasionally is found instead of ־ָה, as רבה Judges 9,29.

3) On the otherhand the forms of the עָתִיד and דֶּרֶךְ הַצִּוּוּי sometimes undergo an *abbreviation* or *change of vowels* for the purpose of expressing a wish (*modus jussivus*).

4) The *abbreviation* only occurs with the verbs נָחִי ל״ה (§ 34), when the ה falls away after the צֵירֵה or סֶגוֹל in the דֶּרֶךְ הַצִּוּוּי or עָתִיד, which omission now and then influences the remaining vowels, as יְצַו from יְצַוֶּה, יֶגֶל from יִגְלֶה, יֵט from יִטֶּה, צַו from צַוֵּה, הֶרֶף from הַרְפֵּה. With the דֶּרֶךְ הַצִּוּוּי it changes a wish into a command.

5) The *change of vowels* only occurs with the forms of the עָתִיד, when the last syllable is חִירֶק or שׁוּרֶק. The former becomes צֵירֶה the latter חוֹלָם, e. g. יַפְקֵד from יַפְקִיד, יָרֵב from יָרִיב, יָקֹם from יָקוּם.

6) Finally an *abbreviation* or *change of vowels* occurs with the 2ᵈ and 3ʳᵈ pers. of the עָתִיד when they are connected with the negative אַל, to express a *prohibition*. The חִירֶק of the last syllable then becomes צֵירֶה with the triliteral stems, and סֶגוֹל with the biliteral stems;

whilst with the נָחִי ל״ה the ה falls away, causing thereby an alteration of vowels; e. g. אַל־תַּשְׁחֵת ,תַּשְׁחִית from אַל־תָּשֵׁת, תָּשִׁית from אַל־תִּפֶן ,תָּפֶן from תִּפְנֶה.

Rem. 4. Exceptions are אַל־יֵשֶׁם 1 Sam. 22,15; 2 Sam. 13,33; and אַל־תָּשֵׁב Ps. 132,10; 2 Chr. 6,42.

§ 46. The Pronominal Suffixes (הַכִּנּוּיִם).

1) When the object of a transitive verb is a personal pronoun, it may be expressed by את with a suffix, as אֹתִי *me*, אֹתְךָ *thee*, אֹתוֹ *him*. Generally however, when the object needs not be particularly emphasised, it is added as a suffix to the verbal form.

2) These suffixes are:

	Plur.		Sing.	
us	־נוּ ־ֵנוּ ־ָנוּ	me	־ִי ־ֵנִי ־ַנִי ־ְנִי	1st
you	־כֶם	thee	־ךָ ־ְךָ	m. } 2d
you (does not occur)	־כֶן or ־ְכֶן	thee	־ךְ ־ֵךְ ־ָךְ ־ִךְ	f.
them	־ם ־ָם ־ֵם ־הֶם	him	־וֹ ־ֵהוּ ־ְהוּ ־ֵו ־ָהוּ	m. } 3d
them	־ן ־ָן ־ֵן	her	־ָהּ ־ָה ־ֶהָ	f.

3) It appears from the preceding table that some suffixes are added without any union-vowel, and others by means of a vowel or half-vowel. The former occur with the forms terminating in a vowel, as יְדָעַתִיו from יְדַעְתִּי ,הֱכוּנִי from הֵכוּ ;. the latter with forms not terminating in a vowel, as מְכָרוּ from מָכַר, שְׂאָהוּ from שָׂא.

4) חוֹלָם or קָמֶץ ,פַּתַח are generally used as union-vowels with the forms of עָבַר ; סְגוֹל or צֵירֶה on the other hand

THE VERBAL SUFFIXES.

with the other verbal forms; e. g. יַעֲמִידֶהָ, נְאָלָם, וְכָדַנִי, כְּבָסֵנִי, יִזְבְּלֵנִי. — פַּתַח or קָמֵץ however sometimes also occur with the forms of עָתִיד as תִּדְבָּקַנִי Gen. 19,19; יִלְבָּשָׁם Ex. 29,30.

5) A נ moreover is sometimes inserted between the verbal form and the suffix (נ *epentheticum*), e. g. יִצְרֶנְהוּ = יִצְרֵהוּ Deut. 32,10; אֶתְקֶנְךָ = אֶתְקֶךָ Jer. 22,24; יְכַבְּדַנְנִי = יְכַבְּדַנִי Ps. 50,23. This נ very frequently is contracted with the first letter of the suffix; thus

יוֹעִידֵנִי	e. g.	־ֵנִי	becomes	־ֶנִּי
תִּבְעֲתַנִי	"	־ַנִי	"	־ֶנִּי
אֲצַוֶּךָ	"	־ְךָ	"	־ֶנְךָ
אֲשִׁיבֶנּוּ	"	־נוּ	"	־ֶנְהוּ
אֲבִיאֶנָּה	"	־ֶנָּה	"	־ֶנְהָ

Rem. 1. כֶם and הֶם often are called *strong suffixes (suffixa gravia)* because they always have the accent. The others on the other hand *light suffixes (suffixa levia)*.

Rem. 2. The suffixes of the 2d person do not occur with the verbal forms of the 2d pers.; nor these of the 1st pers. with verbal forms of the 1st pers. Instead of this a reflexive verb is often used.

§ 47. The alterations of the verbal forms of the regular triliteral stems through the appending of suffixes.

a. The forms of the עָבַר.

1) The ending הָ־ of the fem. sing. becomes ־ַת, e. g. קְרָאַתְנִי [1]).

---

1) Whenever no difference of alteration exists between the regular

Rem. 1. The ה of הו is here often omitted, e. g. גְמָלַתְהוּ and גְּמָלָתְהוּ.

Rem. 2. The suffix ם ָ interchanges its vowel with the union-vowel, e. g. גְּנָבְתֶּם instead of גְּנַבְתָּם.

2) The קָמֵץ under the ת of the 2d pers. masc. sing. often falls away, e. g. חֲקַרְתַּנִי.

3) The ת of the 2d pers. fem. sing. receives again its original form תִּי or ת, e. g. לְבַבְתִּנִי.

Rem. 3. In a few instances the ה of the 2d pers. fem. sing. has צוּרָה instead of חִירֶק, e. g. הוֹרַדְתָּנוּ Jos. 2,18.

4) תֶם becomes תוּ or ת, e. g. הֶעֱלִיתָנוּ.

Rem. 4. תֶן also should probably become תוּ or ת, but of this no instance occurs in the Bible.

5) In the קַל, because of the shifting of the accent, the קָמֵץ of the first stem-letter changes into a half-vowel, (cf. § 18,2) whilst the ע׳ הַפֹעַל gets קָמֵץ, e. g. טְבָחוֹ from טָבַח; לְקָחוּהוּ from (לְקָחוּ לָקְחוּ). The צירה however of the ע׳ הַפֹעַל with the verbs *mediae e* remains, e. g. אֲהֵבוּ.

6) In the פָּעֵל, for the same reason, the צֵירָה of the ע׳ הַפֹעַל changes before suffixes *with* a union-vowel into the half-vowel, and before suffixes *without* a union-vowel into an auxiliary vowel, e. g. וַיִּקְבְּצֵךְ, גְּדָלוֹ.

7) The forms of עָבַר before they are connected with suffixes are:

---

and irregular verbs we shall as a rule take the examples from the latter class.

REGULAR VERBS WITH SUFFIXES.

קל

2	3	1	2	3
פְּקַדְנוּ פְּקָדַתוּ	פְּקָדוּ	פְּקַדְתִּי	פְּקַדְתָּ and פְּקָדַתְ or פְּקַדְתִּי פָּקְדָה	פָּקַד (פְּקָד) פְּקָדַת (פְּקֵדַת)

פִּעֵל

			פִּקַּדְתָּ and פִּקְּדָה or פִּקְּדַתִּי פִּקְּדָה	פִּקֵּד and פִּקַּד פִּקְּדָה
פִּקַּדְנוּ פִּקְּדָתוּ	פִּקְּדוּ	פִּקַּדְתִּי		

הִפְעִיל

			הִפְקַדְתָּ and הִפְקִידָה or הִפְקַדְתִּי הִפְקִידָה	הִפְקִיד הִפְקִידָה
הִפְקַדְנוּ הִפְקִידָתוּ הִפְקִידוּ		הִפְקַדְתִּי		

b. The forms of the עָתִיד.

1) The vowel of the ע' הַפַּעַל becomes a half-vowel before a suffix *with* a union-vowel (cf. § 18,3), as יִרְדְּפוּ, אֲכַבְּדֵהוּ; and is shortened before the other suffixes, e.g. אֲלַמְּדֵכֶם, אֲרוֹמִמְךָ, יִשְׁמָרְךָ. The חִירֶק however in the הִפְעִיל remains (cf. § 18,4), e. g. אַשְׁמִידְכֶם, יַרְכִּיבֵהוּ.

Rem. 5. Yet this חִירֶק also in a very few instances becomes a half-vowel, e. g. תַּעְשְׁרֶנָּה Ps. 65,10.

2) The 2d and 3d pers. fem. plur. take the form of the 2d pers. mas. plur.; e. g. תִּרְאַנִי from תִּרְאֶינָה Cant. 1,6; תַּחְשְׁבֵנִי from תַּחְשֹׁבְנָה Job 19,15; תּוֹכַחְתְּךָ from תּוֹכַחְנָה Jer. 2,19.

3) The forms of עָתִיד, when they are connected with suffixes, are:

קל

		1	2	3
נִפְקֹו and נִפְקֹד תִּפְקְדוּ	יִפְקְדוּ תִּפְקְדוּ	אֶפְקֹד and אֶפְקָד	תִּפְקֹד and תִּפְקָד תִּפְקְדִי	יִפְקֹד and יִפְקָד תִּפְקֹד and תִּפְקָד

6

פָּעַל

יִפָּקֵד an   תְּפָקֵד and תָּפַקֵד   יִפָּקְדוּ   תְּפָקְדוּ   נִפָּקֵד and נִפְקַד
תִּפָּקֵד an   תִּפָּקְדִי   אֲפַקֵד and אֶפָּקֵד

הִפְעִיל

תַּפְקֵד   אַפְקֵד   יַפְקִידוּ   נַפְקִיד
תַּפְקִידִי   תַּפְקִידוּ

c. The forms of the דֶּרֶךְ הַצִּוּוּי.

1) The forms of the masc. plur. and the fem. sing. of the regular verbs undergo no alteration, whilst to those of the fem. plur. no suffixes are appended. If the fem. plur. were connected with a suffix it would probably be similar to the masc. plur. The form of the masc. sing. alone is altered before it is connected with a suffix.

2) With this form the half-vowel of the פ׳הַפֹּעַל in the קַל becomes קָמֵץ חָטוּף· and the vowel of the ע׳הַפֹּעַל falls away, e. g. כָּתְבֵם from כתב.

3) In פָּעֵל, the vowel of the ע׳הַפֹּעַל becomes a half-vowel, as כַּבְּדֵנִי.

4) In הִפְעִיל, the צירה of the ע׳הַפֹּעַל always becomes חִירִק, e. g. הַקְרִיבֵהוּ.

The forms of the masc. sing. of the דֶּרֶךְ הַצִּוּוּי before they are connected with a suffix are:

קַל פָּקֹד   פִּעֵל פַּקֵד   הִפְעִיל הַפְקֵד

d. The nominal forms.

1) When the infinitive expresses an *action* and there-

fore has a *verbal* meaning, it may be connected with the verbal suffixes. The alterations are the same as those of the דֶּרֶךְ הַצִּוּוּי, e. g. לְפָקְדֵנִי *to take care of me*.

2) The participle also sometimes has a verbal meaning and then is connected with the verbal suffixes. Its alterations however are like those of the nomina when they are connected with suffixes, e. g. הַמְאַזְּרֵנִי *who girdeth me*.

§ 48. The alterations of the verbal forms of the irregular triliteral stems through the appending of suffixes.

1) In addition to the alterations spoken of in § 47 we have here the following. With the *verba primae gutturalis* (§§ 26 and 31) the פ׳הפעל has often פַּתַח instead of קָמֵץ חָטוּף, e. g. חַבְלֵהוּ from חָבַל. The פַּתַח of the preformative is sometimes lengthened, e. g. הָעָבְדֵם Ex. 20,5.

2) With the *verba mediae* and *tertiae gutturalis* (§§ 27 and 28) the ע׳הפעל has in an open syllable generally קָמֵץ, in consequence of which the vowel of the פ׳הפעל sometimes becomes a half-vowel, e. g. יְגָאָלוּהוּ from יִגְאָלוּ; בְּחָנוּנִי from בְּחַן; וְיִשְׁלָחֵנִי from וְיִשְׁלַח; שְׁאָלוּנִי from שָׁאֲלוּ; שְׁמָעוּנִי from שִׁמְעוּ.

3) With the verbs נָחִי ל״א (§ 33) the קָמֵץ of the ע׳הפעל remains before the suffixes e. g. יִקְרָאֵנִי.

4) As to the verbs נָחִי ל״ה (§ 34).

(*a*) The ה at the end of the verbal forms falls away with its preceding vowel, and the suffixes are added without any further alteration, e. g. יִפְדְּךָ from צָוָה; יִפְדְּךָ from צוּךְ; רָאָה from רָאָם יַעֲנֶה from יַעֲנֵהוּ; עָשָׂה from עֲשָׂנִי; יִפְדֶּה from פְּצָנִי from פָּצָה.

(b) תָה– is changed before suffixes into תְ–, e. g. רָאַתְךָ from רָאֲתָה.

5) When the חסרי פ' lose the פ'הפעל their connection with suffixes is like that of the נָחִי ל"ה, e. g. יִדְּבֵנוּ from יִדֹּב; תִּגְּהוּ from תֵּן.

§ 49. The alterations of the verbal forms of the *biliteral* stems through the appending of suffixes.

I. When the second stem-letter of the biliteral verbs is doubled, the rules for the triliteral stems are applied.

II. When the stem is restricted to the two stem-letters we have the following alterations.

a. The forms of the עָבַר.

1) The ending הָ– becomes תָ– or תְ–, e. g. בָּאַתְנוּ, שָׂמַתְנוּ.

2) The same alterations, mentioned in § 47ᵃ 2, 3 and 4, occur here, and likewise those of § 48, 2 and 3, whenever they are required, e. g. שַׁתַּנִי from שָׁת; צַמְתַנִי from צמתם.

3) The vowel of the preformative ה in the הִפְעִיל becomes a half-vowel; e. g. הֲפֵרָם from הֵפֵר; הֲבֵאתָנוּ from הֲבֵאתָ; וַהֲמִיתַנִי from הֵמִית; הֱבִיאוּךָ from הֵבִיאוּ.

BILITERAL VERBS WITH SUFFIXES.

Rem 1. The same rule applies to the ה of the infinitive, e. g. לַהֲפִיצֵֽנוּ. In Lev. 26,15 לְהַפְרְכֶם this half-vowel became a vowel because of the first stem-letter losing its vowel.

4) The צירה of the first stem-letter in the הִפְעִיל is shortened, unless a guttural or ר follows; e. g. הֲדַמָּנוּ from הֵדַם; but הֲפֵרָם from הֵפֵר; הֲבֵאתָה from הֵבֵאתָ.

Rem. 2. Likewise in the infinitive, e. g. כַּהֲתִמְּךָ from הָתֵם Jes. 33,1.

b. The forms of the עָתִיד.

1) The vowel of the preformative becomes a half-vowel, e. g. אֲטִילֵךְ, יְבִיאֵנוּ.

Rem. 3. In יְחָנְךָ = יָחְנְךָ Gen. 43,29; Jes. 30,19 the קָמַץ has changed place with the half-vowel.

2) The vowel of the first stem-letter is often shortened, e. g. יְחָגֵּנוּ, יְדֻקֵּנוּ from יָדַק; אֲדֻקֵּם from אָדֻק; יהמם from יָהֹם; יָחָן from יָן. Frequently however it remains, as יְגוּרֵנוּ, תְּדוּשֶׁהָ, יְסִיתְךָ, chiefly before a guttural or ר, e. g. יפרנו, תְּבִיאֵנִי, יִנְהֵהוּ. See further § 47b 2.

c. The forms of the דֶּרֶךְ הַצִּוּוּי.

1) The חוֹלָם is frequently shortened, e. g. חָגֵּנוּ from חֹן; סָלוּהָ from סֹלוּ.

2) The vowel of the preformative in the הִפְעִיל becomes a half-vowel, and the vowel of the first stem-letter generally is חִירֶק (cf. § 47c 4), e. g. הֲבִינֵנִי from הָבֵן.

HEBREW GRAMMAR.

The verbal forms before connection with suffixes are:

קַל

שְׁמָנוּ	שָׂמְתוּ	שָׂמוּ	שַׂמְתִּי	שַׂמְתְּ or שַׂמְתָּ		שָׂם
			שַׂמְתִּי or שָׂמְתִּי	שָׂמְתְּ or שַׂמְתְּ		שָׂמַת or שָׂמַת

Verbal forms with suffixes of the other stem-forms in קַל but rarely occur.

הִפְעִיל

הֲקַמְנוּ	הֲקִמְתּוּ	הֵקִימוּ	הֲקִמֹתִי	הֲקַמְתְּ and הֲקַמְתָּ	הֵקִים
			הֲקִמֹתִי	הֲקַמְתְּ and הֲקִמְתָּ	הֵקִימָת or הֵקִימָה

Rem. 4. חֲטַף פַּתַח may everywhere be used instead of חֲטַף סְגוֹל

Rem. 5. The prolonged forms of the 1st and 2d pers. remain unaltered, e. g. הֲבִיאֹתָ from הֲבִיאֹתָנוּ.

עָתִיד

נגד	תִּגְדוּ	יִגְדוּ	אֶגֹּד	תִּגַּד	יִגַּד	קַל
		תִּגְדוּ		תִּגְדִי	תִּגַּד	

Rem. 6. The שׁוּרֶק may everywhere take the place of the קִבּוּץ.

נְבֹז	תָּבֹזוּ	יָבֹזוּ	אָבֹז	תָּבֹז	יָבֹז	
		תָּבֹזוּ		תָּבֹזִי	תָּבֹז	
נָקִים	תָּקִימוּ	יָקִימוּ	אָקִים	תָּקִים	יָקִים	הִפְעִיל
		תְּקִימוּ		תָּקִימִי	תָּקִים	
נחת	תחתו	יחתו	אחת	תחת	יחת	
		תחתו		תחתי	תחת	
נָפֵר	תָּפֵרוּ	יָפֵרוּ	אָפֵר	תָּפֵר	יָפֵר	
		תָּפֵרוּ		תָּפֵרִי	תָּפֵר	

THE NOMINA.

דֶּרֶךְ הַצִּוּוּי

| קַל | הָן | חָנִי | חָנוּ |
| הִפְעִיל | הָשִׁיב | הָשִׁיבִי | הָשִׁיבוּ |

Rem. 7. As for examples of verbal forms connected with suffixes see Append. 3.

CHAPTER IX.

Nomina שֵׁמוֹת.

§ 50. The various kinds of nomina.

1) The noun (שֵׁם עֶצֶם *substantivum*), to which also belongs the infinitive of the verb (שֵׁם הַפֹּעַל *substativum verbale*).

2) The adjective (תֹּאַר הַשֵּׁם *adjectivum*), to which also belongs the participle (בֵּינוֹנִי *adjectivum verbale, participium*).

3) The pronoun (כִּנּוּי הַשֵּׁם *pronomen*).

4) The numeral (שֵׁם הַמִּסְפָּר *numerale*).

§ 51. The alterations, which the nomina undergo.

The nomina undergo a prolongation, abbreviation or alteration of vowels:

1) through difference of gender (מִין *genus, motio*),

2) through number (מִסְפָּר *numerus*),

3) through connection with another nomen (סְמִיכוּת *status constructus*),

4) through signs of interpunction or accents,

5) through suffixes or prefixes.

The suffixes and prefixes are:

(a) the locative ה,

(b) the pronominal suffixes (הַכִּנוּיִם),

(c) the literae praefixae בהוכלמש וְכָלֵב מֹשֶׁה].

CHAPTER X.

The noun *(substantivum)*.

§ 52. Division of the nouns.

A. According to their meaning.

(a) Proper names (שֵׁם עֶצֶם פְּרָטִי *nomen proprium*),

(b) Appellative names (*nomen appellativum*).

The appellatives again are subdivided into:

1) Names of an entire species of objects (שֵׁם הַמִּין *appellativum* in a stricter sense, as שֻׁלְחָן *table*).

2) Names of a multitude of objects or living beings of the same kind, considered as one whole (שֵׁם הַקִּבּוּץ *nomen collectivum*), as הרר *mountains*, עַם *people*.

Rem. 1. The appellatives are not unfrequently used as collectives. סוּס (*horse*) e. g. sometimes means *cavalry*, רכב (*chariot*) sometimes *chariots*.

3) Names of abstract ideas (שֵׁם הַמִּקְרֶה *nomen abstractum*) e. g. חָכְמָה *wisdom*; and names of concrete ideas (*nomina concreta*).

B. According to their stem.
(a) Stem-nouns, or primitives.
(b) Derived nouns, or derivatives,
(c) Compound nouns.

§ 53. The proper names.

1) The proper names probably are but seldom stem-nouns. It is however difficult to determine their derivation by fixed rules. The stem also from which they are derived is frequently not to be found in the Bible.

2) Many proper names are compounds, chiefly those of persons, e. g. אֶלְקָנָה from אֵל and קָנָה, יְחֶזְקֵאל from חֹזֶק and אֵל.

3) Of the alterations enumerated in § 51 at the utmost only those under 3, 4 and 5 apply to the proper names, as will appear from the §§ on the appellatives.

§ 54. The gender of the nouns [1]).

1) The noun has two genders: *masculine* and *feminine*.

2) The original form is the masc., from which the fem. is derived. This derivation effects a certain alteration of vowels.

---

1) Before entering upon the finer distinctions of the appellatives, we shall first treat of their gender, in order that in the subsequent §§ we may be able at the same time to consider their feminine forms. It should be observed also that, in the following §§ like in the present §, we understand by nouns or substantives the *appellatives*.

3) The derivation is made through the addition of:
- (a) הָ—, e. g. מַלְכָּה from מֶלֶךְ, צְדָקָה from צֶדֶק, פִּרְחָה from אִיל, אַיָּלָה from צְבִי, צְבִיָּה from אכל, אָכְלָה from פֶּחַ.
- (b) ־ת, e. g. אַיֶּלֶת, חוֹתָם from חוֹתֶמֶת, יוֹתֵר from יוֹתֶרֶת, אַיִל from נְבִיר, גְּבֶרֶת from ; chiefly with the infinitive, e. g. בֹּשֶׁת from בֹּשׁ, יבשׁת from יָבֵשׁ, כְּתֹבֶת from כתב.
- (c) —ִית and —וֹת, chiefly to form abstract names, e. g. שְׁבִית from שְׁבִי, אַחֲרִית from אַחַר, רֵאשִׁית from רֹאשׁ; מַלְכוּת from מֶלֶךְ.
- (d) —וֹת uncommon, e. g. אָחוֹת from אָח; חָמוֹת from חָם.
- (e) —ת and ת־ generally poetical, e. g. פּוֹנַת = פּוֹנָה; עֶזְרַת = עֶזְרָה. ת־ is sometimes prolonged into תָה־, e. g. עֶזְרָתָה.

4) There are however fem. nouns which are not derived from masc. nouns, and which have a primitive form; viz.:
- (a) Often the names of fem. beings, e. g. אֵם masc. אָב; רָחֵל masc. אַיִל, אָתוֹן masc. חֲמוֹר, שִׁפְחָה and אָמָה masc. עבד.
- (b) The names of certain inanimate objects and ideas, which are used in the fem., although they have no fem. termination; e. g. the names of the members of the body, and of the powers of nature, as רֶגֶל *foot*, רוּחַ *wind*.

§ 55. The primitives *(substantiva primitiva)*.

There are but few nouns which are not derived from nomina or verba. To these probably belong:

DERIVATION OF THE NOUNS.

1) certain names of living beings, as שֶׂה *lamb*, אֵם *mother*;

2) certain object-names, a אֶבֶן *stone*, אָטָד *thorn*;

3) certain names of members of the body, as רֹאשׁ *head*, אֹזֶן *ear*.

§ 56. The Derivatives *(substantiva derivata)*.

The derivatives are formed from the stem of a verb or from another nomen.

A. The derivatives formed from the stem of a verb.

I. Those derived from the bare stem without addition of letters.

1) The infinitive of the verb, e. g. דֵּעַ, בְּכִי, חֲבֹל, בֹּאשׁ, אוֹר, fem. בָּאְשָׁה, חֲבָלָה, בְּכִית, דֵּעָה or דַּעַת, אוֹרָה; chiefly frequent with the fem. form, as יְכֹלֶת, בֹּשֶׁת, נַאֲוָה, יִרְאָה.

The meaning of these words generally is that of an *abstractum*.

2) The *segolate forms*, so called because the עֲ'הַפֹּעַל of the triliteral stem has סֶגוֹל as auxiliary vowel.

(a) The עֲ'הַפֹּעַל has סֶגוֹל and the פֶּ'הַפֹּעַל has צֵירֶה, סֶגוֹל or חוֹלָם; e. g. סֵפֶר, זֶמֶר, עֶצֶם, fem. סִפְרָה, זִמְרָה, עָצְמָה.

Rem. 1. The auxiliary vowel sometimes is omitted, as חֵטְא along with פֶּלֶא, קֹשְׁטְ along with קֹשֶׁט.

(b) When the עֲ'הַפֹּעַל is a guttural, the auxiliary vowel usually is פַּתַח, e. g. טֹהַר fem. טָהֳרָה; and the צֵירֶה or

סְגוֹל of the פ׳הפעל is often changed into פַּתַח, as נַעַר fem. נַעֲרָה

Rem. 2. We find however also nouns such as אֹהֶל, לֶחֶם, רֶחֶם.

(c) When the ל׳הפעל is a guttural, the auxiliary vowel becomes פַּתַח, e. g. דֶּמַע fem. דִּמְעָה, נַגַּה; except in the stems which only in appearance belong to the נָחִי ל״ה (§ 34), for these retain the סְגוֹל, e. g. הֶגֶה, בֶּכֶה; just as the נָחִי ל״א e. g. פֶּלֶא.

(d) When the ע׳הפעל is י, the auxiliary vowel is חִירֶק and the vowel of the פ׳הפעל always פַּתַח, as חַיִל fem. חַיְלָה.

Rem. 3. In גִיא the auxiliary vowel is omitted.

(e) When the ע׳הפעל is ו, the vowel of the פ׳הפעל is קָמֵץ, e. g. עָוֶל fem. עַוְלָה.

Rem. 4. In שָׁוְא the auxiliary vowel is omitted.

(f) Of the biliteral stems the following agree with the segolate forms, גֵּו, חֹק, מַר fem. גֵּוָה, חֻקָּה, מָרָה.

Although the segolate forms really express an abstract idea, they are often used in a concrete sense.

3) The triliteral stems with a half-vowel under the מ׳הפעל, and סְגוֹל, פתח or a long vowel under the ע׳הפעל, e. g. דָּבָשׁ, שְׁכֶם, קְרָב, בְּאֵר, גְּבִיר, חֲמוֹר, גְּבוּל. Of the latter sorts we also find fem. forms, as גְּבִירָה, חֲמוֹרָה, גְּבוּלָה. These forms generally have a concrete sense.

Rem. 5. When the ע׳הפעל is חוֹלֶם or שׁוּרֶק, and the פ׳הפעל is א, the א sometimes has צֵירָה. e. g. אָפוֹר fem. אֲפוּרָה; אֵמוּן fem. אֱמוּנָה.

DERIVATION OF THE NOUNS.

4) The triliteral stems with קָמַץ under the פ׳הפעל, which becomes a half-vowel, as soon as the word is lengthened at the end. The ע׳הפעל has a long vowel, e. g. גָזֵל, שָׂעִיר, חָגוֹר, חָתוּל fem. אֲשֵׁמָה, גְּדֵלָה, שְׂעִירָה, חֲגוֹרָה, אָשֵׁם, חֲתוּלָה.

<blockquote>
Rem. 6. The stems with חִירְק or שׁוּרְק under the ע׳הפעל often really are participles, and therefore will be spoken of along with the adjectives; see § 67 I A 2—5.
</blockquote>

The same forms we find also with the biliteral stems of which the second stem-letter is doubled; e. g. חָלָל, שְׁמָמָה, מְרֵרָה, חָגִיג, צְחִיחָה.

These also generally have a concrete meaning.

5) The triliteral stems with an immovable short vowel under the פ׳הפעל, e. g. אַיָּל f. אַיָּלָה and אַיֶּלֶת, חֵטְא f. חַטָּאָה or חַטָּאת. When the ל׳הפעל is a guttural the fem. form is like טַבַּעַת, צָרַעַת.

These too generally have a concrete meaning.

6) From the triliteral stems there are many fem. nouns in ־ָה with a half-vowel under the פ׳הפעל, and a long vowel under the ע׳הפעל, which express an operation, e. g. נְקָמָה (also with a guttural as ע׳הפעל in the form בְּהָלָה, שְׂרֵפָה, אֲכִילָה, עֲבוֹדָה, רְפוּאָה.

From the biliteral stems, e. g. סָרָה, לְבָה.

7) A series of concrete words with קָמַץ under the ע׳הפעל, and צֵירֶה or חוֹלָם under the פ׳הפעל; e. g. שׁוֹשָׁן f. שׁוֹשַׁנָּה, חוֹתָם f. חוֹתֶמֶת, שֵׁכָר.

8) Rarer forms are nouns such as, כִּסֵּא, גּוֹמֶץ, אֹסֶר,

סוֹגֵר, כְּלִי, כִּילַי, כּוֹבַע, עַמּוּד, כִּישׁוֹר, פָּגוּל, רָתוֹק, כִּנּוֹר, פַּטִּישׁ, כּוֹתֶל, סְנֶה; and with the accent on the penultimate, as אָחוּ, תֹּהוּ. Also fem. forms, as חֲבוּרָה, תְּמוּרָה, בְּכוֹרָה, תּוֹעֵבָה, and the *pluralia tantum* [1]), as תְּכִיִּים, זֵרוּעִים, שָׂרִגִים, דּוּדָאִים, נְעוּרִים.

The most frequent in use of all these forms are the *pluralia tantum* of the form פָּגוּל, e. g. שְׁלוּחִים, כִּפּוּרִים.

9) Certain forms derived from biliteral stems through duplication of both the stem-letters, e. g. קָרְקֹד, חַתְחַת, גִּלְגָּלָה, שַׁרְשְׁרָה, חַלְחָלָה, fem. בַּקְבּוּק.

From the triliteral stems also a few nouns are formed through duplication of one or more stem-letters, as סַגְרִיר fem. עֲקַלְקַלָּה.

10) Finally the forms which appear to have more than three stem-letters, e. g. שַׁעַטְנֵז, צְפַרְדֵּעַ, עֲטַלֵּף, חֶרְמֵשׁ, חֲנָמָל; all of them generally with a concrete meaning.

II. The derivatives formed by addition of letters.

The letters used to form nouns from verbal stems, are אֲהֵוִימְנַת [הָאֶמַנְתִּיו]. One or more of these letters are for this purpose added either before, after, or between the stem-letters.

1) א before the stem, e. g. אֶזְרָח, אָסוּךְ, אַרְבֶּה, אֶפְעֶה. Fem nouns, e. g. אַשְׁמֹרֶת, אַזְכָּרָה, אַמְתַּחַת.
From the biliteral stems, e. g. אֶפֶס, אֲבַעְבּוּעוֹת (plur.).

2) ה before the stem, e. g. הֵילֵל, הַרְוָחָה.
From the biliteral stems, e. g. הֲנָחָה.

---

1) *Pluralia tantum* are nouns which only occur in plural.

DERIVATION OF THE NOUNS.

3) ו between the stem-letters, e. g. שִׂכְוִי.
From the biliteral stems, e. g. זַעֲוָה, זְוָעָה.

4) י before the stem, e. g. יַלְקוּט, יִצְהָר.
From the biliteral stems, e. g. יָרִיב, יְתוּר.

5) מ

(*a*) before the stem, agreeing with the usual form of the *Chaldee* infinitive, e. g. מוֹצָא, מִחְיָה, מַסַּע, מִקְרָא fem. מוֹצָאָה, and a great many other nouns which later have modified or lost their meaning as infinitive.

(*b*) before the stem, to indicate the place where an action is occurring, e. g. מכלא *kennel, stable* from כלא *to shut in*, מועד *place of destination* from יעד *to determine*.

(*c*) before the stem to express various other meanings, e. g. מכס, מָבוֹא, מָסָךְ, מַחְטוֹר; and fem. nouns, e. g. מְדִינָה, מִגְפָה, מַהְפֵּכָה, מוֹעֵצָה.

(*d*) before the stem to form words which originally were participles, but later got the meaning of nouns, e. g. מוּצָק, מַשְׁחִית, מִקְרֶה, מְבַסֶּה, מִטֶּה, מַטֶּה fem. מוּצָקָה and other fem. nouns, as מָסֹרֶת, מַחְתֶּרֶת, מַאֲכֶלֶת, מְנַקִּית, מְזַמֶּרֶת, (= מְאַסֶּרֶת); and *pluralia tantum*, as מַדְקֵרוֹת.

(*e*) sometimes after the stem to indicate a whole which is composed of many small parts, as כְּנָם, סֻלָּם.

6) נ

(*a*) after the stem, chiefly with the נָחִי ל"ה, to form nouns terminating in וֹן-, יוֹן-, or יָן-, e. g. יָגוֹן,

קָנְיָן ,הִרָיוֹן ,הָרוֹן fem. אֲבִיוֹנָה; yet from other verbs also, as שִׁלְחָן ,קָרְבָּן ,שָׂשׂוֹן ,אֲבַדּוֹן fem. עֶשְׁתּוֹנָה.

(b) before the stem, e. g. נִפְתּוּלִים (plur.).

7) ת

(a) before the stem (generally fem. nouns), chiefly from the נָחֵי ל"ה and from the biliteral stems, e. g. תִּכְלָה, תַּבְנִית ,תְּהִלָּה ,תְּבוּאָה ,תֵּבֵל ,תַּחֲנוּן ,תֹּעַר; and also from other stems, e. g. תּוֹחֶלֶת ,תַּבְעֵרָה ,תִּפְאֶרֶת; masc. nouns, e. g. תַּמְרוּק.

(b) after the stem, chiefly from the נָחֵי ל"ה, e. g. בָּכוֹת, דְּמוּת ,בְּכִית; sometimes also from other stems, e. g. כְּרִיתוֹת ,שְׁאֵרִית ,זֵלוֹת.

B. Nouns derived from nomina.

I. Through alteration of vowels, e. g. מֶלַח from מֶלַח, כֹּרֶם from כֶּרֶם (see § 67 II 1).

II. Through addition of letters.

(a) Through the addition of the letters הָאֱמַנְתִּיו, e. g. אִשָּׁה from אֵשׁ, מַעְיָן from עַיִן, אִישׁוֹן from אִישׁ, צַוָּארֹן from צַוָּאר, צִפְעֹנִי from צֶפַע; chiefly through addition of the endings —וֹת and —ִית for the purpose of forming *abstracts* from *concretes*, e. g. מִסְכְּנוֹת from מִסְכֵּן, רֵאשִׁית from רֹאשׁ.

(b) Sometimes also through the addition of other letters, e. g. שַׁרְבִיט from שֵׁבֶט, כַּרְמֶל from כֶּרֶם, שַׁלְהֶבֶת from לַהַב.

§ 57. Compound Nouns.

1) The Hebrew language possesses but very few com-

pound nouns; e. g. בְּלִיַּעַל (from בַּל *not* and the stem יַעַל *usefulness*) = *worthless*; בְּלִימָה (from בְּלִי = בַּל *not* and מָה *what*, *something*) = *nothing*.

2) When the Hebrew writers wish to express an idea composed of two ideas, they connect the two words, expressing these ideas, by the מַקֵּף, e. g. בְּלִי־שֵׁם *of no significance*.

§ 58. The number of the noun.

The nouns have three numbers, viz. the singular, the dual, and the plural.

A. The dual.

1) Of the monosyllables the dual is formed by adding the termination ־ִים to the sing., e. g. יוֹמַיִם from יוֹם *two days*, יָדַיִם from יָד *two hands*.

2) The words which in the sing. have more than one syllable, for the greater part undergo before the ending ־ִים the same alterations as the plural forms with the pronominal suffixes (see § 64), e. g. אָזְנַיִם from אֹזֶן, עֵינַיִם from עַיִן, נְחֻשְׁתַיִם from נְחֹשֶׁת, לְחָיַיִם from לְחִי. — The instances when they take a different form will be dealt with in § 59 treating of the plural.

3) The words which in the plur. end in ־וֹת take the dual form ־וֹתַיִם, e. g. לוּחַ (plur. לֻחוֹת) לוּחוֹתַיִם; if however their sing. form ends in ־ָה they may also take the dual form ־ָתַיִם, e. g. שְׁנָתַיִם from שָׁנָה, and חוֹמָתַיִם from חוֹמָה (plur. חוֹמוֹת).

Rem. 1. Of מֵאָה *hundred* the dual is מָאתַיִם (contracted from מְאָתַיִם).

4) There are duals which have no singular form *(dualia tantum)*, e. g. מַיִם, שָׁמַיִם, כִּלְאַיִם.

Rem. 2. The ם of the dual ending is sometimes missing, e. g. יָדָי Ez. 13,18.

Rem. 3. The use of the dual is very restricted. Generally the plural is used with the number שְׁנַיִם or שְׁתַּיִם, e. g. יָמִים שָׁנִים = יוֹמִים, שְׁתַּיִם דֻבִּים *two she-bear*s. Objects, however, which either from nature or institution presuppose a *pair*, are regularly used in the dual, e. g. רַגְלַיִם *feet*, מֹאזְנַיִם *balance*, *scale*s. With the former class the dual also serves instead of the plur., e. g. שִׁבְעָה עֵינַיִם *seven eye*s Zech. 3,9.

B. The plural.

1) The plural is formed by adding ‏ִים or ‏וֹת to the sing. according to the following rules.

(a) The names of masc. beings generally have the ending ‏ִים, e. g. בָּנִים *sons* from בֵּן, אִכָּרִים *tillers of the soil* from אִכָּר.

Rem. 4. אָב *father* is in plur. אָבוֹת.

(b) The names of fem. beings generally have the ending ‏וֹת, e. g. בָּנוֹת *daughters* from בַּת, אֲתוֹנוֹת *she-asses* from אָתוֹן.

Rem. 5. The plur. of אִשָּׁה *woman* however is נָשִׁים, of רָחֵל *ewe* רְחֵלִים, of פִּילֶגֶשׁ *concubine* פִּילַגְשִׁים.

(c) Nouns, which in the sing. have a fem. ending, generally take ‏וֹת in the plur., e. g. יְשׁוּעוֹת from יְשׁוּעָה, עֲטָרוֹת from עֲטֶרֶת, מַלְכִיּוֹת from מַלְכוּת.

Rem. 6. The plur. of שִׁבֹּלֶת however is שִׁבֳּלִים, of חִטָּה חִטִּים, of חֲנִית חֲנִיתִים and חֲנִיתוֹת, of זֹנָה זֹנוֹתִים, of מִלָּה מִלִּים; etc.

ALTERATIONS OF THE NOUN IN THE PLUR. 99

2) Uncommon plur. endings are:

(a) ־ִי instead of ־ִים, e. g. עֲמִי Ps. 144,2,

(b) ־ִין instead of ־ִים, e. g. הַיְמִין Daniel,

(c) ־ַי, e. g. חַלּוֹנַי Jer. 22,14.

Rem. 7. The difference of the plur. and dual sometimes denotes a difference of meaning, e. g. יָדַיִם *hand*s and יָדוֹת *handle*s, כַּפַּיִם *hands* and כַּפּוֹת *spoons.*

3) There are a great many words which only occur in plur., e. g. the nouns of the forms כְּפוּרִים and נְעוּרִים; as also the words קוֹצוֹת, מַקְהֵלוֹת, מַצְפּוּנִים and others.

4) The י of ־ִים sometimes falls away, chiefly when the חִירֶק גָּדוֹל precedes, e. g. צַדִּיקִם; and also the ו of ־וֹת when the חוֹלָם precedes, e. g. מְאֹרֹת.

§ 59. The alterations which the noun undergoes before the plural ending is added to it.

A. Nouns *without* a fem. ending.

(a) Monosyllables *without* a preceding half-vowel.

1) The קָמֵץ and צֵירֵה of certain words are shortened into פַּתַח or חִירֶק, whilst in other words they remain, e. g. יָמִים from יָם, דָּמִים from דָּם, קִנִּים from קֵן, אִתִּים and אתִים from אֵת.

Rem. 1. The plur. of בֵּן is בָּנִים, of חטא חַטָּאִים.

2) The other long vowels remain, e. g. צִירִים from צִיר, לוּחוֹת from לוּחַ, דּוֹרוֹת from דּוֹר and דּוֹרִים.

Rem. 2. עִיר is in plur. עָרִים and עֲיָרִים, שׁוֹר pl. דּוֹב, pl. דֻּבִּים,

דוֹדִים pl. דּוֹד, שְׁוָקִים pl. שׁוֹק, חֲוָתִים and חֹחִים pl. חוֹחַ, שׁוּרִים, דּוֹדָאִים and דּוֹדִים.

3) The פַתַח either remains or becomes חִירֶק, e. g. בַּדִּים from בַּד, סִפִּים from סַף (See § 63 A*b*).

Rem. 3. גֵּיא is in plur. גֵּיָאוֹת.

4) The plur. of פֶּה is פִּיוֹת, פֵּיוֹת, and פִּיפִיוֹת.

(*b*) Monosyllables *with* a preceding half-vowel.

1) The plur. endings ־ִים and ־וֹת are added to the sing. causing no alteration of vowel except when the syllable is open and its vowel חִירֶק, e. g. צְבָאוֹת from צְבָא, אֲמוֹנִים from אָמוֹן, גְּדוֹדִים from גְּדוּד, בְּאֵרוֹת from בְּאֵר (cf. § 56 A I 3 Rem. 5), הֲדַסִּים from הֲדַס.

Rem. 4. שַׁלְו is in plur. שַׁלְוִים.

2) When the syllable is open and its vowel חִירֶק, the latter becomes קָמֵץ, e. g. צְבָאוֹת from צְבִי, עֲדָיִים from עֲדִי.

Rem. 5. כְּלִי is in plur. כֵּלִים.

(*c*) Words with two syllables (except the segolate forms).

1) Only the קָמֵץ and צֵירֵה undergo an alteration. When they occur in the first syllable they become a half-vowel. In the second syllable the קָמֵץ either is shortened into פַתַח or remains, and the צֵירֵה remains when the vowel of the first syllable has been changed into a half-vowel, otherwise it becomes a half-vowel, e. g. דְּבָרִים from דָּבָר, גְּמַלִּים from גָּמָל, חֲצֵרִים from חָצֵר, כְּסָאוֹת from כִּסֵּא, לְבָבוֹת from מַחְמָד, מַחְמַדִּים from מָכוֹן, מְכוֹנִים from לֵבָב.

Rem. 6. It appears from these examples that no difference is made whether the letters belong to the stem or not.

Rem. 7. חֶרֶשׁ and פֶּרֶשׁ are in plur. חֲרָשִׁים and פְּרָשִׁים.

Rem. 8. The חוֹלָם of the second syllable sometimes becomes שׁוּרֶק, e. g. צִפֳּרִים from צִפּוֹר; or קָמַץ חָטוּף, e. g. מְגוּרִים from מָגוֹר; שִׁבֳּלִים from שִׁבֹּלֶת.

2) The words however terminating in ה– merely change this ending into ים– or וֹת–, and retain even the קָמַץ of the first syllable, e. g. קָנִים from קָנֶה, חָזוֹת from חָזֶה. — טָלֶה alone is in plur. טְלָאִים.

3) The exceptions to the rule in n° 1 are few, e. g. שָׁבוּעַ is in plur. שָׁבֻעִים or שְׁבֻעִים and שָׁבוּעוֹת and שְׁבוּעוֹת; אֶשְׁכֹּל pl. אַבְנֵטִים; אִיתָן pl. אִיתָנִים; אָחוֹת pl. אֲחָיוֹת; אֶשְׁכֹּלוֹת and אַשְׁכְּלוֹת.

(d) Segolate forms.

1) All the segolate forms, except these of which ע׳הַפֹּעַל is ו or י, change the vowel of the first syllable into a half-vowel, whilst the auxiliary vowel becomes קָמַץ, e. g. זְבָחִים from זֶבַח, רְמָחִים from רֹמַח, חֲלָקִים from חֵלֶק, מְלָכִים from מֶלֶךְ.

Rem. 9. אֹהֶל however is in pl. אֹהָלִים; חֹדֶשׁ pl. חֳדָשִׁים and קֹדֶשׁ pl. קָדָשִׁים. both words with קָמַץ חָטוּף in the first syllable.

2) The segolate forms with ו as ע׳הַפֹּעַל, change the first vowel into חוֹלָם, and lose the auxiliary vowel, e. g. עוֹל from עוּל, עוֹלוֹת from מוֹת, מוֹתִים.

3) The segolate forms with י as ע׳הַפֹּעַל change the first vowel into צֵירֶה, and lose the auxiliary vowel, e. g. אֵילִים from אַיִל, עֵינוֹת from עַיִן.

Rem. 10. בַּיִת is in pl. בָּתִּים, עִיר pl. עָרִים; as for גַּיְא see Rem. 3.

(e) Words with three syllables.

Without the fem. ending these words are only to be found of the form זִכָּרוֹן. They lose the קָמֶץ before the plur. ending and for the rest undergo the same alterations as in the סְמִיכוּת and with suffixes (see § 60 A b 1 and § 63 C b), e. g. עֶשְׂרוֹנִים from עִשָּׂרוֹן, שִׁגְיוֹנוֹת from שִׁגָּיוֹן.

B. Nouns *with* a fem. ending.

1) Nouns ending in הָ‎־ throw off this termination and take in its place ־ִים or ־וֹת, e. g. פָּרוֹת from פָּרָה, מִדּוֹת from מִדָּה, מִלִּים from מִלָּה. Those however which are the fem. of segolate forms undergo before ־וֹת the same alterations as the latter (see above A d), e. g. שְׂמָלוֹת from שִׂמְלָה, עֲלָמוֹת from עַלְמָה, חֲרָפוֹת from חֶרְפָּה.

2) Nouns in ־ֶת and ־ָה form their plur. like the corresponding nouns in הָ‎־, e. g. בֶּהָרוֹת (בֶּהָרָה =) בַּהֶרֶת pl. בְּהָרוֹת, כֻּתֳּנוֹת (כֻּתֳּנָה =) כֻּתֹּנֶת pl. כֻּתֳּנוֹת, מִטְפָּחוֹת (מִטְפָּחָה =) מִטְפַּחַת pl. מִטְפָּחוֹת.

Rem. 11. אִגֶּרֶת is in pl. אִגְּרוֹת, כְּסָמִים pl. כֻּסֶּמֶת.

3) Nouns in ־וֹת form their plur., which very rarely occurs, as if they ended in ־ָיָה, e. g. מַלְכֻיּוֹת pl. מַלְכוּת.

Rem. 12. זְנוּת is in pl. זְנוּתִים, עֵדוּת pl. עֵדְווֹת and עֵדוֹת.

4) Of חֲנִית the plur. is חֲנִיתִים and חֲנִיתוֹת; מַשְׂכִּיּוֹת pl. of מַשְׂכִּית; שְׂחִיתוֹת pl. of (שְׂחִית).

§ 60. The Construct State (סְמִיכוּת *status constructus*).

When two ideas, of which one is the main idea *(nomen regens)* and the other the subordinate idea *(nomen rectum*), are to be connected so as to form one idea, this connection may in English be expressed in different ways; viz. through declension of the *nomen rectum*, e. g. *the man's word*; or through making a compound, e. g. *stone-cutter*, or by means of a preposition, e. g. *they that go into the town*, or by changing the *nomen rectum* into an adjective, e. g. *a golden dish*.

The construction usually employed in Hebrew for expressing such a connection of ideas is the *status constructus (st. constr.)*: i. e. the *nomen regens*, after certain alterations, is placed first, and the *nomen rectum* follows unchanged. The examples above quoted are in in Hebrew דְּבַר הָאִישׁ, חָרַשׁ אֶבֶן, בָּאֵי הָעִיר, קַעֲרַת זָהָב.

The alterations which the *nom. reg.* undergoes are the following.

A. Singular words *without* fem. termination.

a. Of the monosyllables only those with קָמֵץ are altered by changing the קָמֵץ into פַּתַח, e. g. פָּר becomes פַּר, יָד becomes יד.

Rem. 1. אָב and אָח become in the *st. constr.* אֲבִי and אֲחִי; קֵן becomes קַן, גַּיְא נְיָא, שֶׂה שֵׂה, פִּי פֶּה. — יָם remains unaltered except in יַם־סוּף *the Red Sea*.

b. Words of more than one syllable, the segolate forms excepted.

1) The קָמֵץ and צֵירֵה of the penultimate *open* syllable become a half-vowel in words of two syllables, and fall away in words of more than two syllables, e. g. דָּבָר

שִׁבָּרוֹן from שִׁבְרוֹן, קָצִין from קְצִין, רְעָבוֹן from רַעֲבוֹן, דָּבָר from שֵׂעָר from שְׂעַר.

Rem. 2. The קָמֶץ in the penultimate syllable of חָרָשׁ and פָּרָשׁ remains (cf. § 59 Rem. 7), and also the צִירָה in מֵיטָב, נֵכָר, אֵזוֹר. Certain words moreover in ־ָה resemble in the *st. constr.* the corresponding words in ־ָת, e. g. מְלֶאכֶת from מְלָאכָה, מִלְחֶמֶת from מִלְחָמָה.

2) The other vowels of the penultimate syllable remain unaltered independently whether the syllable is open or closed, e. g. אֶצְבַּע, מוֹעֵד, כִּכַּר, אַבִּיר.

3) The קָמֶץ of the last *closed* syllable becomes פַּתַח, e. g. דְּבַר from דָּבָר, חֲרַשׁ from חָרָשׁ, כְּנַף from כָּנָף, שְׂעַר from שֵׂעָר; also the צִירָה in מִזְבֵּחַ, מַקֵּל and in words of the form פָּעֵל, e. g. יְתַד from יָתֵד, חֲצַר from חָצֵר.

In all other instances the vowel of the last *closed* syllable remains unaltered, e. g. אַלּוּף from אַלּוּף, אֲדוֹן from אָדוֹן, נְבִיא from נָבִיא.

Rem. 3. כָּתֵף and יָרֵךְ become כֶּתֶף and יֶרֶךְ. אָבֵל becomes אֲבֶל with מַקֵּף.

4) When the last syllable is *open* the vowel remains, even the קָמֶץ, e. g. צְבָא from צָבָא, נְבִיא from נָבִיא. The words however in ־ָה change this ending into ־ֵה, e. g. שְׂדֵה from שָׂדֶה.

c. The segolate forms.

The segolate forms remain unchanged, e. g. חֶלֶב, אֶבֶן, נַעַר, פֹּעַל, אֹזֶן; except those with ו and י as second stem-

STATUS CONSTRUCTUS.   105.

letter, which undergo the same alterations as before the plur. endings (cf. § 59 A *d* 2. 3) e. g. מוֹת from בֵּית מָוֶת, from בַּיִת; also גַּיְא becomes גֵּיא.

B. Singular words *with* fem. termination.

1) The termination ־ָה becomes ־ַת. The קָמֵץ, and frequently also the צֵירה, of the penultimate syllable become a half-vowel, and in consequence the preceding half-vowel goes over into an auxiliary vowel, e. g. שְׂפַת from שָׂפָה, מַתְּנַת from מַתָּנָה, עֲצַת from עֵצָה, מִצְבַת from מַצֵּבָה, אַדְמַת from אֲדָמָה, בֶּהֱמַת from בְּהֵמָה. — Every other vowel immediately before ־ָה remains unaltered, e. g. אֲמַת, רִנַּת from אָמָה and רִנָּה.

Rem. 4. We find however בְּבַת, עֲקַת, פָּרַת and צָרַת from (בָּבָה), (עֲקָה), פָּרָה, and צָרָה; just as תֵּבַת from תֵּבָה and many others with צירה in the penultimate.

2) Nouns with other fem. endings remain unaltered, e. g. קְטֹרֶת, אַמְתַּחַת *st. constr.* from קְטֹרֶת and אַמְתַּחַת.

Rem. 5. כֻּתֹּנֶת is in the *st. constr.* כְּתֹנֶת.

C. Dual and plural nouns.

The terminations ־ִים and ־ַיִם are shortened into ־ֵי. The ending ־וֹת remains unchanged.

The first part of the word moreover undergoes the following alterations.

(*a*) The קָמֵץ and צֵירה immediately before the plur. termination become a half-vowel, and in consequence the preceding half-vowel changes into an auxiliary vowel, e. g. יְדֵי, דְּמֵי, אֲבוֹת, כְּלֵי, שְׁמוֹת, תּוֹשְׁבֵי,

תּוֹשָׁבִים, שֵׁמוֹת, כֵּלִים, אָבוֹת, דָּמִים, יָדַיִם, from תּוֹעֵבוֹת, צְבָאוֹת from חכמות פֹּעֲלֵי, בְּאֵרוֹת, צְבָאוֹת, and ;תּוֹעֵבוֹת חֲכָמוֹת, פֹּעֲלִים, בְּאֵרוֹת.

The קָמֵץ however remains unchanged before a guttural or ר, e. g. עָרַי, רָעַי, פָּרַי from פָּרִים, רָעִים, עָרִים.

Rem. 6. לְחָיַיִם and חֲטָאִים, גְּדָיִים; בָּתַי is in the *st. constr.* בָּתִים. in *st. constr.* גְדָיַו, חֲטָאֵי, לְחָיֵי. — The צֵירה of the segolate forms always remains, e. g. זֵיתֵי from זֵיתִים.

(b) All the other vowels remain unaltered, e. g. נְדִיבֵי צִפֳּרֵי, מְגוּרֵי from מְגוּרִים, גְּבוּרֵי from גְּבוּרִים, נְדִיבִים from צִפֳּרִים.

Rem. 7. אָהֳלֵי is in the *st. constr.* אֹהָלִים.

D. Rare and only poetic forms of the *st. constr.* are the terminations –ִי and –וֹ, e. g. בְּנֵי אֲתוֹנוֹ = בֶּן אֲתוֹנוֹ; חַיְתוֹ יָעַר = חַיַת יָעַר.

§ 61. The ה locative [1]).

1) The direction *whither* with verbs of motion may be expressed by אֶל or the letter-preposition לְ (cf. §§ 83, 84 B 2), but also by ־ָה appended to the noun.

2) Before this ־ָה the last *short* vowel in a *closed* syllable *not* having the accent is omitted, e. g. בַּיְתָה from בַּיִת, אַרְצָה from אֶרֶץ, אָהֱלָה from אֹהֶל. If however the last vowel is *long* or has the accent, or ־ָה is appended to a noun in the *st. constr.* no alteration is made, e. g. בָּבֶלָה, מִדְבָּרָה, בֵּיתָה, שְׁאוֹלָה from בָּבֶל, שְׁאוֹל, בַּיִת, מִדְבָּר.

---

1) Alterations in consequence of signs of tone or interpunction will be dealt with in §§ 88 II, 89 and 90.

§ 62. The pronominal suffixes of the noun (הַכִּנּוּיִם).

1) When a noun is to be connected with a pronoun *(genitive of subject or object)* suffixes are used just as with the verbs. — The pronominal suffixes therefore take the place of the possessive pronoun.

2) The suffixes appended to a singular noun differ from those which are used for the dual and plural.

3) The suffixes of a singular noun are:

	Plural.		Singular.	
1st pers.	—ֵנוּ, נוּ		—ִי	gem.
2d pers.	—ְכֶם, כֶם		—ְךָ, ךָ	m.
	—ְכֶן, כֶן		—ֵךְ, ךְ	f.
3d pers.	—ָם, הֶם		—ֶה, ־ֹה, וֹ, וּ, הוּ	m.
	—ן, הֶן, הֵן		—ָה, ־ָה, הָ	f.

4) The suffixes without union-vowel or שְׁוָא only occur with those very rare forms of the noun ending in a vowel, e. g. אֲבִיהֶם, פִּינוּ, אָחִיו, פִּיהוּ, אָבִיךָ.

5) The suffixes of a dual or plural noun are:

	Plural.		Singular.	
1st pers.	—ֵינוּ		—ַי	gem.
2d pers.	—ֵיכֶם, כֶם		—ֶיךָ	m.
	—ֵיכֶן, כֶן		—ַיִךְ	f.
3d pers.	—ֵיהֶם, הֶם		—ָיו, יהוּ—	m.
	—ֵיהֶן, הֵן		—ֶיהָ	f.

HEBREW GRAMMAR.

§ 63. Alterations which the singular nouns undergo before they are connected with suffixes.

A. Monosyllables *without* a preceding half-vowel.

(*a*) The קָמֵץ and צֵירה are: — 1) before כֶם and כֶן shortened. — 2) before ךָ and ךְ either shortened or retained. — 3) before the other suffixes they become a half-vowel, or are shortened, or retained; e. g. שְׁמִי, שִׁמְךָ, שִׁמְכֶם from שֵׁם; יָדוֹ, יָדְךָ, יֶדְכֶם from יָד; קְנוֹ from קֵן; בָּנוּ from בֵּן; גֵּוִי, גֵּוָם from גֵּו.

Rem. 1. אָב, אָח and (חָם) with suffixes are, אָבִי, אָבִיךָ, אֲבִיכֶם, אָבִיהוּ etc.

(*b*) The פַּתַח either remains or becomes חִירֶק, e. g. בַּדּוֹ from בַּד, פִּתִי from פַּת (cf. § 59 A *a* 3).

(*c*) Of שֶׂה we find שְׂיוֹ and שְׂיֵהוּ. With פֶּה the suffixes are appended to the form of the סְמִיכוּת, e. g. st. constr. פִּי therefore פִּיו, פִּיהוּ. — *My mouth* is פִּי.

(*d*) All the other vowels remain before the suffixes, e. g. עִירוֹ from עִיר, רִיבְכֶם from רִיב, אוֹרְךָ from אוֹר, סוּסִי from סוּס.

Rem. 2. The חוֹלֶם however of certain nouns is shortened into קִבּוּץ or קָמֵץ חָטוּף, e. g. חֻקִּי, חָקְךָ, חָקְכֶם from חֹק; עֻזִּי and עָזִּי from עֹז.

B. Monosyllables *with* a preceding half-vowel.

(*a*) The חִירֶק in an *open* syllable falls away before the suffixes and the preceding half-vowel becomes an auxiliary vowel (חִירֶק, סְגוֹל, or קָמֵץ חָטוּף), e. g. שְׁבִיוֹ, שִׁבְיְךָ from שְׁבִי; עָנְיִי from עֳנִי.

ALTERATIONS OF THE NOUN WITH SUFFIXES. 109

(*b*) The חוֹלֶם of the infinitive form פְּקֹד is shortened before כֶם and כֶן, e. g. אָכְלְכֶם; before the other suffixes, with exception of ךָ, it becomes a half-vowel, whilst the half-vowel of the פ׳הפעל becomes חִירֶק, or קָמֶץ חָטוּף, e. g. אָכְלוֹ, פָּקְדִי, שָׁכְבָה, בִּגְדוֹ. — Before ךָ the alterations are made in either manner, e. g. עָמָדְךָ and שָׁכְבְּךָ.

(*c*) In the other cases the noun remains unaltered, e. g. יְאֹרְךָ from יְאֹר; גְבוּלְכֶם, גְבוּלְךָ from גְבוּל.

C. Words of more than one syllable *without* fem. termination (the *segolate* forms excepted).

(*a*) The words in ה— throw off this ending, e. g. שָׂדַי, שָׂדֵהוּ from שָׂדֶה; מִקְנְךָ, מִקְנְכֶם from מִקְנֶה.

(*b*) The קָמַץ and צֵירֶה as final vowels are shortened before כֶם and כֶן, e. g. מַקֶּלְכֶם, קָרְבַּנְכֶם, שַׁבַּתְכֶם from מַקֵּל, קָרְבָּן, שַׁבָּת. Sometimes also the חוֹלֶם, e. g. מָעֻזְכֶם from מָעוֹז.

(*c*) With the other final vowels or before the other suffixes, the forms of the *st. constr.* are taken (§ 60 A *b*), of which the final short vowel is either lengthened or changed into its original long vowel, e. g. זָקֵן; חֲצֵרוֹ (חָצֵר) חָצֵר; צְבָאֲךָ (צְבָא) צָבָא; נְבִיאֲכֶם (נָבִיא) נָבִיא; רַעֲבוֹנוּ (רַעֲבוֹן) רָעָבוֹן; אֶצְבְּעוֹ (אֶצְבַּע) אֶצְבַּע; זְקֵנוֹ (זָקֵן).

Rem. 3. Exceptions are יָרֵךְ; שַׁבַּתּוֹ (שַׁבָּת) שַׁבָּת; מִקְלִי (מַקֵּל) מַקֵּל; גְלָלוֹ (גָלָל) גָלָל; כִּתְפָה (כָּתֵף) כָּתֵף; יְרֵכוֹ (יָרֵךְ).

D. The *segolate* forms.

1) The forms with וּ and י as עַהפעל have their suff-

ixes appended to the *st. constr.*, e. g. מוֹתוֹ from מָוֶת (מוֹת); בֵּיתְךָ from זִיתְכֶם (בֵּית) בַּיִת from זַיִת (זִית).

Rem. 4. Exceptions are עֲלוּ עֹל, עִירוֹ עִיר, שִׁיתוֹ שִׁית.

2) The other *segolate* forms lose the auxiliary vowel and shorten the חוֹלָם of the 1st syllable into קִבּוּץ or קָמֵץ חָטוּף, and the צֵירֵה into חִירֶק or סְגוֹל. — The פַּתַח however remains and the סְגוֹל either remains or changes into חִירֶק or פַּתַח; e. g. חָרְשׁוּ from חֹדֶשׁ; קָמְצוּ from קֶמֶץ (קֹמֶץ); יִצְרוֹ from יֵצֶר; חֶלְקוֹ from חֵלֶק; נַעֲרוֹ from נַעַר; נִכְדוֹ from נֶכֶד; בִּגְדוֹ from בֶּגֶד; אַבְנוֹ from אֶבֶן.

Rem. 5. Of נֹכַח we find נִכְחוֹ.

E. Words of more than one syllable *with* fem. termination.

1) The words in ‑ָה have כֶם and כֶן appended to the *unaltered st. constr.*, and the other suffixes to the *st. constr.* with prolonged final vowel; e. g. אִמְרָתִי, אִמְרַתְכֶם from אִמְרָה (אִמְרַת); זְמָתָם, זִמַּתְכֶן from זִמָּה (זִמַּת).

Rem. 6. The words however which in the *st. constr.* end in ת (cf. § 60 Rem. 4) follow the rule of n° 2.

2) The words in ‑ֶת and ‑ַת change the second half just as the *segolate* forms, whilst their first half remains unaltered, e. g. בְּשִׁתָּם from בֹּשֶׁת, לִדְתּוֹ from לֶדֶת, אַדַּרְתּוֹ from אַדֶּרֶת.

3) The words in ‑ִית and ‑וּת remain unaltered, e. g. זְנוּתְכֶם, בְּרִיתִי.

4) אָחוֹת and חָמוֹת are with suffixes אֲחוֹתִי etc. חֲמוֹתָהּ etc.; and in the same manner are altered the infinitives

in וֹת ‒ with two syllables, e. g. רְאוֹתַי from רָאוֹת; those however with more than two syllables remain unaltered, e. g. בִּהְיוֹתְכֶם, בַּהֲבָנוֹתוֹ.

Rem. 7. Examples of nouns connected with suffixes will be given in appendix 4.

§ 64. Alterations of the dual and plural forms before they are connected with suffixes.

(*a*) The forms in ים ‒ and ‒ִים.

1) הֶן הֶם, כֶן, כֶם are appended to the *st. constr.*, e. g. (דְּבָרַי). דְּבָרִים (מַלְכֵי) מְלָכִים from דִּבְרֵיכֶם, מַלְכֵיהֶם.

2) The other suffixes are appended to the dual and plural forms, after ים ‒ and ‒ִים have been cut off, e. g. יָדָיו, מְלָכֶיהָ, דְּבָרֵינוּ.

(*b*) The forms in וֹת ‒ have their suffixes appended to the unaltered *st. constr.*, e. g. שְׁמוֹתֶיךָ from שֵׁמוֹת (שְׁמוֹת), אֲבוֹתָיו from אָבוֹת (אֲבוֹת).

§ 65. The noun with prefixed letters (מֹשֶׁה וְכָלֵב).

Of the letters which are prefixed the ה alone is here considered, because the others will be spoken of in §§ 83, 84 B and 85 B.

The ה prefixed to a noun has two different meanings.

a. As הַיְדִיעָה it has a meaning corresponding with that of our definite article.

1) ה' הַיְדִיעָה has פַּתַח as its vowel, e. g. הַשֵּׁם. Before a guttural or ר it usually has קָמַץ, but before ח it often retains פַּתַח, e. g. הַחוֹמָה, הָרֶכֶב, הָאָדָם.

2) If ח has הַיְדִיעָה 'ה קָמֶץ generally has סְגוֹל, e. g. הֶחָכָם, הֶחָג; so also before ה and ע provided they have not the accent, e. g. הֶהָרִים, הֶעָפָר yet הָהָר, הָעָם.

b. As הַשְּׁאֵלָה 'ה (ה *interrogative*) it introduces a question.

1) The ה *interrogative* has חֲטַף פַּתַח, e. g. הֲגוֹי. Before a guttural which has no קָמֶץ, and before a half-vowel it has פַּתַח, e. g. הַחֵקֶר, הַבְּרָכָה¹).

2) When the guttural has קָמֶץ, the ה *interrogative* has סְגוֹל, e. g. הֶחָכָם Job 15,2; הֶעָלֶה Job 13,25.

CHAPTER XI.

The adjective (תֹּאַר הַשֵּׁם).

§ 66. The gender of the adjectives.

1) All adjectives are capable of receiving a fem. form *(motio)*.

The masculine is the primitive form, from which the feminine is derived.

2) This derivation is made by appending הָ or ת—, and when the masc. form ends in י— a simple ת, under

---

1) The letter following ה *interrogative* has no דָּגֵשׁ that it may be distinguished from הַיְדִיעָה 'ה. Whenever this distinction can be disregarded, for instance with words incapable of ה הַיְדִיעָה, a דָּגֵשׁ is placed in the letter following ה *interrogative*, as is usually done after a short vowel; e. g. הַבְּמִחְתַּנִים, הַלְּבֶן, הַיֵּיטַב.

THE ADJECTIVE.

the same rules for the alteration of vowels as those given for the substantives, e. g. שׁוֹמֵר, מֵבִיא, גָּדוֹל, בָּקָח fem. בָּקְחָה, שׁוֹמֶרֶת, מְבִיאָה, גְּדוֹלָה; שְׁלִישִׁי fem. שְׁלִישִׁית and שְׁלִישִׁיָה.

Rem. When the last stem-letter is a guttural, the סֶגוֹל of ת— is changed into פַּתָח, and this change again affects the preceding סֶגוֹל, e. g. מַגִּיעַ, בּוֹרֵחַ from מַגַּעַת, בּוֹרַחַת.

3) Masc. forms in ה— become fem. by changing their termination into ־ָה, e. g. יָפָה, גּוֹלָה from יָפֶה, גּוֹלֶה.

4) The adjectives of the form פָּעוֹל with א or ע as 1st stem-letter shorten their חוֹלָם before the fem. termination, e. g. עֲנֻגָה, אֲיֻמָה. In the same manner (נְקֻדָה) from נָקֹד. — מָתוֹק is in fem. מְתוּקָה.

§ 67. The derivation of the adjectives.

All adjectives are derived either from the stem of a verb or from a nomen.

Primitive or compound adjectives are not found.

I. Adjectives derived from a verbal stem.

A. *Without* addition of letters.

1) The participles of the קַל and the נִפְעַל, e. g. יוֹשֵׁב, נָכוֹן, בָּא, שָׁב, צַר, טוֹב, מֵת, גֶעֱזָב, עָצוּר, קָטֹן, זָקֵן.

2) The בֵּינוֹנִי פָּעוּל of the קַל of the triliteral stems has as adjective the collateral form פָּעִיל, e. g. שָׂנִיא and שָׂנוּא Deut. 21,15. — This collateral form is frequently used as a substantive, e. g. מָשִׁיחַ *the anointed*, sometimes with an intransitive sense as צָעִיר *young* and sometimes even

8

with an active sense, as נָבִיא *prophet*. — The primitive forms also now and then have similar meanings, e. g. בָּחוּר *lad*; שָׁכוּן *dwelling* Judges 8,11; אָחוּז *holding* Cant. 3,8.

3) With the בֵּינוֹנִי פָּעוּל is closely connected the form פָּעוֹל e. g. שָׂכוּל, רַחוּם. This form is generally used to denote a certain characteristic quality, a meaning which the form פָּעוּל also now and then expresses, e. g. חָרוּץ *a diligent man*.

4) Also the form פָּעִיל is closely connected with the בֵּינוֹנִי פָּעוּל. This form has the alterations of both n° 2 and 3, as אסיר and אָסִיר; and is used as substantive e. g. אָסִיר and as adjective, e. g. צַדִּיק.

5) The form פָּעֵל of the triliteral stems, e. g. חָכָם, עָנָו, with a purely adjective meaning. With the verbs ל"ה this form has a סגול under the second stem-letter e. g. קָשֶׁה.

6) Closely connected with the preceding is the form פָּעָל, e. g. חַטָּא, גַּנָּב. This form denotes a quality as a habit.

Rem. 1. A rare collateral form of פָּעָל is קַנּוֹא Nah. 1,2.

7) The form פָּעוֹל of the triliteral stems, e. g. קָרוֹב, עָנֹג.

8) The forms פָּעוּל and פָּעֵל of the triliteral stems, e. g. עִקֵּשׁ, גִּבּוֹר. The latter form is chiefly used to qualify certain organic operations, as אִלֵּם *deaf*, פִּקֵּחַ *sharp of sight or hearing*, חרשׁ *deaf* (cf. § 4 Rem. 5).

B. *With* the addition of letters prefixed or appended.

1) All the participles except those of the קַל and נִפְעַל, e. g. מְחוֹלָל, מֵצַר, מִתְנַקֵּם, מַשְׁחִית, מְמוּרָט, מְזֻבָּח.

2) Adjectives of the form פַּעֲלוּל, e. g. נַבְנוּן.

3) Adjectives formed by duplication of the last two stem-letters of the triliteral stems, e. g. פְּתַלְתֹּל; chiefly in use with colours, to express a modification of the original colour, e. g. אֲדַמְדָּם *deep red, crimson* from אָדֹם *red*.

II. Adjectives derived from a nomen.

1) Like the בֵּינוֹנִי פֹּעֵל of the קַל various adjectives are formed without addition of letters. They are however generally used as substantives, e. g. כּוֹרֵם *vine-dresser* from כֶּרֶם *vineyard*.

2) By appending the termination ‎ִי— (fem. ‎ִיָּה—) adjectives are formed·

(*a*) from proper names to denote ones origin, e. g. יִשְׂרְאֵלִי *Israelite* from יִשְׂרָאֵל *Israel*; אֲרָמִית *Aramaic* from אֲרָם *Aram*.

(*b*) from the cardinal numbers to make the ordinals, e. g. שִׁשִּׁי *the sixth* from שֵׁשׁ *six*.

Rem. 2. When these adjectives are formed from a compound proper name, the component parts of the proper name are first separated, e. g. אֲבִי הָעֶזְרִי *the Abiezerite* from אֲבִיעֶזֶר *Abiezer*.

§ 68. The number of the adjective.

1) The adjective has two numbers, viz. the *singular* and the *plural*.

2) The plur. of *all* the masc. adjectives ends in ‎ִים— and that of *all* the feminine in ‎וֹת—, e. g. יָפִים from יפה and יָפוֹת from יָפָה.

3) The plur. is formed from the sing. according to the

same rules as those for the substantives, e. g. חֲכָמִים, שׁוֹמְרִים, שׁוֹמְרוֹת from שׁוֹמֶרֶת, שׁוֹמֵר, חָכָם (cf. § 59). — The adjectives, however, spoken of in § 66,4, undergo here the same alteration as has been explained there, e. g. מְתוּקִים, נְקֻדִּים, אֲדֻמִּים; whilst the fem. forms in ־ִית form their plur. like the corresponding forms in ־ִיָה e g עִבְרִיּוֹת from עִבְרִית (עִבְרִיָּה).

§ 69. Other causes for which the adjectives are altered.

(*a*) The *st. constr.* and the *literae praefixae* affect the adjectives in the same manner as the substantives, e. g. גָּדוֹל, מְאִירָה, יָפָה, יְפַת, מְאִירַת, יְפֵה from גָּדוֹל, יָפֶה; הַגָּדוֹל, הָאַדִּיר from אַדִּיר, גָּדוֹל. — The plurals however of monosyllabic participles retain in the *st. constr.* even the קָמַץ and צֵירה, e. g. מֵתֵי, צָרֵי from מֵתִים, צָרִים.

(*b*) Adjectives may be connected with suffixes like the substantives, whenever they are used as such. This occurs chiefly with the participles.

The appending of suffixes takes place according to the following rules.

1) The monosyllables always retain their vowel, e. g. צָרַי, גֵּרוֹ (cf. *a*).

2) The sing. masc. of the בינוני פּוֹעֵל of the קַל changes the צֵירה of the הִפְעִיל before ךָ, כֶם, כֶן into סֶגוֹל, e. g. חֹתֶנְךָ; and when ע or ח of לְהִפְעִיל is a guttural into פַּתַח, e. g. שֹׂנַאֲךָ, גֹּאֲלְךָ. Before the other suffixes צֵירה becomes a half-vowel, e. g. שׁוֹמְרֵי, גֹּאֲלָם, שֹׂנְאוּ.

THE PRONOUNS.

3) The sing. masc. of the בֵּינוֹנִי of the פָּעֵל changes the צירה of the עׇ֫הפעל before כן ,כם, ךָ into סגול or חִירֶק, e. g. מְקַלֶּלְךָ, מְקַדְּשְׁכֶם, מְקַדְּשָׁם. When, however, the ל׳הפעל is a guttural the צִירֶה remains, e. g. מְשַׁלֵּחֲךָ. Before the other suffixes it becomes a half-vowel, e. g. מְקַדְּשׁוּ, מְקַבְּצָם.

4) All other forms follow the rules of the substantives, e. g. מַפְרְךָ, מְיֻדָּעַי, אֲהוּבִי, קְרוֹבוֹ, מַעֲרִיצְכֶם.

CHAPTER XII.

The pronoun (כנוי).

§ 70. 1) The pronouns which are expressed by a separate words are:

(a) The *personal pronoun* (כנוי הגוף) as *subject*.
(b) The *demonstrative pronoun* (כנוי הָרוֹמֵז).
(c) The *relative pronoun* (כנוי הַמִּצְטָרֵף).
(d) The *interrogative pronoun* (כנוי הַשְּׁאֵלָה).

2) The *personal pronoun* as *object* has been treated of as suffix appended to the verb (§§ 46—49).

The *possessive pronoun* (כנוי הַקִּנְיָן) has been treated of as a suffix appended to the noun (§§ 62—64 and 69).

The *reflexive pronoun* (כנוי הַחוֹזֵר) is expressed in the following manner:

(a) by means of certain conjugations of the verb, chiefly by the הִתְפַּעֵל, e. g. הִתְנַכֵּר *to make oneself unknown*, הִתְרָאוֹת *to behold one another*, but also by the נִפְעַל

especially with a reciprocal sense, e. g. הִסָּתֵר *to hide oneself*, הִתְוַכֵּחַ *to strive with one another*

(b) by אֵת with suffixes, e. g. וְהִשִּׂיאוּ אוֹתָם *and they will burden themselves*. Lev. 22,16.

(c) by pronominal suffixes with certain prepositions, e. g. וַיַּעַשׂ לוֹ *and he made for himself*

(d) by certain nouns such as לֵב and others, e. g. בְּלִבּוֹ *unto himself*.

§ 71. The personal pronoun.

1) The personal pronouns are:

	Plural.		Singular.	
we	אֲנַחְנוּ, נַחְנוּ, אָנוּ	I	אֲנִי, אָנֹכִי	gem.
you	אַתֶּם	thou	אַתָּה	m.
you	אַתֵּן, אַתֶּן	thou	אַתְּ	f.
they	הֵם	he	הוּא	m.
they	הֵן	she	הוּא, הִיא	f.

Rem. 1. Instead of the 2ᵈ pers. masc. sing. the fem. form אַתְּ occurs three times in the Bible.

2) All these forms are used as substantives and only as subject of the sentence. They cannot therefore be connected with the literae praefixae בכלם which represent the inflections of the noun, but only with the letters הוש, viz. with the ה merely as הַשְׁאֵלָה 'ה e. g. הָאָנֹכִי, הַאַתָּה, and with שׁ and ו according to the rule of § 85 B.

Rem. 2. Concerning the use of certain of those pronouns as adjectives see the following §.

Rem. 3. The pers. pronoun is sometimes employed to repeat the pronominal suffix in a separate form, e. g. לִבִּי גַם אָנִי Prov. 23,15.

THE PRONOUNS.

3) To express the inflections of the pers. pronoun, אֵת with suffixes is used to express the object, and בכלם with suffixes for the other cases.

4) The alteration of the vowels of the pers. pronouns is only occasioned by the signs of tone or of interpunction. See § 89.

§ 72. The demonstrative pronoun.

1) The demonstrative pronouns are:

	Plural.		Singular.	
these	זוֹ, אֵלֶּה, אֵל	this	זֶה	m.
those		that	זֹאת, זֹה, זוֹ	f.
			זוֹ	gem.

2) All these forms are used as adjectives, and may be connected with the literae praefixae מֹשֶׁה וְכָלֵב.

3) Connected with ה' הידיעה we find the collateral form הַלָּזֶה for the masc. sing. and הַלֵּזוּ for the fem. sing. Both forms may be shortened into הַלָּז.

4) The personal pronouns of the 3ᵈ pers., connected with ה' הַיְדִיעָה may take the place of the demonstrative pronouns, e. g. הָהֵן, הָהֵם, הַהִיא, הַהוּא.

Rem. זוּ also generally implies the meaning of a relative pronoun, e. g. זוּ = *which*.

§ 73. The relative pronoun.

1) There is but one relative pronoun for all genders and numbers, viz. אֲשֶׁר.

2) אֲשֶׁר is used as a substantive. It takes the place

of the subject and object, and with the assistance of one of the letters בכלם expresses also the other cases.

3) It is evident from the use of the ה and שׁ (§§ 65 and 85 B 2) that these two letters cannot be connected with אֲשֶׁר.

§ 74. The interrogative pronoun.

1) The interrogative pronouns are מִי for persons, and מָה and מה for things, with no difference of number and gender.

2) They are used as substantives. They take the place of the subject and object, and express the other cases with the help of one of the letters בכלם.

Rem. מָה connected with מַקָּף becomes מה.

CHAPTER XIII.

The number (מִלַּת הַמִּסְפָּר).

§ 75. 1) There are in Hebrew two kinds of numbers.
(*a*) The *cardinal* (מִסְפְּרֵי הַיְסוֹד).
(*b*) The *ordinal* (מִסְפְּרֵי הַסֵּדֶר).

2) Both kinds may undergo all the alterations to which the nomen is subject. Here the alterations alone are spoken of in which they deviate from the substantive and adjective.

§ 76. The Cardinals.

1) The cardinals from *one* to *ten* may be connected with the nouns, to which they belong, in a twofold manner, viz. as *substantives* and as *adjectives*.

2) Used as substantives they express a *unit, triad, decade* etc., and are then in the *st. constr.* connected with the noun to which they belong.

3) The cardinals are:

	as substantives.		as adjectives.	
	Fem.	Masc.	Fem.	Masc.
	אַחַת	אֶחָד	אַחַת	אֶחָד
	שְׁתֵּי	שְׁנֵי	שְׁתַּיִם	שְׁנַיִם
3	שְׁלֹשׁ	שְׁלֹשֶׁת	שָׁלֹשׁ	שְׁלֹשָׁה
4	אַרְבַּע	אַרְבַּעַת	אַרְבַּע	אַרְבָּעָה
5	חֲמֵשׁ	חֲמֵשֶׁת	חָמֵשׁ	חֲמִשָּׁה
6	שֵׁשׁ	שֵׁשֶׁת	שֵׁשׁ	שִׁשָּׁה
7	שְׁבַע	שִׁבְעַת	שֶׁבַע	שִׁבְעָה
8	(שְׁמֹנַת)	שְׁמֹנַת	שְׁמֹנֶה	שְׁמֹנָה
9	תְּשַׁע	תִּשְׁעַת	תֵּשַׁע	תִּשְׁעָה
10	עֶשֶׂר	עֲשֶׂרֶת	עֶשֶׂר	עֲשָׂרָה

Rem. 1. It is curious that the numbers from 3—10 are connected *also as adjectives* in the *fem. form* with *masc.* nouns and vice versa, e. g. חָמֵשׁ יָדוֹת, חֲמִשָּׁה יָמִים.

Rem. 2. אַרְבָּעָה and שִׁבְעָה have a dual form שִׁבְעָתַיִם, אַרְבַּעְתַּיִם with the meaning *fourfold, sevenfold*.

Rem. 3. As plural forms of the cardinals we find אֲחָדִים *some, a few, the same, united into one*, עֲשָׂרוֹת *tens*.

Rem. 4. A number connected with a suffix appears in שְׁלָשְׁתְּכֶם (*your triad*) *the three of you*. Num. 12,4.

4) The numbers from 11—19 are used as adjectives only. They are formed by connecting the units as substantives with עָשָׂר for the masc. and with עֶשְׂרֵה for the fem. With עֶשְׂרֵה the units are connected in the *st. constr.*, with עָשָׂר those from 13—19 generally in the *st. absolutus*.

They are:

	Fem.	Masc.
11	אַחַת עֶשְׂרֵה or עַשְׁתֵּי עֶשְׂרֵה	אַחַד עָשָׂר or עַשְׁתֵּי עָשָׂר
12	שְׁתֵּים עֶשְׂרֵה (somet. שְׁתֵּי עֶשְׂרֵה)	שְׁנֵים עָשָׂר (somet. שְׁנֵי עָשָׂר)
13	שְׁלֹשׁ עֶשְׂרֵה	שְׁלֹשָׁה עָשָׂר
14	אַרְבַּע עֶשְׂרֵה	אַרְבָּעָה עָשָׂר
15	חֲמֵשׁ עֶשְׂרֵה	חֲמִשָּׁה עָשָׂר (חֲמֵשֶׁת עָשָׂר rarely)
16	שֵׁשׁ עֶשְׂרֵה	שִׁשָּׁה עָשָׂר
17	שְׁבַע עֶשְׂרֵה	שִׁבְעָה עָשָׂר
18	שְׁמֹנֶה עֶשְׂרֵה	שְׁמֹנָה עָשָׂר (שְׁמֹנַת עָשָׂר rarely)
19	תְּשַׁע עֶשְׂרֵה	תִּשְׁעָה עָשָׂר

5) *Twenty* is עֶשְׂרִים, the plur. of עֶשֶׂר, and the other tens from 30—90 are expressed by the plur. of the corresponding units, thus שְׁלֹשִׁים 30, אַרְבָּעִים 40, חֲמִשִּׁים 50, שִׁשִּׁים 60, שִׁבְעִים (not שְׁבָעִים) 70, שְׁמֹנִים 80, תִּשְׁעִים (not תְּשָׁעִים) 90.

6) *One hundred* is מֵאָה, a fem. noun. מָאתַיִם (instead of מְאָתַיִם) 200 is the dual of מֵאָה.

The hundreds from 300—900 are expressed by the plur. of מֵאָה preceded by the fem. form of a unit in the

THE NUMERALS. 123

st. constr., thus שְׁלֹשׁ מֵאוֹת 300, אַרְבַּע מֵאוֹת 400, חֲמֵשׁ מֵאוֹת 500, שֵׁשׁ מֵאוֹת 600, שְׁבַע מאות 700, שְׁמֹנֶה מֵאוֹת 800, תְּשַׁע מֵאוֹת 900.

7) *One thousand* is אֶלֶף, a masc. noun. 2000 is אַלְפַּיִם. The thousands from 3000—9000 are expressed by the plur. of אֶלֶף preceded by the masc. form. of a unit in the *st. constr.*, thus שְׁלֹשֶׁת אֲלָפִים 3000, אַרְבַּעַת אֲלָפִים 4000, חֲמֵשֶׁת אֲלָפִים 5000, שֵׁשֶׁת אֲלָפִים 6000, שִׁבְעַת אֲלָפִים 7000, שְׁמֹנַת אֲלָפִים 8000, תִּשְׁעַת אֲלָפִים 9000.

8) *Ten thousand* is רְבָבָה, but connected with units it is רבוא, רבו or רִבּוֹת. All these are fem. nouns, e. g. שְׁתֵּי רִבּוֹא or שְׁתַּיִם עֶשְׂרֵה רִבּוֹ 20,000, אַרְבַּע רִבּוֹא 40,000, רִבּוֹתַיִם or רִבּוֹת 120,000. — The more usual expressions however are מֵאָה וְעֶשְׂרִים אֶלֶף, ארבעים אלף, עֶשְׂרִים אֶלֶף. — 10,000 may also be expressed by עֲשֶׂרֶת אֲלָפִים.

9) *One hundred thousand* is מֵאָה אֶלֶף or מְאַת אֶלֶף; 200,000 מָאתַיִם אֶלֶף; 300,000 שְׁלֹשׁ מֵאוֹת אֶלֶף etc.

10) When units are to be connected with tens they may be placed either before or after the tens, e. g. אֶחָד וְשִׁשִּׁים or שִׁשִּׁים וְאֶחָד 61. — With the hundreds and thousands the units stand first, or last, or between the tens and the hundreds, e. g. שֵׁשׁ מֵאוֹת חָמֵשׁ וְשִׁבְעִים or שֵׁשׁ מֵאוֹת וְשִׁבְעִים וְחָמֵשׁ 675. — If however no units are named the numbers are by preference placed in a descending order, e. g. 601,750 שֵׁשׁ מֵאוֹת אֶלֶף וָאֶלֶף שְׁבַע מֵאוֹת וַחֲמִשִּׁים In all cases the ו conjunctive is placed before the second number and also generally before the other numbers.

Rem. 5. The letters of the alphabet are used as ciphers in the following manner: א—י = 1—10; כ—צ = 20—90; ק = 100, ר = 200, ש = 300, ת = 400, ך = 500, ם = 600, ן = 700, ף = 800, ץ = 900. The last five letters are at present less in use. We generally write תק = 500, תר = 600 etc.; התק = 900 etc. — Further, a letter marked with ¯ or ˙, placed over it, indicates as many thousands as the letter expresses units, e. g. א or אֿ 1000, ד or דֿ 4000. — הֿ תרנח or ה תרנח = 5658.

§ 77. The Ordinals.

1) The ordinals are adjectives and only occur with the numbers from 1—10.

2) The ordinals are made from the cardinals by adding ־ִי for the masc. and ־ִית or ־ִיָּה for the fem., along with a quite peculiar alteration of vowels. In אַרְבַּע moreover the א falls away. *The first* is always expressed by רִאשׁוֹן, רִאשׁוֹנָה from the noun רֹאשׁ *head, beginning.*

The ordinals are:

Masc. רִאשׁוֹן, שֵׁנִי, שְׁלִישִׁי, רְבִיעִי, חֲמִישִׁי or חמשי, שִׁשִּׁי, שְׁבִיעִי, שְׁמִינִי, תְּשִׁיעִי, עֲשִׂירִי or עָשׂוּר.

Fem. רִאשׁוֹנָה, שֵׁנִית, שְׁלִישִׁית or שְׁלִישִׁיָּה, רְבִיעִית, חֲמִישִׁית, שִׁשִּׁית, שְׁבִיעִית, שְׁמִינִית, תְּשִׁיעִית, עֲשִׂירִית or עֲשִׂירִיָּה.

3) The ordinals above ten have no appropriate forms, but are expressed by the cardinals, e. g. יוֹם עָשָׂר בחמשה *on the 15th day.* — Even with the units the cardinals are more than once used instead of the ordinals, e. g בתשעה לַחֹדֶשׁ *on the 9th day of the month.*

§ 78. Manner of expressing the other kinds of numerals.

1) The *distributiva* (*singuli, bini, terni* etc.) are expressed by repetition of the cardinals, e. g. שְׁנַיִם שְׁנַיִם *two by two*.

2) The *adverbia numeralia* (*twice, thrice, four times*) are expressed by the cardinals with a noun implying the idea *times*, e. g. פַּעַם אֶחָת *once*, פַּעֲמַיִם *twice*, עֶשֶׂרֶת מנים *ten times*, שָׁלֹשׁ רְגָלִים or שָׁלֹשׁ פְּעָמִים *three times* (cf. § 80, 1*f*).

Rem. *Four times* and *seven times* may also be expressed by אַרְבַּעְתַּיִם and שִׁבְעָתַיִם. (§ 76 Rem. 2).

3) Fractions are expressed by the ordinals in the fem., e. g. שְׁלִישִׁית הַהִין *the third of a Hin*. — $1/4$ is also expressed by רֶבַע or רְבַע; $1/5$ also by חֹמֶשׁ; $1/10$ also by עִשָּׂרוֹן pl. עֶשְׂרֹנִים. — $1/2$ is in Hebrew חֲצִי (in pausa חֵצִי), מֶחֱצָה or מַחֲצִית.

CHAPTER XIV

The Particles (מִלּוֹת).

§ 79. 1) The particles are:
(*a*) the *adverb* (תֹּאַר הַתֹּאַר or תֹּאַר הַפֹּעַל),
(*b*) the *preposition* (מִלַּת הַיַּחַס),
(*c*) the *conjunction* (מִלַּת הַחִבּוּר),
(*d*) the *interjection* (מִלַּת הַקְּרִיאָה).

2) There are but very few primitive particles. They generally are nomina or verba, which in course of time have acquired the peculiar meaning of particles.

§ 80. The Adverb.

1) As adverbs the nomina (amongst which also the infinitive) are used *with* or *without* a preposition.

   (*a*) Substantives connected with a preposition, e. g. מִבַּיִת *within* (from בַּיִת *house*), בִּמְאֹד *with strength* = *very* (from מְאֹד *strength*).

   (*b*) Substantives without a preposition, e. g. מְאֹד *very*, בֶּטַח *(security) safely*, הַיּוֹם *(the day) now* Lat. *hodie*.

   (*c*) The infinitive, as הַרְבֵּה *(the multiplying) much.* Sometimes also with prepositions, e. g. לְהַרְבֵּה Neh. 5,18.

   (*d*) Adjectives, chiefly in the fem. form, e. g. רַבָּה or רַבַּת *much*, אֲרָמִית *in Aramaic manner*

   (*e*) Pronouns, e. g. הֵנָּה *hither*.

   (*f*) Numerals, e. g. שֶׁבַע *seventimes*, שֵׁנִית *a second time*, רִאשׁוֹנָה *in the first place, first of all.* — Sometimes also connected with prepositions, e. g. בָּרִאשׁוֹנָה, לְמַבָּרִאשׁוֹנָה, לָרִאשׁוֹנָה 1 Chron. 15,13.

2) Further, adverbs are formed from substantives through the addition of ־ָם or ־ֹם, e. g. חִנָּם *gratis*, from חֵן *favour*, פִּתְאֹם (instead of פִּתְעָם) *suddenly* from פֶּתַע *moment;* or of other terminations, e. g. קְמָמִיּוּת *straight*.

3) There are a few adverbs which probably are primitive, or of which at least it is difficult to trace the derivation, e. g. לֹא *no, not*, מָתַי *when*.

4) There are also a few compound adverbs e. g. מדוע

ADVERBS AND PREPOSITIONS.

(from מַה and דוּעַ = דֵּעַ) *why;* בִּלְעֲדֵי (from בַּל and עֲדֵי) *besides;* — chiefly those compounded with אִי, as אִיפֹה or אֵיכֹה ,אֵיפוֹ or אֵיכוֹ.

§ 81. Adverbs with suffixes.

Certain adverbs, *implying the idea of the verb to be*, may be connected with the verbal suffixes, and by preference through means of the נ *epentheticum* (see § 46, 5). e. g.:

אֵינֶנִּי *I am not*, אֵינְכֶם *you are not*, from אַיִן, אֵין.
אַיֶּכָה *where art thou*, אַיּוֹ *where is he*, from אַיֵּה *where.*
הִנְנִי *here am I*, הננו *here are we*, from הֵן or הִנֵּה *(behold!).*
עוֹדֶנִי *as yet I am* from עוֹד *yet.*

In addition to these we find other adverbs which are connected with the nominal suffixes, e. g. בִּלְעָדַי *besides me*, בִּלְעָדוֹ *without him* from בִּלְעֲדֵי *without, besides.*

§ 82. The preposition.

The prepositions are divided into two classes:

A. *Letter-prepositions.* They are the letters בכלמ, which prefixed to a noun take the place of a preposition, e. g. בְּרֵאשִׁית *in the beginning* from רֵאשִׁית *beginning;* לִשְׁתּוֹת *for the purpose of drinking, to drink.*

B. *Word-prepositions.* As such are used:

1) Substantives in the *st. constr.*, e. g. עַל *upon* (from עָל *height*), אֵצֶל *at the side of, close by* (from אֵצֶל *side*).

2) Letter-prepositions connected with:

(a) a substantive in the *st. constr.*, e. g. לִפְנֵי *(before the face of)* before, בִּגְלַל *because of* (from גָּלָל).

(b) an adverb, e. g. מֵאַיִן *without* (from אַיִן *not*), בְּדֵי *enough for* (from דַּי *sufficiency*).

(c) a word-preposition, e. g. מִתַּחַת *under*, מֵעַל *over, above* (from תַּחַת and עַל).

3) Word-prepositions connected with a substantive in the *st. constr.*, e. g. אֶל־פְּנֵי *before*, עַל־אוֹדוֹת *because of.*

§ 83. The Vowels of the Letter-prepositions.

1) The letters בכל when prefixed to other words have the half-vowel, e. g. לְקֵץ, כְּאַיִן, בְּרָב. This half-vowel becomes a חִירֶק whenever the word itself to which it is prefixed commences with a half-vowel, e. g. כִּזְכֹר, בִּבְנִי, לִנְפֹל, and if the first letter of the word is a י with the half-vowel, the latter falls away after the חִירֶק, e. g. בִּימֵי, לִימִין, כִּימוֹת. — Before a guttural however with חֲטָף the letter-preposition takes the vowel of which the חֲטָף is composed, e. g. לֶאֱכֹל, כַּאֲרִי, בַּאֲנִי.

Rem. There are however the exceptions לֵאלֹהוּ, כֵּאלֹהִים, בֵּאלֹהִים, לֵאמֹר.

2) With the ה' הַיְדִיעָה the letter-prepositions are usually contracted, with the consequence that they take the vowel of the ה which is then omitted, e. g. בְּהַיּוֹם = בַּיּוֹם, לְהֶעָפָר = לֶעָפָר, כְּהָאֶבֶן = כָּאֶבֶן. — In a similar manner we sometimes find the ל contracted with the ה of the infinitive, e. g. וּלְהַאֲדִיב = וְלַאֲדִיב, לְהַרְאֹתְכֶם = לַרְאֹתְכֶם.

PREPOSITIONS.

3) The ל generally has קָמַץ immediately before the accent, e. g. לָשֶׁבֶת, לָנֶצַח, לָתֵת, unless the word is closely connected with the subsequent word, e. g. לְשֶׁבֶת אַבְרָם Gen. 16,3.

With certain monosyllabic pronouns even the בּ and כּ have the קָמַץ e. g. כָּזֶה, בָּזֶה.

Before מָה or מֶה the בּ and כּ have פַּתַח, e. g. בַּמֶּה, כַּמֶּה; but the ל has קָמַץ, e. g. לָמָה, לָמֶה.

4) The מ is an abbreviation of מִן. As prefix therefore it has חִירֶק and ought to be followed by a דָגֵשׁ to supplement the missing נ, e. g. מִן בוֹא = מִבּוֹא. The חִירֶק becomes צֵירֶה before אהחער, e. g. מֵאָדָם, מֵרָאוֹת. Before ה or ח however the חִירֶק is sometimes retained, e. g. מִחוּט, מִהְיוֹת. The דָגֵשׁ is now and then also omitted when the first letter has the half-vowel, e. g. מִלְמַעְלָה. Hence the half-vowel falls away under the י, e. g. מִידֵי.

§ 84. The prepositions with pronominal suffixes.

A. The word-prepositions.

1) Since the word-prepositions originally were substantives they are capable of being connected with the pronominal suffixes, e. g. לְפָנַי from לִפְנֵי, אַחֲרַי, אַחֲרָיו from אַחֲרֵי, בֵּינִי from בֵּין, תַּחַת from תַּחְתָּם, אֶצֶל from אֶצְלִי.

2) Of אֶל, עַד and עַל the poetic plural forms עֲלֵי, עֲדֵי and עֱלֵי are used for the connection with suffixes, e. g. עֲלֵיהֶם, עָלֶיךָ, עָלֵינוּ, אֵלָיו, אֵלַי. — Also of other prepositions the *st. constr.* of the plur. form is used by preference,

e. g. סָבִיב ,סְבִיבָיו (אַחֲרָיו (אַחֲרַי) and סְבִיבֹתָיו (not סְבִיבוֹ) from סָבִיב; אַחֲרָיו (אַחֲרַי) from אַחַר. — Of בֵּין, although בֵּינְךָ, בֵּינִי, yet always בֵּינוֹתָם and בֵּינוֹתֵינוּ, now and then even בֵּינֵינוּ, בֵּינֵיכֶם, בֵּינֵיהֶם.— With תַּחַת the suffixes appear to have been appended to the form תַּחְתִּי, e. g. תַּחְתָּיו, תַּחְתֵּינוּ etc. תַּחְתָּם alone, however, is yet found along with תַּחְתֵּיהֶם.

3) עִם, on the other hand, is connected with suffixes like an ordinary monosyllabic substantive, as עִמָּה, עִמּוֹ etc. Instead of עִמִּי we find also עִמָּדִי.

Rem. הִנֵּה occurs a few times with a verbal suffix, e. g. תַּחְתֵּנִי 2 Sam. 22,37.40.48.

4) אֵת. generally indicates the object of an action and as such is left untranslated. It has however also the meaning *with*.

In the first case it is connected with suffixes as if these were appended to the form אוֹת, e. g. אוֹתִי, אוֹתְךָ etc. Along with אוֹתָן, אוֹתָם and אוֹתְכֶם we find the collateral forms אֶתְהֶן, אֶתְהֶם and אֶתְכֶם; whilst of אֶתְכֶן no other form occurs.

In the second case its connection with suffixes is quite regular, e. g. אִתְּךָ, אִתִּי etc.

B. The letter-prepositions with suffixes.

1) בְּ with suffixes; *sing.* בִּי, בְּךָ, בָּךְ, בּוֹ, בָּהּ; *plur.* בָּנוּ, בָּכֶם, בָּכֶן, בָּהֶם or בָּם (בְּהֵמָּה) בָּהֶן, בָּהֵן, בָּהֵנָּה).

2) לְ with suffixes; *sing.* לִי, לְךָ, לָךְ, לוֹ, לָהּ; *plur.* לָנוּ, לָכֶם, לָכֶן, לָהֶם, לָהֵמָּה, לָמוֹ), לָהֶן, לָהֵן, לָהֵנָּה).

3) כְּ is strengthened by the addition of מוֹ before it takes the suffixes.

CONJUNCTIONS. 131

sing. כָּמוֹנִי, כָּמוֹךָ, ... כָּמֹהוּ, כָּמוֹהָ

plur. כָּמוֹנוּ, כְּמוֹכֶם (generally כָּכֶם) .... כְּמוֹהֶם (equally frequent כָּהֶם), [כָּהֵם], כָּהֵן (כָּהֵנָה).

4) מ is lengthened into מִן and connected with suffixes in the following manner.

sing. מִמֶּנִי (poet. מִנִּי), מִמְּךָ (in pausa מִמֶּךָּ), מִמְּךָ, מִמֶּנּוּ מִמֶּנָּה (מִנְהוּ, מִנֶּהָ).

plur. מֵהֶנָּה, (מֵהֵמָּה) מֵהֶם, מִכֶן, מִכֶּם, מִמֶּנּוּ.

§ 85. The Conjunctions.

The conjunctions are twofold; *word-conjunctions* and *letter-conjunctions*.

A. The *word-conjunctions*.

1) Many *word-conjunctions* are substantives, e. g. יַעַן *(in answer to) because*, אוּלָם *(strengthening) but*.

2) There are also conjunctions which appear to be primitive, e. g. אוֹ *or*, אַף *also*.

3) Certain conjunctions are formed by connecting a subst. or other word with one of the letters בכלם, e. g. לְמַעַן (from מַעַן = מַעֲנֶה *answer*) *to the end that*, מִטֶּרֶם (from טֶרֶם *before* = *not yet*) *before*, בְּיַעַן (from יַעַן) *because*.

4) Further, conjunctions are formed by connecting a preposition with אֲשֶׁר, כִּי or אִם, e. g. עֵקֶב *instead of* אֲשֶׁר *because;* עַל *upon, because,* עַל אֲשֶׁר *because;* עַד *until* עַד אִם *until*.

5) Finally, the prepositions by themselves are used as conjunctions, e. g. בַּעֲבוּר *(by reason of) to the end that*.

B. The *letter-conjunctions*.

1) The most frequently used of all conjunctions is the ו (ו' הַחִבּוּר *conjunctive*).

(a) The ו *conjunctive* is placed before the word and has the half-vowel, e. g. וְטַף ,וְרָאָה. Before a labial or a letter with a half-vowel it becomes וּ, e. g. וּמֶלֶךְ ,וּדְבַר; and for the rest it follows the rules of § 83, 1 and 3; e. g. וַאֲנִי ,וַאֲנִי ,וְיָקָר ,וָאֱמֶת ,וָמֵת ,וָבֹהוּ.

(b) Prefixed to a verb the ו has yet another function, and then is called ו *conversive* (ו' הַמְהַפֵּךְ). — With the forms of the עָבַר it changes their meaning into that of the עָתִיד; e. g. וְרָאָה (from רָאָה *he has seen*) may also mean *he sees*, or *he will see*. — When prefixed to the forms of the עָתִיד, it changes their meaning into that of the עָבַר, and has פַּתַח, e. g. יִפְקֹד *he appoints*, or *he will appoint*, וְיִפְקֹד *and he appoints*, or *and he will appoint*, וַיִּפְקֹד *and he appointed*.

(c) With the forms of the עָתִיד the ו' הַמְהַפֵּךְ often shortens the vowel of the last syllable, when this is closed and preceded by an open syllable. The accent in consequence is shifted from the last syllable to the penultimate, e. g. יָקוּם (מִלְרַע) *he arises*, וַיָּקָם (מִלְעֵיל) *he arose*; נָסַב (מִלְרַע) *we turn* וַנָּסָב (מִלְעֵיל) *we turned*; יֹאמַר (מִלְרַע) *he says* וַיֹּאמֶר (מִלְעֵיל) *he said*; יִשָּׁבֵר (מִלְרַע) *it is broken* וַיִּשָּׁבֵר (מִלְעֵיל) *it was broken*.

Rem. 1. A similar shortening of the vowel also occurs with certain forms of the עָבַר, viz. דִּבֶּר (דבר only *in pausa*) וְדִבֶּר, וְכִבֶּם, כִּפֶּר, כִּבֶּם, דִּבֶּר from וְכִפֶּר.

(d) As in the 1st pers. sing. of the עָתִיד the ו stands before an א, the vowel which it has as ו׳ הַמְהַפֵּךְ is lengthened, e. g. וָאֶפְקֹד (cf. § 4 Rem. 5). The last syllable in this case is not shortened, nor is the accent shifted; e. g. וָאָקוּם *I arose* from אָקוּם *I arise*; וָאֹמַר *I said* from אֹמַר *I say* (cf. § 88 I 4 c).

(e) With the נָחִי ל״ה the ו׳ הַמַהְפֵּךְ causes the ה in the עָתִיד-forms to fall away, which occasions a certain alteration of vowels and a shifting of the accent, e. g. וַיֶּגֶל from יִגְלֶה, וַיְהִי from יִהְיֶה from יהיה, וַיַּרְא from אֶפְנֶה, וַיֵּפֶן from יִפְנֶה, וַיֵּט from יִטֶּה, וַיְחִי from יִרְאֶה, וַיְצַו from יְצַוֶּה.

2) The only letter besides ו used as conjunction is שׁ with the meaning of אֲשֶׁר *that* = כִּי. This שׁ moreover is sometimes substituted for אֲשֶׁר as pronoun.

In both cases שׁ has סֶגוֹל, e. g. שֶׁעִטְּרָה *that she crowned with*, שֶׁלִּשְׁלֹמֹה *which belongs to Solomon*; and sometimes פתח before a letter with פַּתַח or קָמֶץ, e. g. שַׁקַּמְתִּי, שַׁלְמָה.

Rem. 2. Occasionally it has קָמֶץ, as in שָׁאַתָה Judg. 6,17; or the half-vowel as in שְׁהֵם Eccl. 3,18.

§ 86. The Interjections.

They are:

(a) sounds involuntarily uttered because of an emotion; e. g. *of grief* אֲהָהּ *ah!* אוֹי *wo!* — *of joy* הֶאָח *aha!* הֵידָד *hurrah!*

(b) forms of verbs placed outside all connection with the context, e. g. הָבָה *(give) come on!* לְכָה *(go) come on!* רְאֵה *(see)* = הֵן and הִנֵּה *behold!*

(c) forms of other words uttered with emphasis, e. g. חָלִילָה *(ad profana) for shame, far be it.* — It is generally construed with the לְ of the person who would have committed the offence and with מִ of the person or object who would have been offended e. g. חָלִילָה לִי מֵה׳.

Rem. The interjections mentioned in (b) may be inflected, e. g. לְכוּ *come on!* הַס (to one) *silence!* (to many) הַסוּ *silence!*

CHAPTER XV.

The place of the accent with words of Hebrew origin, having two or more syllables.

§ 87. General rules.

1) A *closed* syllable with a long vowel has by preference the accent. Deviations from this rule are rare, e. g. אֹתָךְ.

2) Next in order for the accent is an *open* syll. with a *long* vowel, then an *open* syll. with a *short* vowel, and finally a *closed* syll. with a *short* vowel. — The deviations are occasioned by circumstances for which *particular* rules are given.

3) With syllables of equal rank, the ultimate has pre-

THE ACCENTS.   135

ference above the penultimate. — Here also the deviations are regulated by particular rules.

§ 88. The particular rules (as to *pausa* see § 89).

I. The verbs.

1) The terminations ון, תֶן, תֶם always have the accent.

2) When a suffix forms a separate syllable, the word to which it is appended is מִלְעֵיל (i. e. accent on the penultimate), otherwise it is מִלְרַע (i. e. accent on the ultimate); except ךָ-, כֶם, כֶן and הֵם which always have the accent, e. g. אַפְאֵיהֶם, בְּרָאָם, וַתִּקְבְּצוֹ, יִרְאֻנִי.

3) The triliteral stems.

(a) The ע' הַפֹעַל has the accent when it has a vowel, e. g. נֶעֶבְדָה, אָשְׁמְעָה, קָמְלוּ, אֲשָׁבַּע, הִשְׁכֵּם, יָשַׁבְתִּי, שָׁמַר.

(b) In the עָבַר the וְ הַמְהַפֵּךְ causes the accent to shift from the penultimate *closed* syllable to the ultimate, e. g. וְהִגְבַּלְתָּ, וּבֵרַכְתָּ, וְאָכַלְתָּ, except in *pausa* when the vowel is lengthened, e. g. וְשָׁבָעְתָּ. If on the other hand the penultimate is *open*, it retains the accent, e. g. וְעָשִׂיתָ, וְקָרָאתִי; except when it has a conjunctive accent, at least in the פָּעַל and הִפְעִיל, and is immediately followed by a א or ה, e. g. וְצִפִּיתָ אֹתוֹ Ex. 25,11; וְהִשְׁקִיתָ אֶת־הָעֵדָה Num. 20,8; וְהִבְדִּילָה הַפָּרֹכֶת Ex. 26,33 (cf. 4 *b*).

Rem. 1. In the קַל also we find וְאָפִיתָ אֹתָהּ Lev. 24,5.

(c) With the other verbal forms, on the contrary, the accent is shifted from the ultimate to the penultimate, when the ultimate closed syllable is shortened and preceded by an open syllable with a long vowel, e. g. הִשָּׁמֶר. This is often occasioned by the יו' הַמְהַפֵּךְ as וַיֹּאמֶר, וַיֵּלֶךְ, or by the omission of ה in the ל"ה נָחִי, e. g. תֵּפֶן, וַיִּפֶן (cf. § 45,5.7 and § 85 B).

Rem. 2. The forms mentioned in § 85 Rem. 1 are excepted.

4) The biliteral stems.

(a) When the second stem-letter is doubled they follow the rules of the triliteral stems. — If the second stem-letter is not doubled, the first stem-letter has the accent, e. g. הֵחֵל, יָקֻם, בָּאתִי, הֵחֵלּוּ, זַכּוּ unless of course the first stem-letter had ceased to belong to the ultimate or penultimate syllable, for then it *cannot* have the accent, e. g. בִּינוֹתִי, הֱעִירֹתָהּ (cf. § 7,4).

(b) The forms of the עָבַר which are מלעיל often become מלרע because of יו' הַמְהַפֵּךְ, e. g. וְשָׁבְתָּ֛; except when the syllable of the first stem-letter is *open*, e. g. וּבָאתָ (cf. 3 b). — The מִלְעֵיל-forms often also become מִלְרַע when they have a conjunctive accent and are followed by a guttural or half-vowel, e. g. עוּרִי עוּרִי כִּי־שָׁמְעוּ אֹתִי Gen. 40,15; גִּילִי מְאֹד Zech. 9,9; דְּבוֹרָה Judges 5,12.

THE ACCENTS. 137

(c) The forms of the עָתִיד, on the other hand, which are מִלְרַע become מִלְעִיל because of the וֹ׳ הַמְהַפֵּךְ, except the 1st pers. sing., e. g. וָאָקוּם ,וַנָּסָב ,וַיָּקָם (cf. § 85 B 1 c and d).

II. The nomina.

1) All the nomina are מִלְרַע, e. g. רוֹנֵעַ (= רוֹגֵעַ), מִזְרָח, עֲרָפֶל; except:

(a) the segolate forms, and others having a similar termination (cf. § 60 Rem. 4), e. g. מַחֲשֶׁבֶת, מָוֶת, צֹהַר (st. constr. of מַחֲשָׁבָה) אֲמִתַּחַת, תִּפְאֶרֶת.

(b) the fem. (prolonged) forms in ־ָתָה, e. g. אֵימָתָה.

(c) the duals, e. g. יָדַיִם.

2) Nomina with pronominal suffixes follow the rules of the verbs with suffixes (see I 2), and also here ־ְךָ, הֶם, כֵן, הֵם and הֵן always have the accent.

3) All other suffixes exercise no influence on the accents of the nomina, e. g. אֱלִימָה, סֻכָּתָה, בֵּיתָה, לַיְלָה, except ־ִי which often has the accent, e. g. הַמַּשְׁפִּילִי, מְקִימִי.

III. The particles.

The particles follow the rules of the nomina. The word לָמָה alone becomes מִלְרַע before a guttural, e. g. לָמָה הֲרֵעֹתָ.

§ 89. The alteration of vowels and the shifting of the tone because of the distinctive accents of higher rank. (הֶפְסֵק [מַאֲמָר] *pausa*).

A. The verbs.

1) The half-vowel changes into the vowel which occurs

in the stem-form, e. g. יָכְלוּ (from יָכֹל); דָּבְקָה (from
דָּבֵק); דָּבְקָה, וַאֲדַבְּרָה (from אֲדַבֵּר); דִּבְרוּ (from
דִּבְּרוּ. — The פַּתַח of the stem-form however is here
lengthened unto קָמֵץ, e. g. וְשָׁמְרוּ (from שָׁמַר); like
the פַּתַח generally changes into קָמֵץ when it stands in
pausa, e. g. יָמֹקּוּ and יָמַקּוּ. Lev. 26,37.

2) The short vowel changes into the vowel of the
stem-form, e. g. וַיֹּאמֶר (from יֹאמַר); וְיָאכֶל (from יֹאכַל) וַיֹּאכַל
וַיֹּאמֶר.

3) The שְׁוָא before the suff. ךָ becomes סֶגוֹל, which
change more than once exercises an influence upon the
first part of the word, e. g. אֲצַוְּךָ becomes אֲצַוֶּךָּ; עֶזְבְךָ
becomes עָזְבֶךָ; — the פַּתַח before נִי becomes קָמֵץ e. g.
צַוֵּנִי becomes צַוֵּנִי.

B. The nomina.

1) The short vowel having the accent is lengthened,
viz. both סֶגוֹל and פַּתַח into קָמֵץ, e. g. בֶּגֶד from בָּגֶד, זַיִת,
אַתְּ, אַתָּה, לַיְלָה, דְּבַשׁ from דָּבָשׁ, לָיְלָה, אָתָה, אָתְּ; זָיִת.

2) The nomina of the form כְּלִי change the half-vowel
into סֶגוֹל, e. g. כְּלִי becomes כֶּלִי; whilst the pers. pronouns
אֲנִי and אֲנוּ become אָנִי and אָנוּ.

3) The שְׁוָא before the suff. ךָ becomes סֶגוֹל, and this
change frequently influences the first part of the word,
e. g. בְּךָ from בֶּךָ, גַּאֲלָךְ from גְּאָלֵךְ, בְּכָאֲךָ from בְּכָאֶךָ.

4) The termination ־ַי becomes ־ָי, e. g. שָׂרַי and שָׂרָי
Gen. 17,15; בְּנַי and בָּנָי.

THE מַקֵּף.

C. The particles.

The particles, both with suffixes and without, undergo in *pausa* the same alterations as the nomina, e. g. מְתָחַת from מִתַּחַת, אֵלָי from אֱלַי. — לְךָ, בְּךָ and מִמְּךָ are in *pausa* לָךְ, בָּךְ, and מִמֶּהָ.

§ 90. The alteration of vowels in consequence of the מַקֵּף.

1) Since the מַקֵּף connects two words in the closest manner possible (cf. § 7,3), the last vowel of the first word is sometimes shortened, even in those cases where such an abbreviation is not called for by other reasons.

2) This shortening of the vowel occurs with צֵירֵה, קָמֵץ and חוֹלָם, e. g. יַם from יָם in יַם־סוּף; שֶׁם from שֵׁם in שֶׁם־בְּנוֹ; יִפְרָץ־בָּם from כָּל־ ;יִפְרָץ from כֹּל ;כְּתָב־לְךָ from כְּתֹב ;כַּאֲבֶל־אֵם from כַּאֲבֵל בֶּן־יִשׁ, הָן from בֵּן, יֵשׁ, הֵן ;יַבְדֵּל־חֹשֶׁךְ from יַבְדֵּל.

Rem. 1. Of קֵן we find קַן־צִפּוֹר Deut. 22,6.

Rem. 2. A similar abbreviation without the מַקֵּף occurs in דְּבַר of which the original form is only found in *pausa*, and in הִשָּׁמֶר from הִשָּׁמֵר in the sense of *to beware*.

Rem. 3. A word connected by מַקֵּף with the preceding word may in the same manner be connected with a subsequent word, and this again with another word. Thus we find four words connected by מַקֵּף and having but one accent, e. g. וְאֶת־כָּל־אֲשֶׁר־לוֹ Gen. 12,20.

APPENDIX I.

The names and forms of the signs of interpunction.

A. All the books of the Bible with the exception of the *Psalms, Proverbs* and *Job*.

1) The *distinctive* signs are of different rank in proportion to the division which they indicate [1]).

a The highest in rank are: אֶתְנַחְתָּא ;סִלּוּק or סוֹף פָּסוּק or אֶתְנָח *(Imperatores)*.

b Then follow: רְבִיעַ ,זָקֵף גָּדוֹל ,זָקֵף קָטֹן, סְגוֹל, and שַׁלְשֶׁלֶת *(reges)*.

c Next in rank come: תְּבִיר ,פַּשְׁטָא ,זַרְקָא ,טִפְחָא and יְתִיב *(duces)*.

d Finally: גֵּרְשַׁיִם ,גֶּרֶשׁ ,תְּלִישָׁא גְדוֹלָה ,קַרְנֵי פָרָה ,פָּזֵר and פָּסִיק *(comites)*.

2) The *conjunctive* signs are: מֵרְכָא ,מֵרְכָא ,דַּרְגָּא ,קַדְמָא ,מוּנַח מְהֻפָּךְ ,יֶרַח בֶּן יוֹמוֹ ,תְּלִישָׁא קְטַנָּה ,כְּפוּלָה.

---

1) The signs indicating the accents are placed in their proper positions under, over, or by the side of their respective names.

NAMES OF THE ACCENTS.   141

Rem. 1. The סוֹף פָּסוּק generally denotes the end of a sentence.

The אֶתְנָח is used at the end of a subordinate sentence. For the same purpose are used זָקֵף גָּדוֹל, זָקֵף קָטָן, סֶגוֹל and רְבִיעַ. — The שַׁלְשֶׁלֶת which is always followed by a פָּסִיק is employed when at the beginning of a verse an idea is expressed by a single word.

The other distinctives generally stand at the end of the various portions of a sentence.

Rem. 2. Of the conjunctives the מֵרְכָא and מֵרְכָא כְפוּלָה serve exclusively, and the קַדְמָא and קְטַנָּה תְּלִישָׁא almost exclusively, the distinctive signs of inferior rank. The last two are not unfrequently subordinate even to other conjunctive signs.

The דַּרְגָּא almost exclusively stands before תְּבִיר; the מַהְפָּךְ only before the פַּשְׁטָא, and the יֶרַח בֶּן יוֹמוֹ only before the קַרְנֵי פָרָה. The מוּנַח serves as well the distinctives of higher and lower rank as the conjunctives.

Rem. 3. The signs of interpunction are placed either *above* or *under* the word. The פָּסִיק alone stands at the side of a word [2]). The distinctives stand all *above* the word, except the אתנח, סוֹף פָּסוּק, תְּבִיר, טִפְחָא, and יְתִיב. The conjunctives stand all *under* the word, except the קַדְמָא and קְטַנָּה תְּלִישָׁא.

Rem. 4. As signs of tone they stand above the syllable which has

---

[2]) The פָּסִיק also serves other purposes; e. g. it stands between a twice repeated name, of which the 1st has a conjunctive accent, e. g. אַבְרָהָם ׀ אַבְרָהָם Gen. 22,11; or between two words of which the first ends with the same letter with which the 2d begins, e. g. הַגּוֹיִם ׀ מִנְחָה Jes. 66,20 (cf. § 6 note 2).

the accent. Yet the פַּשְׁטָא, תְּלִישָׁא קְטַנָּה, סְגוֹל, זַרְקָא always stand above the *last* letter of the word *(postpositivi)*. If therefore the word is מִלְעֵיל, in fairly good editions the sign is repeated above the syllable which has the accent, e. g. וְכָּכָה Ex. 12,11; בַּבֹּקֶר Ex. 16,18. — The תְּלִישָׁא גְדוֹלָה, on the contrary, always stands on the *first* letter of the word *(praepositivus)*, and must therefore be repeated when the word is מִלְרַע, e. g. כִּמְעָט Gen. 27,10. — The *praepositivus* יְתִיב, which stands on the right of the first letter of the word, need never to be repeated, because it only occurs with monosyllables, or with words of two syllables that are מִלְעֵיל.

3) The names of the accents as given above are in use with the so called Ashchenazic Jews (אַשְׁכְּנַזִּים), who form by far the majority of the Jews in the western countries of Europe. The so called Portuguese Jews (סְפָרַדִּים) have different names for most of the accents. — Enumerated in the same order as above their names are:

Distinctives זָקֵף, זָקֵף קָטָן, סְגוֹלְתָּא, אַתְנָח, סִלּוּק of סוֹף פָּסוּק, פָּזֵר גָּדוֹל, יְתִיב, תְּבִיר, קַדְמָא, זַרְקָא, טַרְחָא, שַׁלְשֶׁלֶת, רְבִיעַ, גָּדוֹל פְּסִיק ן, שְׁנֵי גְרִישִׁין, גֵּרֵישׁ, תַּרְצָא, קַרְנֵי פָּרָה

Conjunctives יֶרַח בֶּן, תַּלְשָׁא, תְּרֵי טַעֲמֵי, מַאֲרִיךְ, דַּרְגָּא, אַזְלָא שׁוֹפָר הוֹלֵךְ, שׁוֹפָר מְהֻפָּךְ, יוֹמוֹ.

B. The signs of interpunction in the *Psalms, Proverbs* and *Job* [אֱמֶת].

The *Distinctives* are:

שַׁלְשֶׁלֶת גְדוֹלָה ן, רְבִיעַ מוּגְרָשׁ, רְבִיעַ גָּדוֹל, אַתְנָח, עוֹלֶה וְיוֹרֵד, סִלּוּק, אַזְלָא לגרמיה ן, מַהְפָּךְ לגרמיה ן, פָּזֵר, דְּחִי, רְבִיעַ קָטָן, צִנּוֹר.

NAMES OF THE ACCENTS.

The *Conjunctives* are:

שַׁלְשֶׁלֶת קְטַנָּה, אַזְלָא, מַהְפַּךְ, יֶרַח בֶּן יוֹמוֹ, טַרְחָא, עִלּוּי, מוּנַח, מֵרְכָא.

Rem. 1. The distinctives מַהְפַּךְ לְגַרְמֵיהּ, שַׁלְשֶׁלֶת גְדוֹלָה and the אַזְלָא לְגַרְמֵיהּ are distinguished from the conjunctives of the same name by the פָּסִיק. — The רְבִיעַ קָטָן *always*, but the רְבִיעַ גָדוֹל *never* immediately precedes the עוֹלֶה וְיוֹרֵד.

Rem. 2. Also here there is a *postpositus* the צִנּוֹר, and a *praepositus* the דְחִי. The דְחִי is by its place of *praepositus* distinguished from the טַרְחָא which stands on the syllable having the accent.

APPENDIX II.

The more common stems of the פ״י נֶחָי which occur in the Bible borrow their forms partly from A and partly from B § 32.

Of these the stems ועל, יסף, יסר, וכח, ודע, וגה, וכל, ואל, וצא, וקש, ורד, ושב, ושע and ותר alone have no verbal forms according to the conjugation B, and *vice versa* the stems יפה, ינק, ילל, יטב, יחש and יקץ have no verbal forms according to A.

The following stems on the contrary take their forms both from A and B.

1) יבש, ינע and ינה are conjugated in the קַל according to B, but in the הִפְעִיל according to A.
2) ידה in the קַל according to B, but in the הִפְעִיל and התפעל according to A.
3) יחל in the נפעל acc. to A and B, but in the הפעיל acc. to A.
4) ילד in all the forms acc. to A, but in the הִתְפַּעֵל acc. to B.
5) יסר in the הפעיל acc. to B, but in the נפעל and התפעל acc. to A.

THE נָחֵי פ"י.

6) יער in the קַל acc. to B, but in the הִפְעִיל and הָפְעַל acc. to A.

7) יעץ in the קַל and הִתְפַּעֵל acc. to B, but in the נִפְעַל acc. to A.

8) יצק in the קל acc. to A and B, but in the הָפְעַל acc. to A.

9) ישן, ירא, יצר in the קַל acc. to B, but in the נִפְעַל acc. to A.

10) יקד in the קַל acc. to A and B, but in the הָפְעַל acc. to A.

11) יקר in the קל acc. to A and B, but in the הפעיל acc. to A.

12) ירה in the קַל and נפעל acc. to B, but in the הִפְעִיל acc. to A.

13) ירש in the קַל acc. to A and B, but in the נִפְעַל and הפעיל acc. to A.

14) ישר in the קַל acc. to B, but in the הִפְעִיל acc. to A and B.

15) יכל is only found in the קַל. It has the infinitive יכלה acc. to B, and the יוכל עָתִיד, a strange and irregular form for יַוְכַל or יִיכַל

APPENDIX III.

Verbal forms with pronominal suffixes.

Example of a triliteral verb with pronominal suffixes §§ 46—48.

(The numbers 1, 2, 3 and the letters *m. f.* denote the person and gender of the suffixes).

קל of the עָבַר

1
פָּקַד

| פְּקָדוּ | פְּקָדְךָ | פְּקָדַנִי | פְּקָדָם | פְּקַדְכֶם | פְּקָדָנוּ |
| פְּקָדָהּ | פְּקָדֵךְ | פְּקָדֵךְ | פְּקָדָן | פְּקַדְכֶן | |

פָּקְדָה

| פְּקָדַתְהוּ or פְּקָדַתּוּ | פְּקָדַתְךָ | פְּקָדַתְנִי | פְּקָדָתַם | פְּקָדַתְכֶם | פְּקָדַתְנוּ |
| פְּקָדָתָהּ or פְּקָדַתָּה | פְּקָדָתֵךְ | | פְּקָדָתָן | פְקַדְתְּכֶן | |

פָּקַדְתָּ

| פְּקַדְתּוֹ or פְּקַדְתְּהוּ | פְּקַדְתַּנִי | פְּקַדְתָּם | | פְּקַדְתָּנוּ |
| פְּקַדְתָּהּ | | פְּקַדְתָּן | | |

פָּקַדְתְּ

| פְּקַדְתִּיהוּ | פְּקַדְתִּינִי | פְּקַדְתִּים | | פְּקַדְתִּינוּ |
| פְּקַדְתִּיהָ | | פְּקַדְתִּין | | |

VERBAL FORMS WITH SUFFIXES.

פְּקַדְתִּי

| פְּקַדְתִּיכֶם פְּקַדְתִּים | פְּקַדְתִּיךָ | פְּקַדְתִּיו or פְּקַדְתִּיהוּ | m. |
| פְּקַדְתִּיכֶן פְּקַדְתִּין | פְּקַדְתִּיךְ | פְּקַדְתִּיהָ | f. |

פָּקְדוּ

| פְּקָדוּכֶם פְּקָדוּם | פְּקָדוּךָ | פְּקָדוּנִי | פְּקָדוּהוּ | m. |
| פְּקָדוּכֶן פְּקָדוּן | פְּקָדוּךְ | | פְּקָדוּהָ | f. |

פְּקַדְתֶּם and פקדתֶּן

| פְּקַדְתּוּם | פְּקַדְתּוּנִי | פְּקַדְתּוּהוּ | m. |
| פְּקַדְתּוּן | | פְּקַדְתּוּהָ | f. |

פְּקַדְנוּ

| פְּקַדְנוּכֶם פְּקַדְנוּם | פְּקַדְנוּךָ | פְּקַדְנוּהוּ | m. |
| פְּקַדְנוּכֶן פְּקַדְנוּן | פְּקַדְנוּךְ | פְּקַדְנוּהָ | f. |

עָבַר of פְּעַל.

פָּקַד

| פְּקָדְכֶם פְּקָדָם | פְּקָדְךָ | פְּקָדַנִי | פָּקְדוּ | m. |
| פְּקָדְכֶן פְּקָדָן | פְּקָדֵךְ | | פְּקָדָהּ | f. |

פְּקָדָה

פְּקָדַתְהוּ or פְּקָדַתּוּ etc. m.

עָבַר of הִפְעִיל.

הִפְקִיד

| הִפְקִידְכֶם הִפְקִידָם | הִפְקִידְךָ | הִפְקִידַנִי | הִפְקִידוּ | m. |
| הִפְקִידְכֶן הִפְקִידָן | הִפְקִידֵךְ | | הִפְקִידָהּ | f. |

הִפְקִידָה

הִפְקִידַתְהוּ or הִפְקִידַתּוּ etc. m.

קַל of עָתִיד.

יִפְקֹד

יִפְקֹד	יִפְקְדֶם יִפְקְדְכֶם	יִפְקְדָם יִפְקְדֶן	יִפְקְדֵנִי	יִפְקָדְךָ יִפְקָדֵךְ	יִפְקְדֵהוּ or יִפְקְדוּ יִפְקְדָהּ or יִפְקְדָה

so also תִּפְקֹד with alteration of י into ת.

תִּפְקְדִי

תִּפְקֹד	תִּפְקְדִים תִּפְקְדִין	תִּפְקְדִינִי		תִּפְקְדֵיהוּ תִּפְקְדֶיהָ

אֶפְקֹד

	אֶפְקְדֵם אֶפְקְדְכֶם	אֶפְקְדָם אֶפְקְדֶן	אֶפְקָדְךָ אֶפְקָדֵךְ	אֶפְקְדֵהוּ or אֶפְקְדוּ אֶפְקְדָהּ or אֶפְקְדָה

יִפְקְדוּ

יִפְקְדוּ	יִפְקְדוּכֶם יִפְקְדוּם	יִפְקְדוּן יִפְקְדוּם	יִפְקְדוּנִי	יִפְקְדוּךְ יִפְקְדוּךָ	יִפְקְדוּהוּ יִפְקְדוּהָ

so also תִּפְקְדוּ and תִּפְקֹדְנָה with alteration of י into ת.
„ „ „ „ א into נ. אֶפְקֹד like נִפְקֹד

פִּעֵל of עָתִיד.

יְפַקֵּד

יְפַקֵּד	יְפַקְּדֶם יְפַקֶּדְכֶם	יְפַקְּדָם יְפַקְּדֶן	יְפַקְּדֵנִי	יְפַקֶּדְךָ יְפַקְּדֵךְ	יְפַקְּדֵהוּ or יְפַקְּדוּ יְפַקְּדָהּ or יְפַקְּדָה

etc.

הִפְעִיל of עָתִיד.

יַפְקִיד

יַפְקִי	יַפְקִידֶם יַפְקִידְכֶם	יַפְקִידָם יַפְקִידֶן	יַפְקִידֵנִי	יַפְקִידְךָ יַפְקִידֵךְ	יַפְקִידֵהוּ or יַפְקִידוּ יַפְקִידָה or יַפְקִידָה

etc.

VERBAL FORMS WITH SUFFIXES.

․דֶּרֶךְ הַצִּוּוּי

פְּקֹד

פָּקְדֵנוּ	פָּקְדֵם / פָּקְדֵן		פָּקְדֵנִי	m. פָּקְדֵהוּ / f. פָּקְדֶהָ

פַּקֵּד

פַּקְּדֵנוּ	פַּקְּדֵם / פַּקְּדֵן		פַּקְּדֵנִי	m. פַּקְּדֵהוּ / f. פַּקְּדֶהָ

הַפְקֵד

הַפְקִידֵנוּ	הַפְקִידֵם / הַפְקִידֵן		הַפְקִידֵנִי	m. הַפְקִידֵהוּ / f. הַפְקִידֶהָ

Example of a biliteral stem with pronominal suffixes §§ 46 and 49.

․קל of עָבַר

שָׂם

שָׂמָנוּ	שָׂמְכֶם / שָׂמְכֶן	שָׂמָם / שָׂמָן	שָׂמַנִי	שָׂמְךָ / שָׂמֵךְ	m. שָׂמוֹ or שָׂמָהוּ / f. שָׂמָהּ

שָׂמָה

שָׂמַתְנ	שָׂמָתַם / שָׂמָתֶן שָׂמַתְכֶם / שָׂמַתְכֶן	שָׂמָתַן	שָׂמַתְנִי	שָׂמָתְךָ or שָׂמַתֶךָ / שָׂמָתֵךְ	m. שָׂמַתְהוּ or שָׂמָתְהוּ / f. שָׂמָתָה

All other forms are like those of פָּקַד with omission of the first stem-letter.

The forms of the עָבַר in the הִפְעִיל are like those of the triliteral verbs, after the 1st stem-letter and ה have been omitted, and the preform. הֲ or הֵ has been substituted, e. g. הֲקִימָה or הֵקִימָה; הֲקִימוּ or הֵקִימוּ.

HEBREW GRAMMAR.

The forms of יָשִׂים are like those of יַפְקִיד, except for a small alteration of vowels; viz. י, ת etc. are prefixed after the 1st stem-letter and its preformative have been cut off.

יָגֵד

| | m. | יָגְדֵהוּ יָגְדְךָ | יִגְדֵנִי | יִגְדֵם יָגְדְכֶם | יִגְדֵנוּ |
| | f. | יָגְדָהּ יָגְדֵךְ | | יִגְדֵן יָגְדְכֶן | |

Instead of the קִבּוּץ the שׁוּרֻק may be used, and often also the חוֹלָם.

₁   ₂

יָבֹז

| | m. | יָבְזֵהוּ יָבְזְךָ | יִבְזֵנִי | יִבְזֵם יָבְזְכֶם | יִבְזֵנוּ |
| | f. | יָבְזָהּ יָבְזֵךְ | | יִבְזֵן יָבְזְכֶן | |

עָתִיד of הִפְעִיל.

The forms of יָקִים are like those of יָשִׂים.

יֵחַת or יָחַת

| | m. | יַחְתֵנוּ יַחְתְךָ | יַחְתֵנִי | יַחְתֵם יחתכם | יַחְתֵנוּ |
| | f | יָחְתֶנָּה יַחְתֵךְ | | יַחְתֵן יָחְתְכֶן | |

יָפֵר

| | m. | יְפָרֵנוּ יְפָרְךָ | יְפָרֵנִי | יְפָרֵם יְפָרְכֶם | יְפָרֵנוּ |
| | f. | יְפָרֶנָּה יְפָרֵךְ | | יְפָרֵן יְפָרְכֶן | |

יָסִית

| | m. | יַסִיתֵנוּ יַסִיתְךָ | יְסִיתֵנִי | יַסִיתֵם יסיתכם | יסיתנו |
| | f. | יסיתנה יַסִיתֵךְ | | יַסִיתֵן יַסִיתְכֶן | |

דֶרֶךְ הַצִוּוּי

שִׂים

| | m. | שִׂימֵהוּ | שִׂימֵנִי | שִׂימֵם | שִׂימֵנוּ |
| | f. | שִׂימָהּ | | שִׂימֵן | |

VERBAL FORMS WITH SUFFIXES. 151

m.	חָנֵהוּ		חָנֵנִי	חֹן
f.	חָנֶהָ			חָנֻם	חָנֵנוּ
				חָנֻן	
			הָקֵים		
m.	הֲקִימֵהוּ		הֲקִימֵנִי	הֲקִימֵם	הֲקִימֵנוּ
f.	הֲקִימֶהָ			הֲקִימֵן	

APPENDIX IV

L st of nouns ın he *st. constr* and with pronominal suffixes.

		:.	sing. suff. 1	sing. suff. 2 m.	sing. suff. 2 f.	sing. suff. 3 m.	sing. suff. 3 f.	plur. suff. 1	plur. suff. 2 m.	plur. suff. 2 f.	plur. suff. 3 m.	plur. suff. 3 f.
s.	יָד	יַד,	יָדִי,	יָדְךָ,	יָדֵךְ,	יָדוֹ,	יָדָהּ,	יָדֵנוּ,	יֶדְכֶם,	יֶדְכֶן,	יָדָם,	יָדָן
d.	יָדַיִם,	יְדֵי,	יָדַי,	יָדֶיךָ,	יָדַיִךְ,	יָדָיו,	יָדֶיהָ	יָדֵינוּ,	יְדֵיכֶם	־כֶן	־הֶם,	־הֶן
p.	יָדוֹת,	יְדוֹת,	יְדוֹתַי	־תֶיךָ,	־תַיִךְ,	־תָיו,	־תֶיהָ,	־תֵינוּ,	־תֵיכֶם,	־תֵיכֶן,	־תֵיהֶם or יְדֹתָם	־תֵיהֶן or יְדוֹתָן
s.	שֵׁם(בֵּן)	שֵׁם(שֶׁם)	שְׁמִי	שִׁמְךָ,	שְׁמֵךְ,	שְׁמוֹ,	שְׁמָהּ,	שְׁמֵנוּ,	שִׁמְכֶם,	שִׁמְכֶן,	שְׁמָם,	שְׁמָן
p.	שֵׁמוֹת	שְׁמוֹת,	־תַי	etc.								
s.	אָב,	אֲבִי,	אָבִי	אָבִיךָ,	אָבִיךְ,	אָבִיו,	אָבִיהָ,	אָבִינוּ,	אֲבִיכֶם,	־כֶן,	־הֶם,	־הֶן

Of אָחָת and פֶּה, st. ds. אֲחִי and פִּי, the forms are according ιo the same lde.

p.	אָבוֹת	אֲבוֹת	Further like those of שֵׁמוֹת									
p.	אַחִים,	אֲחֵי	אַחַי,	אַחֶיךָ	אַחַיִךְ,	אֶחָיו,	אַחֶיהָ	אַחֵינוּ,	אֲחֵיכֶם,	־כֶן,	־הֶם,	־הֶן
s.	עָם,	עַם,	עַמִּי,	etc.								
p	עַמִּים,	עַמֵּי,	עַמַּי,	etc.								
s.	לֵב(אֵם)	לֵב,	לִבִּי,	te.								

			sing. suff.					plur. suff.				
			1	2		3		1	2		3	
		t.		m.	f.	m.	f.		m.	f.	m.	f.
-	גֵּו,	גֵּו,	גֵּוִי,	etc.								
p.	בָּנִים (דָּמִים)	בְּנֵי,	בָּנַי,	בָּנֶיךָ,	בָּנַיִךְ,	בָּנָיו,	בָּנֶיהָ,	בָּנֵינוּ,	בְּנֵיכֶם,	־כֶן,	־הֶם,	־הֶן
p.	אִמּוֹת,	אִמּוֹת,	אִמּוֹתַי,	etc.								
s	דָּם,	דַּם,	דָּמִי,	דָּמְךָ,	דָּמֵךְ,	דָּמוֹ,	דָּמָהּ,	דָּמֵנוּ,	דִּמְכֶם,	־כֶן,	דָּמָם,	דָּמָן
s.	חֵטְא,	חֵטְא,	חֶטְאִי	חֶטְאֲךָ	חֶטְאֵךְ,	חֶטְאוֹ,	חֶטְאָהּ	חֶטְאֵנוּ,	חֶטְאֲכֶם	־כֶן,	חֶטְאָם	־אָן
p.	חֲטָאִים,	חַטָּאֵי,	חֲטָאַי	etc.								
s.	בַּת (פַּת)	בַּת,	בִּתִּי,	te.								
s	בַּד,	בַּד,	בַּדִּי,	te.								
p.	בַּדִּים,	בַּדֵּי,	בַּדַּי,	etc.								
s.	עִיר,	עִיר,	עִירִי,	etc.								
s.	אוֹר,	אוֹר,	אוֹרִי,	etc.								
s.	חֹק,	חק(חָק	חֻקִּי,	חֻקְּךָ,	חֻקֵּךְ,	חֻקּוֹ,	חֻקָּהּ,	חֻקֵּנוּ,	חָקְכֶם,	־כֶן,	חֻקָּם,	חֻקָּן
p.	חֻקִּים,	חֻקֵּי,	חֻקַּי,	etc.								
s.	סוּס,	סוּס,	סוּסִי,	etc.								
p.	סוּסִים,	סוּסֵי,	סוּסַי,	etc.								
s.	שְׁבִי,	שְׁבִי,	שִׁבְיִי	שֶׁבְיְךָ,	שִׁבְיֵךְ,	שִׁבְיוֹ,	שִׁבְיָהּ,	שִׁבְיֵנוּ,	שִׁבְיְכֶם,	־כֶן,	שִׁבְיָם,	־יָן

HEBREW GRAMMAR.

		st. c.	sing. suff. I	sing. suff. 2 m.	sing. suff. 2 f.	sing. suff. 3 m.	sing. suff. 3 f.	plur. suff. I	plur. suff. 2 m.	plur. suff. 2 f.	plur. suff. 3 m.	plur. suff. 3 f.
p.	מָגִנִּים,	מָגִנֵּי,	מָגִנַּי,	etc.								
s.	שָׂדֶה,	שְׂדֵה,	שָׂדִי,	שָׂדְךָ,	שָׂדֵךְ,	שָׂדֵהוּ,	שָׂדָהּ,	שָׂדֵנוּ,	שְׂדֵכֶם,	־כֶן,	שָׂדָם,	שָׂדָן
p.	(שָׂדִים,	שְׂדֵי,	שָׂדַי,	שָׂדֶיךָ,	שָׂדַיִךְ,	שָׂדָיו,	שָׂדֶיהָ,	שָׂדֵינוּ,	שְׂדֵיכֶם,	־כֶן,	־הֶם,	־הֶן
s.	בֶּגֶד,	בֶּגֶד,	בִּגְדִי,	־דְךָ,	־דֵךְ,	־דוֹ,	־דָהּ,	־דֵנוּ,	־דְכֶם,	־דְכֶן,	־דָם,	־דָן
s.	חֹדֶשׁ,	חֹדֶשׁ,	חָדְשִׁי·	חָדְשְׁךָ,	־שֵׁךְ,	־שׁוֹ,	־שָׁהּ,	־שֵׁנוּ,	־שְׁכֶם,	־שְׁכֶן,	־שָׁם,	־שָׁן
p.	חֳדָשִׁים	חָדְשֵׁי	חֳדָשַׁי,	חֳדָשֶׁיךָ,	־שַׁיִךְ,	־שָׁיו,	־שֶׁיהָ,	־שֵׁינוּ,	חָדְשֵׁיכֶם	־כֶן,	־הֶם,	־הֶן
s.	נַעַר,	נַעַר,	נַעֲרִי,	נַעַרְךָ,	נַעֲרֵךְ,	־רוֹ,	־רָהּ,	־רֵנוּ,	נַעַרְכֶם,	־כֶן,	נַעֲרָם,	־רָן
p.	נְעָרִים,	נַעֲרֵי,	נְעָרַי,	־רֶיךָ,	־רַיִךְ,	־רָיו,	־רֶיהָ,	־רֵינוּ,	נַעֲרֵיכֶם,	־כֶן,	־הֶם,	־הֶן
s.	מָוֶת,	מוֹת,	מוֹתִי,	etc.								
s.	בַּיִת,(זַיִת)	בֵּית,	בֵּיתִי,	־תְךָ,	־תֵךְ,	־תוֹ,	־תָהּ,	־תֵנוּ,	בֵּיתְכֶם,	־כֶן,	בֵּיתָם,	־תָן
p.	בָּתִּים,	בָּתֵּי,	בָּתַּי,	בָּתֶּיךָ,	־תַּיִךְ,	־תָיו,	־תֶיהָ,	־תֵינוּ,	־תֵיכֶם,	־תֵיכֶן,	־תֵיהֶם,	־תֵיהֶן
p.	זֵיתִים,	זֵיתֵי,	זֵיתַי,	־תֶיךָ,	־תַיִךְ,	־תָיו,	־תָי ,	־תֵי נוּ,	־תֵיכֶם,	־תֵיכֶן,	־הֶם,	־הֶן
s.	קָרְבָּן,	קָרְבַּן,	קָרְבָּנִי,	קָרְבַּנְךָ,	־בָּנֵךְ,	־בָּנוֹ,	בָּנָהּ,	־בְּנֵנוּ,	קָרְבַּנְכֶם,	־כֶן,	קָרְבָּנָם,	־נָן
p.	(קָרְבָּנִים,	קָרְבְּנֵי,	קָרְבָּנַי,	־נֶיךָ,	־נַיִךְ,	־נָיו,	־נֶיהָ,	־נֵינוּ,	קָרְבְּנֵיכֶם,	־כֶן,	־הֶם,	־הֶן
s.	מִזְבֵּחַ,	מִזְבַּח,	מִזְבְּחִי,	מִזְבַּחֲךָ,	מִזְבְּחֵךְ,	־חוֹ,	־חָהּ,	־חֵנוּ,	מִזְבַּחֲכֶם,	־כֶן,	מִזְבְּחָם,	־חָן
p.	מִזְבְּחוֹת,	מִזְבְּחוֹת,	־חוֹתַי,	etc.								

		st c.	s ng. suff. 1	s ng. suff. 2 m.	s ng. suff. 2 f.	s ng. suff. 3 m.	s ng. suff. 3 f.	plur. suff. 1	plur. suff. 2 m.	plur. suff. 2 f.	plur. suff. 3 m.	plur. suff. 3 f.
s.	צְדָקָה,	צִדְקַת,	צִדְקָתִי,	־תְךָ,	־תֵךְ,	־תוֹ,	־תָהּ,	־תֵנוּ,	־קַתְכֶם,	־כֶן,	צִדְקָתָם,	־תָן
p.	צְדָקוֹת	צִדְקוֹת,	צִדְקוֹתַי,	etc.								
s.	גְּבֶרֶת,	גְּבֶרֶת,	גְּבִרְתִּי,	־תְּךָ,	־תֵּךְ,	־תּוֹ,	־תָּהּ,	תֵּנוּ,	־תְּכֶם,	־תְּכֶן,	גְּבִרְתָּם,	־תָּן
s.	אִוֶּלֶת,(שׁוֹמֶרֶת)	אִוֶּלֶת,	אִוַּלְתִּי,	־תְּךָ,	־תֵּךְ,	־תּוֹ,	־תָּהּ,	־תֵּנוּ,	־תְּכֶם,	־תְּכֶן,	־תָּם,	־תָּן
s.	חַטָּאת,	חַטַּאת	חַטָּאתִי	חַטָּאתְךָ,	חַטָּאתֵךְ,	־תוֹ,	־תָהּ,	־תֵנוּ,	חַטַּאתְכֶם,	־כֶן,	חַטָּאתָם	־תָן
p.	חַטָּאוֹת	חַטֹּאת	־תַי,	etc.								
of	חַטָּאוֹת											
s.	שׁוֹמֵר,	שׁוֹמֵר,	שׁוֹמְרִי,	־מֶרְךָ,	־מְרֵךְ,	־מְרוֹ,	־מְרָהּ,	־מְרֵנוּ,	־מֶרְכֶם,	־מֶרְכֶן,	־מְרָם,	־מְרָן
p.	שׁוֹמְרִים,	שׁוֹמְרֵי,	שׁוֹמְרַי,	־רֶיךָ	־רַיִךְ,	־רָיו,	־רֶיהָ,	־רֵינוּ,	־רֵיכֶם,	־רֵיכֶן,	־רֵיהֶם,	־רֵיהֶן
s.	אָהוּב,	אֲהוּב,	אֲהוּבִי,	etc.								
p.	אֲהוּבִים,	אֲהוּבֵי,	אֲהוּבַי,	etc.								
s.	אֲהוּבָה,	אֲהוּבַת,	אֲהוּבָתִי,	־בַתְךָ,	־בָתֵךְ,	־בָתוֹ,	־בָתָהּ	־בָתֵנוּ,	־בַתְכֶם,	־בַתְכֶן,	־בָתָם	־בָתָן
s.	מַחֲשָׁבָה	מַחֲשֶׁבֶת,	מַחְשַׁבְתִּי	etc.								
of	מַחֲשֶׁבֶת,											
p.	מַחֲשָׁבוֹת,	מַחְשְׁבוֹת	מַחְשְׁבוֹתַי,	te.								

APPENDIX V.

The letters.

א		אָלֶף	*alef*
ב	v or b	בֵּית	*beth*
ג	g	גִימֶל	*gimel*
ד	d	דָלֶת	*daleth*
ה	h	הֵא	*he*
ו	w	וָו	*waw*
ז	z	זַיִן	*zain*
ח	ch	חִית	*cheth*
ט	t or th.	טֵית	*teth*
י	y	יוֹד or יוּד	*yod* or *yud*
כ (ך)	ch or k	כַּף	*kaf*
ל	l	לָמֶד	*lamed*
מ (ם)	m	מֵם	*mem*
נ (ן)	n	נוּן	*nun*
ס	s	סָמֶךְ	*samech*
ע	ng or unsounded	עַיִן	ʿ*ain*
פ (ף)	f	פֵּא	*phe*
צ (ץ)	ts	צָדִי	*tsadey*
ק	k	קוֹף or קוּף	*kof* or *kuf*
ר	r	רֵישׁ	*resh*
ש	sh or s	שִׁין or שִׂין	*shin* or *sin*
ת	s, th or t.	תָּו	*thaw*

See § 2 Remarks.

The vowels.

The long vowels: (Portuguese or Sephardaic pronunciation) ָ (ā) קָמַץ *kamats*; ֵ (ē) צֵירֶה *tsereh*; ִי (ī) חִירִק נָדוֹל *chirik-gadol*; וֹ or ֹ (ō) חוֹלָם *cholam*; שׁוּרֻק וּ (ū) *shuruk*.

The short vowels:

(ă) פַּתַח *pathach*; ֶ (ĕ) סֶגוֹל *segol*; ִ (ĭ) חִירִק קָטָן *chirik-katan*; ָ (ŏ) קָמַץ חָטוּף *kamats-chatuf*; ֻ (ŭ) קִבּוּץ *kibbuts*.

In the not-Portuguese or Ashchenazic pronunciation קָמַץ is pronounced ō (as in *rode*); צֵירֶה ī (as in *white*); חוֹלָם *ou* (as in *loud*).

Just Published:

WIJNKOOP (J. D.) — Manual of Hebrew Syntax. Translated from the Dutch by C. van den Biesen. 8vo. Cloth. pp. XXII, 152 and Index.

Price 5s.

A COMPLETE LIST

OF

BOOKS AND PERIODICALS

PUBLISHED AND SOLD BY

LUZAC & CO.

Oriental and Foreign Booksellers,

*Official Agents and Publishers to
The Royal Asiatic Society of Great Britain and Ireland ·
The University of Chicago;
The Imperial Academy of Sciences, St. Petersburg;
Comité de l'Asie française; Siam Society, Bangkok;
·Theosophical Publishing Co., New York;
Vedanta Publication Committee, New York;
Anthropological Society of Bombay;
etc., etc., etc.*

INDIAN GOVERNMENT PUBLICATIONS SUPPLIED TO ORDER.

LONDON
LUZAC & CO.,
46, GREAT RUSSELL STREET (OPPOSITE THE BRITISH MUSEUM).
1905.

AUTHORS *and* PUBLISHERS *of new Oriental books desirous of making their works known to Oriental Students, Scholars, and Librarians in all parts of the world, can best attain that object by sending a copy to the Editor of* LUZAC'S ORIENTAL LIST, *46, Great Russell Street, London, who will give it special and early notice.*

Advertisements are also received in LUZAC'S ORIENTAL LIST, *which can now safely be said to be the best medium extant for advertising books on all Oriental subjects. Terms to be had on application to the Publishers.*

ORIENTAL STUDENTS *are invited to submit their* MANUSCRIPTS *to* MESSRS. LUZAC & CO. *for publication before sending them elsewhere.*

LUZAC & CO.'S

COMPLETE

LIST OF BOOKS AND PERIODICALS.

Abhedânanda (Swâmi).—Divine Heritage of Man. 12mo, pp. 215, cloth. With portrait of author, frontispiece. 4s. 6d. net.

- I. Existence of God.
- II. Attributes of God.
- III. Has God any Form?
- IV. Fatherhood and Motherhood of God.
- V. Relation of Soul to God.
- VI. What is an Incarnation of God?
- VII. Son of God.
- VIII. Divine Principle in Man.

Abhedânanda (Swâmi).—How to be a Yogi. 12mo, pp. 188, cloth. 4s. 6d. net.

- I. Introductory.
- II. What is Yoga?
- III. Science of Breathing.
- IV. Was Christ a Yogi?

" For Christians interested in foreign missions this book is of moment, as showing the method of reasoning which they must be prepared to meet if they are to influence the educated Hindu. To the Orientalist, and the philosopher also, the book is not without interest. . . . Swâmi Abhedânanda preaches no mushroom creed and no Eurasian hybrid 'theosophy.' He aims to give us a compendious account of Yoga. Clearly and admirably he performs his task. In form the little book is excellent, and its English style is good."—*New York Times Saturday Review of Books*, Dec. 6th, 1902.

" 'How to be a Yogi' is a little volume that makes very interesting reading. The book contains the directions that must be followed in physical as well as in mental training by one who wishes to have full and perfect control of all his powers."—*Record-Herald*, Chicago, Feb. 28th, 1903.

Abhedânanda (Swâmi).—The Sayings of Sri Râmakrishna. Compiled by SWÂMI ABHEDÂNANDA. 234 pages. Flexible cloth, gilt top, 3s. 6d. net.

Râmakrishna was a great Hindu saint of the nineteenth century who has already had an influence on the religious thought of America and England through the teachings of his disciples, Swâmi Vivekânanda, Swâmi Abhedânanda, and others. His Sayings are full of broad, practical, non-sectarian instructions concerning the spiritual life which cannot but give help and inspiration to the followers of all creeds. The present volume contains a larger number of Sayings than has yet appeared in any one English collection. For the first time also they have been classified into chapters and arranged in logical sequence under marginal headings, such as "All creeds paths to God," "Power of Mind and Thought," "Meditation," "Perseverance." As an exposition of the universal truths of Religion and their application to the daily life this book takes its place among the great scriptures of the world.

Abhedânanda (Swâmi).—Reincarnation. 8vo, pp. 61. Paper cover, 1s. 3d. ; cloth, 2s. net.
> I. Reincarnation. II. Evolution and Reincarnation.
> III. Which is Scientific, Resurrection or Reincarnation?

Abhedânanda (Swâmi).—Philosophy of Work. 8vo, pp. 93. Paper cover, 1s. 6d. ; cloth, 2s. 6d. net.
> I. Philosophy of Work. II. Secret of Work.
> III. Duty or Motive in Work.

Abhedânanda (Swâmi).—Spiritual Unfoldment. 8vo, pp. 97. Paper cover, 1s. 3d. ; cloth, 2s. net.
> I. Self-control II. Concentration and Meditation.
> III. God-consciousness.

Abhedânanda (Swâmi).—Single Lectures. 8vo, paper covers. 6d. each net.

- The Way to the Blessed Life.
- Scientific Basis of Religion.
- Cosmic Evolution and its Purpose.
- The Philosophy of Good and Evil.
- Does the Soul exist after Death?
- The Relation of Soul to God.
- The Word and the Cross in Ancient India.
- The Motherhood of God.
- Why a Hindu is a Vegetarian.
- Religion of the Hindus.
- Divine Communion.
- Who is the Saviour of Souls?
- Woman's Place in Hindu Religion.
- Why a Hindu accepts Christ and rejects Churchianity
- Christian Science and Vedanta.
- Spiritualism and Vedanta.

Ad Damîrî.—Hayat al-Hayawân (Life-History of Animals). Translated from the Arabic by Lieut.-Colonel A. S. G. JAYAKAR, I.M.S. (Retired). 2 vols., 8vo. 15s. net.

To the student of Islamic literature and sciences, and Arab folklore, the work is of immense importance, whilst its value as a guide to Semitic scholars in studying the primitive culture of the Semites is unquestionable, for they will find in it, in a readily accessible form, some of the principal materials necessary for such an enquiry ; as, for instance, the numerous proverbs, poetical allusions, and traditional sayings which are profusely quoted in the book, and which, while preserving in a remarkable degree the freshness of the language of the wild Arabs of the desert, throw an important light on the mode of thought and life of that great branch of the Semitic race.

Adler (E.N.) et M. Seligsohn.—Une Nouvelle Chronique Samaritaine. Texte Samaritan transcrit et édité pour la première fois avec une traduction française. Roy. 8vo, pp. ix, 116. 3s. net.

Adler (M. N.).—Chinese Jews. A Lecture delivered at the Jews College Literary Society on June 17th, 1900. 8vo, pp. 24. 1s. net.

Alabaster (Ernest).—Notes and Commentaries on Chinese Criminal Law and Cognate Topics. With Special Relation to Ruling Cases. Together with a Brief Excursus on the Law of Property. Chiefly founded on the Writings of the late Sir Chaloner Alabaster, K.C.M.G., etc. By ERNEST ALABASTER, of the Inner Temple, Barrister-at-Law ; and Christ's College, Cambridge ; Advanced Student, Chinese Customs Service. With a Copious Index. Roy. 8vo, pp. lxii, 675, cloth. 18s. net.

"It fulfils its purpose of giving a full trustworthy account of Chinese criminal practice."—*Athenæum*.

"This work is decidedly of a high order, and can be thoroughly trusted as a popular guide to the principles of Chinese Law."—*Asiatic Quarterly Review*.

"To students of the judicial problems presented by the Far East we can suggest no better Introductory Manual than Mr. Alabaster's book."—*Law Journal*.

Allen (F. S.).—Studies in Popular Poetry. Reprint. 4to, pp. xxiii, paper covers. 1s. 6d.

American Journal of Semitic Languages and Literature (continuing Hebraica). Edited by WILLIAM R. HARPER and the Staff of the Semitic Department of the University of Chicago. Published quarterly. Vol. xxi in progress. Annual subscription, including postage, 18s.

American Journal of Sociology. Published quarterly. Vol. x in progress. Annual subscription, including postage, 10s. 6d.

American Journal of Theology. Edited by Members of the Divinity Faculty of the University of Chicago. Quarterly. Vol. ix in progress. Annual subscription, including postage, 15s. Single numbers, 4s. 6d.

"The theologians of America are attempting to supply a real need . . . it aims at a complete presentation of all recent theological work . . . we give it a hearty welcome, as a scheme likely to prove of real utility to theological students and to the cause of truth."—*Guardian.*

Andersen (D.).—A Pāli Reader. With Notes and Glossary. Part I: Text and Notes. 4to, pp. 191, cloth. 6s. net.

—— **The Same.** Part II : First Half of Glossary. 4to, pp. 112. 5s. net.

Anne, Countess of Winchilsea, The Poems of. Edited from the Original Edition of 1713 and from Unpublished Manuscripts, with an Introduction and Notes. By MYRA REYNOLDS. 8vo, pp. cxxxiii, cloth, 436. 15s. net.

Aston (W. G.).—Grammar of the Japanese Written Language. Third Edition. Revised and Corrected. 8vo, pp. 198, lxxiv, 1905, cloth. 12s. net. [Luzac's Oriental Grammars Series, V.]

Aston (W. G.).—Grammar of the Japanese Spoken Language. Fourth Edition. 8vo, pp. 212, cloth. 7s. 6d. net.

'Awfi Muhammad.—The Lubábu'l-Albab. Part II. Edited in the Original Persian, with Preface, Indices, and Variants. By EDWARD G. BROWNE, M.A., M.B., M.R.A.S. 8vo, pp. 78, 472, cloth. 18s. net. [Persian Historical Series, Vol. II.]

"The work is of very considerable interest ; only two MSS. are known to exist. . . . Its value depends not so much on the biographical notices of the poets mentioned in it as on the fact that it has preserved for us selections from the works of men of whom we should otherwise know little or nothing."—*Spectator.*

Bāna's Harsa Carita.—An Historical Work, translated from the Sanskrit, by E. B. COWELL and F. W. THOMAS. 8vo, pp. xiv, 284, cloth. 10s. net.

Bana's Kadambari.—Translated, with Occasional Omissions, with a full Abstract of the Continuation of the Romance by the Author's Son Bhushanabhatta, by C. M. RIDDING. 8vo, pp. xxiv, 232, cloth. 10s. net.

Bartholomaei (J.).—Lettres Numismatiques et Archéologiques, relatives à la Transcaucasie. Avec 4 pl. 4to, pp. ix, 116. 4s. 6d.

Bastian (A.). See **Satvótpatti** and **Buddhistic Essays.**

Beal (Rev. S.).—Two Papers. Reprint. 8vo, pp. 88. 1s.
    I. Brief Remarks on some Japanese Titles.
    II. Account of the Shui Lui, or Infernal Machine.

Belléli (L.).—Un Nouvel Apocryphe. Etude sur un Fragment de Manuscrit du Vieux Caire. Roy. 8vo, pp. 23. 2s. 6d. net.

Belléli (L.).—Greek and Italian Dialects, as spoken by the Jews in some places of the Balkan Peninsula. Reprint. 8vo, pp. 8. 1s. net.

Bemmelen (T. F. van) and Hooyer (G. B.).—Guide to the Dutch East Indies. Composed by invitation of the Royal Steam Packet Company. Translated by B. T. BERRINGTON. 32mo, pp. viii, 202, cloth. 1s. 6d.

Beveridge (A. S.).—The History of Humāyūn. By Gul-Baden Begam (Princess Rose-Body). Translated, with Introduction, Notes, Illustrations, and Biographical Appendix; and reproduced in the Persian from the only known manuscript of the British Museum, by A. S. BEVERIDGE. 8vo; pp. xiv, 332, and 96 pages of Persian text, with 10 Plates; cloth. 10s. net.

Bezold (Ch.).—Oriental Diplomacy: being the transliterated Text of the Cuneiform Despatches between the King of Egypt and Western Asia in the Fifteenth Century before Christ, discovered at Tell el Amarna, and now preserved in the British Museum. With full Vocabulary, Grammatical Notes, etc., by CHARLES BEZOLD. Post 8vo, pp. xliv, 124, cloth. 18s. net.

"For the Assyriologist the book is a serviceable and handy supplement to the British Museum volume on the Tell el Amarna tablets. The author is specially skilled in the art of cataloguing and dictionary-making, and it is needless to say that he has done his work well."—*The Academy.*

"Die in dem Hauptwerke (The Tell el Amarna Tablets in the British Museum with autotype Facsimiles, etc) vermisste Transcription des Keilschrift-textes der Tafeln, sowie ein sehr ausführliches, mitunter die Vollstandigkeit einer Concordanz erreichendes Vocabulary bietet die Oriental Diplomacy von C. Bezold, das eben deshalb gewissermassen als Schlüssel zu dem Publicationswerke betrachtet werden kann."—*Liter. Centralblatt.*

Bhagavad-Gita. — The Book of Devotion. Dialogue between Krishna, Lord of Devotion, and Arjuna, Prince of India. In English. By W. G. JUDGE. Small 8vo, pp. 133, limp leather. 3s. 6d. net.

Biblia. A Monthly Journal of Oriental Research in Archæology, Ethnology, Literature, Religion, History, Epigraphy, Geography, Languages, etc. Vol. xviii in progress. Annual subscription, 5s. net.

Biblical World (The). Edited by WILLIAM R. HARPER. Published monthly. Vol. xxvi in progress. Annual subscription, including postage, 12s.

"The *Biblical World* makes a faithful record and helpful critic of present Biblical work, as well as an efficient, practical, and positive independent force in stimulating and instructing the student, preacher, and teacher."

Bibliographical List of Books on Africa and the East. Published in England. 2 vols. Vol. I: Containing the Books published between the Meetings of the Eighth Oriental Congress at Stockholm in 1889 and the Ninth Congress in London in 1892. Vol. II: Containing the Books published between the Meetings of the Ninth Oriental Congress in London in 1892 and the Tenth Oriental Congress at Geneva in 1894. Systematically arranged, with Preface and Author's Index, by C. G. LUZAC. 12mo. Each vol. 1s.

De Boer (Dr. T J.).—The History of Philosophy in Islam. Translated, with the sanction of the Author, by E. R. JONES, B.D. Roy. 8vo, pp. 216, cloth. 7s. 6d. net. [Luzac's Oriental Religions Series, Vol. II.]

'It is, we believe, the most useful work of its kind that has ever yet appeared in our language, and it will undoubtedly be found to be of the greatest possible value to missionaries, historians, and all students of subjects relating to the Arabians of sub-Islamic times."—*Asiatic Quarterly Review.*

Böhtlingk (O.).— Sanskrit Chrestomathie. Zweite, ganzlich umgearbeitete Auflage. Roy. 8vo, pp. 1, 372. 4*s.* 6*d.* net.

Böhtlingk (O.) and R. Roth.—Sanskrit Worterbuch, herausgegeben von der Kaiserlichen Akademie der Wissenschaften, St. Petersburg. 7 parts, 4to. £8 17*s.* 6*d.* net.

—— **The Same.** Smaller Edition. 7 parts, 4to. £3 3*s.* net.

Bolognese (Dr. S.).—The Economical Interpreter. English and Italian. With a Treatise on Italian Pronunciation and the Conjugation of Italian Verbs. Second Edition. Oblong, pp. 268. 2*s.* net.

Book of Consolations, or the Pastoral Epistles of Mâr Ishô-Yahbh of Kûphlanâ in Adiabene. Edited with an English Translation by P. SCOTT-MONCRIEFF, B.A. (Assistant in the Department of Egyptian and Assyrian Antiquities, British Museum). Part I : Syriac Text. 8vo, pp. lvi. 101, cloth. 10*s.* 6*d.* net. [Luzac's Semitic Text and Translation Series, Vol. XVI.]

Borel (H.).—Wu-Wei. A Phantasy based on the Philosophy of Lao-Tse. Translated from the Dutch by M. IANSON. 8vo, pp. 69, cloth. 3*s.* net.

Brhadâranjakopanishad. In der Mâdhjamdina Recension. Herausgegeben und übersetzt von OTTO BÖHTLINGK. 8vo, pp. iv, 72, 100. 5*s.* net.

Brönnle (Paul).—Contributions towards Arabic Philology. Part I: The Kitāb al-maksūr wa'l-mamdūd. By Ibn WALLĀD. Being a Treatise, Lexicographical and Grammatical, from Manuscripts in Berlin, London, Paris. Edited with Text, Critical Notes, Introduction, Commentary, and Indices. By Dr. PAUL BRÖNNLE. I : Arabic Text. Roy. 8vo, pp. xii, 128, cloth. 7*s.* 6*d.* net ; paper covers, 6*s.* net.

" This is the first of a series of ten parts, in which it is intended to publish some important works of the earliest Arabic authors, together with systematic investigations into the various branches of Arabic Philology."

" In the second part, which contains the Introduction and Commentary to the Arabic text given in the first part, along with a Preface and Bibliography to the whole series, the Author will have opportunity of enlarging at some length upon the principles by which he has been guided in embarking upon this scheme."

Browne (E. G.). See **Persian Historical Series.**

Browne (E. G.).—Account of a rare Manuscript History of Ispahan. 8vo, pp. 90. 1*s.* 6*d.* net.

Browne (E. G.).—Biographies of Persian Poets. Contained in Chapter V, Section 6, of the Tárikh-i-Guzída, or "Select History," of Hamdu'lláh Mustawfi of Qazwín. Translated by E. G. BROWNE. 8vo, pp. 80. 2*s.* net.

Browne (E. G.).—The Chahár Maqála (Four Discourses) of Nidhámi-i-'arúdí-i-samarqandí. Translated into English by E. G. BROWNE. Demy 8vo, pp. 139, cloth. 4*s.* net.

Buck (C. D.).—A Sketch of the Linguistic Conditions of Chicago. Reprint. 4to, pp. 20, paper covers. 1*s.* 6*d.* net.

Buddhaghosuppatti, or Historical Romance of the Rise and Career of Buddaghosa. Edited and translated by JAMES GRAY, Professor of Pali, Rangoon College. Two parts in one. 8vo, pp. viii, 75, and 36, cloth. 6s.

Buddhism. An Illustrated Quarterly Review. Vol. I. Rangoon, 1904. Annual subscription, 10s. 6d. post free.

Buddhist Pali Texts. Edited under the direction of W. A. DE SILVA. In Pali with Singhalese Translation by W. A. SAMARASEKARA. Vols. I and II: The Digha Nikaya. 10s. each net.

> The Digha Nikaya will be complete in 3 vols.

Buddhistic Essays referring to the Abhidharma. With Introduction in German. By A. BASTIAN. 8vo, pp. 21. 1s. net.

Budge (E. A. Wallis). — Oriental Wit and Wisdom, or the "Laughable Stories." Collected by Mâr Gregory John Bar-Hebraeus, Maphrian of the East from A.D. 1264 to 1286. Translated from the Syriac by E. A. WALLIS BUDGE, M.A., Litt.D., D.Lit. Roy. 8vo, pp. xxvii, iv, 204, cloth. 6s. net.

' In the Preface to the present publication the satisfactory remark is made that the volume containing both the Syriac Text and the Translation, published 1897, price 21s. (see the notice in the *Athenæum* for March 13th, 1897), 'has been well received, both in England and on the Continent,' and that 'in answer to many requests from students of literature generally' Messrs. Luzac & Co. 'have decided to issue the English Translation of it separately in a handy form.

" In such circumstances the new volume is likely to succeed, and we need only add that, although many of the sayings are at war with the finer æsthetic taste of the present day, the collection is fairly representative, and of considerable value. Of some special interest appears to us to be the twentieth chapter, ' Physiological Characteristics described by the Sages.' "—*Athenæum.*

Budge (E. A. Wallis).—The History of the Blessed Virgin Mary and **The History of the Likeness of Christ** which the Jews of Tiberias made to mock at. The Syriac Texts edited with English Translations by E. A. WALLIS BUDGE, M.A., Litt.D., D.Lit., Keeper of the Egyptian and Assyrian Antiquities in the British Museum. Vol. I: The Syriac Texts. pp. xi, 224. 12s. 6d. net. Vol. II: English Translations. pp. xvii, 246. 10s. 6d. net. [Luzac's Semitic Text and Translation Series, Vols. IV and V.]

" To Mr. Budge belongs, however, the great merit of having very materially enriched no fewer than four different branches of Oriental Literature. Several of his editions will no doubt serve as the groundwork for future publications. The general aspect of the volumes is all that could be desired."—*Athenæum.*

" It may be regarded as an exceptionally excellent commentary on the New Testament, the main lines of which it closely follows, for in dealing with the same facts it lets in a great deal of light on the manners, customs, and ideas of the country and the period. . . . The translations are in admirable English, and evince singular ability."—*Catholic Times.*

Budge (E. A. Wallis).—The Histories of Rabban Hôrmîzd, the Persian and Rabban Bar-'Idta. The Syriac Text, edited with English Translations by E. A. WALLIS BUDGE, M.A., Litt.D., Keeper of the Egyptian and Assyrian Antiquities in the British Museum. Two vols. in three. Vol. I: The Syriac Texts. pp. xv, 202. 12s. 6d. net. Vol. II, Part 1: English Translations. pp. xlii, 304. 12s. 6d. net. Vol. II, Part 2: The Metrical Life of Rabban Hôrmîzd, by Mâr Sergius of Adhorbâijân. English Translations. 8vo, pp. ix, 207. 10s. 6d. net. [Luzac's Semitic Text and Translation Series, Vols. IX, X, XI.]

" We have in these handsome volumes valuable records of two of the most remarkable Nestorians who ever lived."—*Expository Times.*

Budge (E. A. Wallis).—The Laughable Stories collected by Bar-Hebraeus. The Syriac Text, with an English Translation, by E. A. WALLIS BUDGE, Litt.D., F.S.A., Keeper of the Department of Egyptian and Assyrian Antiquities, British Museum. 8vo, cloth. 21s. net. [Luzac's Semitic Text and Translation Series, Vol. I.]

' Dr. Budge's book will be welcome as a handy reading-book for advanced students of Syriac, but in the meantime the stories will be an addition to the literature of gnomes and proverbs, of which so many are found in India, and in Persian, Hebrew, and Arabic, although not yet published. We are happy to say that Dr. Budge's new book is well edited and translated, as far as we can judge."—*Athenæum.*

" The worthy Syrian Bishop's idea of humour may excite admiration when we hear that he collected his quips in the grey dawn of the middle ages."—*Pall Mall Gazette.*

Buhler (J. G.).—On the Indian Sect of the Jainas. Translated from the German, and Edited with an Outline of Jaina Mythology by J. BURGESS, C.I.E., LL.D. 8vo, pp. 79, cloth. 3s. 6d. net.

Burnell.—The Sâmavidhânabrâhmana. Being the Third Brahmana of the Sama Veda. Edited by A. C. BURNELL. Vol. I : Text and Commentary, with Introduction. 8vo, pp. xxxviii, 104, cloth. (Publ. 12s.) 5s. net.

Buttenwieser (M.).—Outline of the Neo-Hebraic Apocalyptic Literature. Roy. 8vo, pp. 45. 2s. 6d. net.

Cappeller (Carl).—A Sanskrit-English Dictionary. Based upon the St. Petersburg Lexicons. Roy. 8vo, pp. viii, 672, cloth. (Published 21s.) Reduced to 10s. 6d. net.

The book is certainly the cheapest, and, for a beginner, in some respects the best, of existing Sanskrit-English dictionaries."—*Academy.*

Castren (M. A.).—Nordische Reisen und Forschungen. Herausgegeben von A. SCHIEFNER. 12 vols. £2 16s. net.

Ceylon, A Tale of Old. See **Sinnatamby.**

Ceylon Handbook (The), and Directory, and Compendium of Useful Information, to which is prefixed a Review of the Planting Enterprise and Agriculture of the Colony ; with Statistical Information referring to the Planting Enterprise in other Countries. Compiled and Edited by J. FERGUSON. Thick royal 8vo, cloth. 24s. net.

Chakrabarti (J. Ch.).—The Native States of India. 8vo, pp. xiv, 274, cloth. With Map. 5s. net.

Chapman (Major F. R. H.).—English Hindustani Pocket Vocabulary (containing 1500 Useful Words in Classified Lists). Romanized. 32mo, pp. 92, cloth. 1s. 6d. net.

Chatterjee (B. C.).—Chandra Shekhar. Translated from the Bengali by MANMATHA NATH ROY CHOWDHURY, of Santosh, a distinguished writer and orator of Bengal. With Illustrations. 8vo, pp. viii, 318, cloth gilt. 6s. net.

" 'Chandra Sekhar' is one of the greatest of B. C. Chatterjee's works, and Anglo-Indians who have not hitherto been acquainted with either the author or his writings may now read in their own language a work which will give pleasure in its perusal. The author has been called the ' Sir Walter Scott of India,' and anyone who would like to verify this high tribute of praise cannot do better than procure a copy of the work, and peruse it. We trust the book will prove a success, and will stimulate the accomplished translator to give us more of this kind of work."—*Capital.*

" 'Chandra Shekhar,' by the late Bankim Chandra Chatterjee, has been ably translated into English by Kumar Manmatha Nath Roy Chowdhury. . . . English readers who do not know the original will be glad of this opportunity to catch a glimpse of the writings of the most popular novelist of Bengal."—*Englishman.*

Chattopadhyaya (A.).—The Original Abode of the Indu-European or Arya Races. 8vo, pp. iii, 224. 2s. 6d. net.

Chiplūnkar (Vishnu K. S.).—Kavi-panchaka. Essays on the Sanskrit Classical Poets. Translated into Sanskrit from the Marathi. 8vo, pp. 271. 3s. 6d. net.

—— The same, cloth. 4s. 6d. net.

Chotzner (J.) —Hebrew Humour, and other Essays. Roy. 8vo, pp. 186, cloth. 5s. net.

These essays deal somewhat extensively with the humour and satire that is not infrequently to be found in the works both of ancient and modern Hebrew writers.

Codrington (O.). — A Manual of Musalman Numismatics. 8vo; pp. 239, with 2 Plates, cloth. 7s. 6d. net.

Collins (M.). — The Idyll of the White Lotus. 8vo, pp. 131, cloth. 4s. 6d. net.

Comité de l'Asie Française.—Bulletin Mensuel. Single numbers, 2s. each net.

Annual subscription of 25 frs. (£1) entitles the subscriber to membership, and the Bulletin is supplied free. Messrs. Luzac & Co., having been appointed Agents to the above, can receive subscriptions.

Cool (W.).—With the Dutch in the East. An Outline of the Military Operations in Lombock, 1894, giving also a Popular Account of the Native Characteristics, Architecture, Methods of Irrigations, Agricultural Pursuits, Folklore, Religious Customs, and a *History of the Introduction of Islamism and Hinduism into the Island.* By Capt. W. COOL (Dutch Engineer). Translated from the Dutch by E. J. TAYLOR. Illustrated by G. B. HOOYER, late Lieutenant-Colonel of the Dutch Indian Army. Royal 8vo; pp. viii, 365, x, with numerous Plates, Illustrations, and Plans, and a Map of Lombock; cloth. (Published 21s.) Reduced to 7s. 6d. net.

"The book contains an interesting account of the Balinese and Sassak customs, and throws some light on the introduction of the Mahomedan and Hindu religions into Lombok. . . . The translation by Miss E. J. Taylor is satisfactory, and some of the illustrations are excellent."—*The Times.*

Cordier (H.).—Les Origines de deux Etablissements Français dans l'Extrême-Orient: Chang-Hai –Ning-Po. Documents Inédits publiés avec une Introduction et des Notes. 4to, pp. xxxix, 76. 6s. net.

Cowell (E. B.). See Bana's Harsa Carita.

Cowper (B. H.).—Principles of Syriac Grammar. Translated and abridged from the work of Dr. HOFFMANN. 8vo, pp. 184, cloth. 7s. 6d. net.

Crow (F. E.).—Arabic Manual. A Colloquial Handbook in the Syrian Dialect. For the use of visitors to Syria and Palestine, containing a simplified Grammar, a Comprehensive English and Arabic Vocabulary and Dialogues. The whole in English Characters, carefully transliterated, the Pronunciation being fully indicated. Crown 8vo, pp. viii, 334, cloth. 7s. 6d. [Luzac's Oriental Grammars Series, Vol. IV.]

"Messrs. Luzac have now issued a manual of colloquial Syrian Arabic, which will be of the greatest use to visitors, merchants, and consular officers. . . . Mr. Crow, formerly one of the most brilliant linguists of the student-interpreters of Constantinople, afterwards Vice-Consul at Beyrut."—*The Spectator.*

Cust (R. N.).—Linguistic and Oriental Essays. Third Series. 1891. 8vo, pp. 611, cloth. 7s. 6d. net.

—— The Same. Fourth Series. 1895. 8vo, pp. 634, cloth. 7s. 6d. net.

—— The Same. Fifth Series. 1898. 2 vols. 8vo, cloth. 15s. net.

—— The Same. Sixth Series. 1901. 8vo, pp. 485, cloth. 7s. 6d. net.

—— The Same. Seventh Series. 1904. 8vo, pp. 408, 237, cloth. 7s. 6d. net.

Cust (R. N.).—Essay on the Common Features which appear in all Forms of Religious Belief. 8vo, pp. xxiv, 194, cloth. 5s. net.

Cust (R. N.).—The Gospel Message, or Essays, Addresses, Suggestions, and Warnings of the different aspects of Christian Missions to Non-Christian Races and Peoples. 8vo, pp. 494. Paper, 6s. 6d.; cloth, 7s. 6d. net.

'The scheme is so comprehensive as to include almost every detail of the missionary enterprise. Every essay is stamped, of course, with the personality of its author, whose views are expressed with characteristic force and clearness."—*The Record.*

Cutting (S. W.).—Concerning the Modern German Relatives 'Das' and 'Was' in Clauses dependent upon substantivized Adjectives. Reprint. 4to, pp. 21, paper covers. 1s. 6d. net.

Dawlatsháh. — The Tadhkiratu'sh - Shu'ará ("Memoirs of the Poets") of Dawlatsháh Bin 'Ala'u'd - Dawla Bakhtisháh Al - Ghazi of Samarqand. Edited in the original Persian with Prefaces and Indices by EDWARD G. BROWNE, M.A., M.B., M.R.A.S. 8vo, pp. xvi, 10, 622, cloth. 18s. net. [Persian Historical Series, Vol. I.]

"Critical editions of the chief historical and biographical works of reference in Persian are much wanted, and it is earnestly to be hoped that the series projected by Prof. Browne will receive encouraging support. . . . . As regards the editing little need be said. Mr. Browne's name is a pledge that it has been done in the most exact and scholarly fashion."—*Athenæum.*

"It would be ungracious not to recognise the advantage which this edition possesses over all Oriental publications, not only in the correctness of the text, but in carefully prepared indices of the names of persons, places, and books mentioned in the text."—*Asiatic Quarterly Review.*

Dhamma-Sangani.—A Buddhist Manual of Psychological Ethics of the Fourth Century B.C. Being a Translation, now made for the First Time, from the Original Pali of the First Book in the Abhidhamma Pitaka, entitled Dhamma-Sangani (Compendium of States or Phenomena). With Introductory Essay and Notes by CAROLINE A. F. RHYS DAVIDS, M.A., Fellow of University College. 8vo, pp. xcv, 393, cloth. 10s. net.

Dighā Nikaya. See **Buddhist Pali Texts.**

Distracted Love. Being the translation of Udbhranta Prem. By D. N. SHINGHAW. 8vo, pp. 97. 2s. 6d. net.

Dorn (B.).—Muhammedanische Quellen zur Geschichte der Südlichen Küstenländer des Kaspischen Meeres. Herausgegeben, übersetzt, und erläutert von B. DORN. 4 vols. 8vo. £1 18s. net. The volumes are also sold separately. Vol. I, 15s.; Vol. II, 6s. 6d.; Vol. III, 4s. 6d.; Vol. IV, 12s.

Dsanglu.—Der Weise und der Thor. Aus dem Tibetischen übersetzt und mit dem original texte herausgegeben von I. J. SCHMIDT. 2 vols. 4to. 15s. net.

Dunkley (M.).—Nature's Allegories and Poems. Illustrated. 8vo, pp. 167, cloth. 2s. 6d. net.

Dvivedi (Mahāvīra-prasada).—Kāvya-manjushā. A Collection of Poems. In Sanskrit and Hindi. 8vo, pp. 243. 3s. net.

Economy of Human Life. Complete in two Parts. Translated from an Indian Manuscript written by an ancient Bramin. To which is prefixed an account of the manner in which the manuscript was discovered, in a letter from an English gentleman then residing in China to the Earl of Chesterfield. New Edition, prepared with a Preface, by DOUGLAS M. GANE. Small 8vo. pp. 164, cloth gilt. 2s. 6d. ; parchment covers, 3s. net.

Little more than 100 years ago this work enjoyed a wide popularity, not only in Great Britain, but throughout Western Europe, and passed through numerous editions in each country in which it appeared. In the British Museum alone there are copies of more than fifty different English editions.

" Somewhat similar in form to the Proverbs of Solomon. The 'Economy of Human Life' is even more interesting, inasmuch as the precepts are not disconnected, but display a method in arrangement. Together they form one complete system, perfect as a whole, and the parts exquisite condensations of wisdom."—*Sunday Special.*

Edkins (Joseph).—China's Place in Philology. An attempt to show that the Languages of Europe and Asia have a Common Origin. Demy 8vo, pp. xxiii, 403, cloth. (Published 10s. 6d.) 7s. 6d. net.

Edkins (Joseph).—Chinese Architecture. Contents: (1) Classical Style; (2) Post-Confucian Style; (3) Buddhist Style; (4) Modern Style. 8vo, pp. 36. 1s. net.

Edkins (Joseph).—Chinese Currency. Roy. 8vo, pp. 29. 1s. net.

Edkins (Joseph).—Introduction to the Study of the Chinese Characters. Roy. 8vo, pp. xix, 211, 101, boards. (Published 18s.) 12s. 6d. net.

Edkins (Joseph).—Nirvana of the Northern Buddhists. 8vo, pp. 21. 6d. net.

Edkins (Joseph).—Ancient Symbolism among the Chinese. 8vo, pp. 26. 6d. net.

Efes Damîm.—A Series of Conversations at Jerusalem between a Patriarch of the Greek Church and a Chief Rabbi of the Jews, concerning the Malicious Charge against the Jews of using Christian Blood. By J. B. LEVINSOHN. Translated from the Hebrew by Dr. L. LOEWE. Roy. 8vo, pp. xvi, 208, cloth. (Published 8s.) Reduced price 2s. 6d. net.

Eitel (E. J.).—Europe in China. The History of Hongkong. From the Beginning to the year 1882. 8vo; pp. vii, 575, with Index: cloth. 15s. net.

' His work rises considerably above the level commonly attained by Colonial histories written from a Colonial point of view."—*Times.*

Ettinghausen (Maurice L.).—L'histoire et la vie de Harsavardhana. Roy. 8vo, about 180 pp. (In the Press.)

Far East (The). A Monthly Illustrated Periodical. Edited by C. FINK. Vol. I now in progress. Annual subscription, 16s. net.

Faridu'ddin 'Attar.—Tadhkiratu'l-Awliya (Memoirs of the Saints) of Muhammad Ibn Ibrahim Fariduddin 'Attar. Part I. Edited in the original Persian, with Preface, Indices, and Variants, by R. A. NICHOLSON, M.A., Lecturer in the University of Cambridge. With a Critical Introduction by Mirza Muhammad B. 'Abdu'l - Wakha'b I. Qazwini. 8vo, pp. 66, 357, cloth. 18s. net. [Persian Historical Texts Series, Vol. III.]

Fausböll (V.).—Indian Mythology according to the Mahabharata, in Outline. Roy. 8vo, pp. xxxii, 208, cloth. 9s. net. [Luzac's Oriental Religions Series, Vol. I.]

" This is a very learned work, and should be interesting—nay, will be found essential—to all English students of the Mahábhárat. It is a model of beautiful printing."—*Asiatic Quarterly Review.*

Fausböll (V.).—The Dhammapada, being a Collection of Moral Verses in Pāli. Edited a second time with a literal Latin Translation, and Notes for the use of Pāli Students. By V. FAUSBÖLL. 8vo, pp. xvi, 96, cloth. 7s. 6d. net.

" In its present form the 'Dhammapada' makes an admirable text-book for the use of those who are commencing the study of Pali, and it is with this object that the present edition has been issued in an abbreviated form."—*Asiatic Quarterly Review.*

" Il Dhammapada resta sempre il libro più adatto e per molti riguardi conveniente ai principcanti, come a tutti gli studiosi di cose buddistiche è indispensabile."— (P. E. P.) *Cultura.*

Ferguson (A. M.).— All about Pepper ; including Practical Instructions for Planting, Cultivation, and Preparation for Market, giving Cost of Cultivation, Estimate of Expenditure, and much other useful information from a variety of sources. Roy. 8vo, pp. 90. 2s. net.

Ferguson (A. M.).—All about Cinnamon; including Practical Instructions for Planting, Cultivation, and Preparation for Market, with Information from a variety of sources. Roy. 8vo, pp. 43. 2s. net.

Ferguson (A. M.).—" Inge Va ! " or the Sinna Durai's Pocket Tamil Guide. Fourth Edition. 8vo, pp. viii, 156, boards. 2s. 6d. net.

Ferguson (A. M.).—" Mehe Varen," or the Sinna Durai's Pocket Sinhalese Guide, being a Sinhalese Translation of A. M. Ferguson's " Inge Va." 8vo, pp. ii, 44, boards. 2s. net.

Ferguson (J.).—Limited Companies in Ceylon for Tea and other Plantations (in Rupee Currency), with full particulars, compiled and published to supplement Messrs. GOW, WILSON, & STANTON's " Tea-Producing Companies (Sterling) of India and Ceylon." 8vo, pp. viii, 96, cloth. (Published 7s. 6d.) 1s. 6d. net.

Ferguson (J.).—Ceylon in 1903. Describing the Progress of the Island since 1803, its Present Agricultural and Commercial Enterprises, and its Unequalled Attractions to Visitors. With Statistical Information, a Map of the Island, and upwards of one Hundred Illustrations. 8vo, pp. 154, 183, cloth. 10s. net.

Ferguson (J.).—All about Coconut Planting. Including Practical Instructions for Planting and Cultivation with Estimates specially prepared for Expenditure and Receipts ; a special chapter on Desiccating Coconut, and other suitable information referring to the industry in Ceylon, South India, the Straits Settlements, Queensland, and the West Indies. Third Edition. 8vo, pp. 87, cxcii, cloth. 5s. net.

Ferguson (J.). The Coffee Planter's Manual for both the Arabian and Liberian Species. Compiled from the Original Manual by the late A. BROWN, and a variety of other Authorities, by J. F. Fourth Edition. With Illustrations. 8vo, pp. vii, 320, boards. 4s. 6d. net.

Ferguson (J.).—All about Rubber and Gutta-Percha. The India Rubber Planter's Manual, with the latest Statistics and Information, more particularly in regard to Cultivation and Scientific Experiments in Trinidad and Ceylon. Third Edition, Revised and Enlarged. 8vo, pp. 350, boards. 6s. net.

Flagg (W. J.). — Yoga, or Transformation. A Comparative Statement of the various Religious Dogmas concerning the Soul and its Destiny, and of Akkadian, Hindu, Taoist, Egyptian, Hebrew, Greek, Christian, Mohammedan, Japanese, and other Magic. Roy. 8vo, pp. 376, cloth gilt. 13s. 6d. net.

Franson (Rev. F.).—The Religion of Tibet and the True Religion. For English-speaking Tibetans. Roy. 8vo, pp. 47. 1s. 6d. net.

Gaster (M.).—The Chronicles of Jerahmeel, or the Hebrew Bible Historiale. A Collection of Jewish Legends and Traditions. Translated for the first time from an unique manuscript in the Bodleian Library. With an Introduction, Notes, and full Index, and five Facsimiles. Roy. 8vo, pp. cxii, 341, cloth. With 5 plates. 10s. net.

Gates (Professor E.).—The Relations and Development of the Mind and Brain. Square 8vo, pp. 56, paper covers. 1s. 6d. net.

—— The same, cloth. 2s. 6d. net.

Geber.—The Discovery of Secrets attributed to Geber, from the MS. In Arabic. With a rendering into English by R. A. STEELE, F.C.S. 8vo, pp. 8. 1s. net.

Ghosal (J.).—Celebrated Trials in India. Compiled by J. GHOSAL. Vol. I. Roy. 8vo, pp. 332, cloth. 4s. 6d. net.

Ghosh (Rakhaldas). — A Treatise on Materia Medica and Therapeutics. Including Pharmacy, Dispensing, Pharmacology, and Administration of Drugs. Edited by C. P. LUKIS, M.B., F.R.C.S. 8vo, pp. 684, cloth. 7s. net.

Gibb (E. J. W.).—A History of Ottoman Poetry. By the late E. J. W. GIBB, M.R.A.S. Edited by E. G. BROWNE, M.A., M.B. Vols. I, II, III, IV. Roy. 8vo, cloth. 21s. each net.

"How complete was the author's mastery of their language and literature is abundantly attested by the spontaneous evidence of Turkish men of letters, one of whom asserts that neither in the Ottoman Empire nor amongst the Orientalists of Europe does anyone exist who has more profoundly studied the Ottoman language and literature than he."—*Asiatic Quarterly Review.*

"The premature death of that profound Orientalist Mr. E. J. W. Gibb would have proved an irreparable loss had not the unfinished MS. of his monumental work been entrusted for publication to Professor E. G. Browne. . . . . We heartily congratulate Professor Browne on the brilliant manner in which he has performed this portion of his task, and eagerly look forward to the remaining volumes."—*Westminster Review.*

Gladstone (Right Hon. W. E.).—Archaic Greece and the East. 8vo, pp. 32. 1s. net.

Gray (James). See **Buddhaghosuppatti** and **Jinalankara.**

Great Trial Series.—The Great Baroda Case. Being a full Report of the Proceedings of the Trial and Deposition of His Highness Mulhar Rao Gaekwar of Baroda for instigating an attempt to poison the British Resident at his Court. Roy. 8vo, pp, xxxv, 544, 75, cloth. Price 6s. net.

The whole of the proceedings and a full report with Sergeant Ballantine's fearless and sensational speeches and incontrovertible arguments, etc., etc., *verbatim*.

Sergeant Ballantine's speeches and art of cross-examination are uncommon and in themselves a monument of learning and forensic ability unsurpassed in the annals of criminal trials in the world, and are worthy of special study.

Great Wahabi Case.—A Full and Complete Report of the Proceedings and Debates in the matters of Ameer Khan and Hashmadad Khan. In the Crown Side of the High Court of Judicature at Fort William in Bengal. In the year 1870. 2s. 6d. net.

Gribble (J. D. B.).—A History of the Deccan. With numerous Illustrations, Plates, Portraits, Maps, and Plans. Vol. I. Roy. 8vo, cloth. 21s.

" In a style easy and pleasant the author tells the story of the Mohammedan occupation of the Deccan . . . . the general style of the book and the admirable photographs and drawings with which it is enriched leave nothing to be desired." *Athenæum.*

Grierson (G. A.).—A Handbook to the Kayathi Character. Showing the actual Handwriting in current use in Bihár. 4to, pp. vi, 4, cloth. With 30 plates. (Published 18s.). 6s. net.

The plates are in the Kayathi Character with the transliteration and translation opposite.

Grierson (G. A.). — **Notes on Tul'si Das.** 4to, pp. 62. Reprint. 2s. 6d. net.

Grierson (G. A.).—Notes on Ahom. 8vo, pp. 59. Reprint. 2s. net.

Grierson (G. A.).—Curiosities of Indian Literature. Selected and translated by G. A. G. Small 8vo, pp. 24. 6d.

Grierson (G. A.).—Essays on Bihári Declension and Conjugation. 8vo, pp. 34. Reprint. 1s. 6d. net.

Grierson (G. A.).—Essays on Kāçmīrī Grammar. Roy. 8vo, pp. 257, xciii, paper covers. 13s. 6d. net.

Guides Madrolle. Chine, Ports du Japon. 8vo. 10s. net.

CONTENTS.—*Grammaire Chinoise, par A. Vissiere.—Voyageurs Chinois, par Ed. Chavannes.—* Notices historiques des Cités de Chine, par A. Vissiere.—*Art Chinois.—Histoire de la Chine.—Populations autochtones de la Chine, etc., etc.

—— **The Same.** Pekin, Corée, le Trans-sibérien. 8vo. 8s. 6d. net.

CONTENTS.—* Histoire de la Corée, par M. Courant.—Notices historiques des Cités de Chine, par A. Vissiere.

This Guide takes the traveller to Shanghai, and accompanies him during excursions around Pekin and Northern China, and describes the journey back to Europe by way of Tien-Tsin, Pekin, Seoul, Moscow, Berlin.

—— **The Same.** Indo-Chine. Harar, Indies, Ceylon, Siam, Chine Méridionale. 8vo. 15s. net.

This Guide describes every point of interest from Marseilles to Canton, the sumptuous temples of India, as well as the Sanatoria of Ceylon. Describes also the dead cities of Siam, and takes the traveller to Canton by way of the Red River.

* Reprints of these to be had separately at various prices.

Guiraudon (F. G. de).—Manuel de la langue foule, parlée dans la Sénégambie et le Soudan. Grammaire, textes, vocabulaire. 8vo, pp. 144, cloth. 6s. net.

Guthrie (Rev. K. S.).—Of the Presence of God. Being a Practical Method for beginning an Interior Life. Square 8vo, pp. 106, cloth gilt. 4s. 6d. net.

Guthrie (Rev. K. S.).—Regeneration Applied. Being the Sequel and Practical Application of Regeneration, the Gate of Heaven. 8vo, pp. 154, cloth. 4s. 6d. net.

Guthrie (Rev. K. S.). — The Gospel of Apollonius of Tyana. According to Philostratos. 8vo, pp. 73, cloth. 3s. 6d. net.

Guthrie (Rev. K. S.).—The Ladder of God, and other Sermons. 8vo. pp. 88, cloth. 4s. 6d. net.

Guthrie (Rev. K. S.).—Of Communion with God. Small 8vo, pp. 62, cloth. 2s. 6d. net.

Halcombe (Charles J. H.).—The Mystic Flowery Land. A Personal Narrative. By CHARLES J. H. HALCOMBE, late of Imperial Customs, China. Second Edition. 8vo; pp. 226, with numerous Illustrations and Coloured Plates; cloth gilt. 7s. 6d.

The valuable and handsome volume contains thirty long chapters, a frontispiece of the author and his wife—the latter in her Oriental costume—numerous fine reproductions from photographs, and several beautiful coloured pictures representing many scenes and phases of Chinese life, etchings, and comprehensive notes by the author.

" His pages are full of incident, and his narrative often vivid and vigorous."—*Times.*

" The illustrations are good and numerous. Many are facsimiles of coloured Chinese drawings, showing various industrial occupations; others are photogravures representing buildings and scenery."—*Morning Post.*

" The illustrations are all good, and the Chinese pictures reproduced in colours interesting. We have not seen any of them before."—*Westminster Review.*

Harding (Beecham).—Brotherhood: Nature's Law. 8vo, pp. 110, cloth. 2s. net.

Hardy (R. Spence).—The Legends and Theories of the Buddhists. Compared with History and Science. 8vo, pp. 244, cloth. 7s. 6d. net.

Harîri.—The Assemblies of al Harîri. Translated from the Arabic, with an Introduction and Notes, Historical and Grammatical, by TH. CHENERY and F. STEINGASS. With Preface and Index, by F. F. ARBUTHNOT. 2 vols. 8vo, pp. x, 540, and xi, 395, cloth. 30s. net.

Harper (R. F.).—The Code of Hammurabi, King of Babylonia (about 2250 B.C.). The most ancient of all codes. In 2 Vols. Vol. I: Map, Text, Transliteration, Glossary, Historical and Philological Notes, and Indices. By ROBERT FRANCIS HARPER, Professor of Semitic Languages and Literatures in the University of Chicago; Director of the Babylonian Section of the Oriental Exploration Fund of the University of Chicago; Fellow of the Royal Geographical Society. 8vo, 103 plates and 192 pages, cloth. 18s. net. Part II (in preparation). By WILLIAM RAINEY HARPER, Ph.D., President of the University of Chicago; Professor and Head of the Department of Semitic Languages and Literatures.

In this volume it is proposed to present in succinct form the more important laws and usages of the Hebrew Codes considered historically, and to compare therewith the parallel material contained in the Hammurabi Code and in other Assyro-Babylonian writings. In view of the great influence of the Mosaic Code upon subsequent legislation, a competent inquiry into the relations of this code with that of Hammurabi and other contemporary or possibly antecedent enactments is at the present time pertinent and sure to yield results of great historic value. This book, published as the complement of Part I, will be a work that must of necessity find a place in the library of every man interested in ancient Oriental civilization and desirous of apprehending the great debt of the present to the past.

"This handsome volume, which must have been produced at great expense, is a credit to the University of Chicago Press, and not less to the distinguished Professor of Semitic languages at the same University . . . the special feature of the book is the series of plates giving the autographed text reproduced from the photographs published by Scheil in 1902. . . . The student who wishes to read the original text is thus put in possession of all the necessary materials. . . . A word of special praise is due to the clearness of the plates, which should satisfy the most fastidious eyes."—*Manchester Guardian.*

"The student will welcome the lists of proper names, signs, numerals, and complete glossary; to the ordinary reader, especially, the comprehensive index of subjects covered by the Code will be a useful guide. This edition may be styled 'The Student's Hammurabi.' It forms a compact and handy volume, which will serve as a helpful introduction to the study of Babylonian texts; and to every student of Assyriology the concise arrangement of its contents and the fulness of its information should make it a constant companion."—*Expository Times.*

Harper (R. F.).—Assyrian and Babylonian Letters, belonging to the K Collection of the British Museum. By ROBERT FRANCIS HARPER, of the University of Chicago. Vols. I to VIII. Post 8vo, cloth. Price of each vol., 25*s*. net.

"The Assyriologist will welcome them with gratitude, for they offer him a mass of new material which has been carefully copied and well printed, and which cannot fail to yield important results."—*Athenæum.*

"The book is well printed, and it is a pleasure to read the texts given in it, with their large type and ample margin."—*Academy.*

Hartmann (F.).—Magic, White and Black. The Science of Finite and Infinite Life. Containing Practical Hints for Students of Occultism. Seventh Edition. Revised. 8vo, pp. 292, cloth. 9*s*.; paper covers, 7*s*. 6*d*. net.

Hartmann (Martin).—The Arabic Press of Egypt. By MARTIN HARTMANN. 8vo, pp. ii, 93, cloth. 3*s*. 6*d*. net.

A learned critical list of Arabic publications."—*The Athenæum.*

Such compilations as the present are valuable as works of reference, and as showing the intellectual activity of all those people who fall under British influence."—*Asiatic Quarterly Review.*

Heeres (J. E.).—The Part borne by the Dutch in the Discovery of Australia, 1606–1765. By J. E. HEERES, LL.D., Professor at the Dutch Colonial Institute, Delft. In English and Dutch. With 19 Maps, Charts, and Illustrations. Folio, pp. vi, xvii, 106, cloth. 21*s*. net.

"This handsome work is considerately printed both in English and Dutch. After the publication of the present work, writers of Australia will have no excuse for ignorance of the splendid achievements of the Dutch navigators between 1606 and 1765. The work is illustrated with several of the quaint maps and charts of the early Dutch explorers, an inspection of which will interest our Australian fellow-countrymen."—*Scottish Geographical Magazine.*

"Professor Heeres has rendered another service to historical geography by editing a complete series of documents bearing on the Dutch Voyages to Australia from 1606 to 1765. Among the documents perhaps the most valuable are the Journal kept by Jan Carstensz on his voyage of 1623 to the Gulf of Carpentaria with the Pera and Arnhem, and the various papers relating to the voyage of Pool and Pieterszoon in 1636. While allowing that the Dutch discoveries in the west were the result of accident, Professor Heeres points out that those in the north were the outcome of a systematic endeavour on the part of the Dutch officials to extend the sphere of their operations."—*Geographical Journal.*

Hemakandra.—Abhidhanakintamani, ein systematisch angeordnetes synonymisches Lexicon. Herausgegeben, übersetzt, und mit Anmerkungen begleitet von O. BÖHTLINGK et C. RIEU. 8vo, pp. xii, 443. 12s. net.

Hendrickson (G. L.).—The Proconsulate of Julius Agricola in Relation to History and to Encomium. Reprint. 4to, pp. 33, paper covers. 2s.

Hirschfeld (Dr. H.).—New Researches into the Composition and Exegesis of the Qoran. 4to, pp. 155. 5s. net.

Imperial and Asiatic Quarterly Review and Oriental Record (founded January, 1886). Third Series, Vol. XIX, now in progress. Annual subscription, 20s. net.

Irvine (W.).—The Army of the Indian Moghuls; its Organisation and Administration. Roy. 8vo, pp. 324, cloth. 8s. 6d. net.

"This book is a mine of curious information, collected with great labour and pains from recondite sources; and it deals with a subject of supreme importance to the student of that period of Indian history which immediately preceded the British domination of the country."—*Asiatic Quarterly Review.*

"The subject-matter of the volume is certain to prove of deep interest to all students of Indian history, as well as to military experts, who are here provided with an excellent opportunity of comparing and considering the points of resemblance and difference between the military organisations of the East and West."—*Aberdeen Daily Journal.*

Jacolliot (L.).—Occult Science in India and among the Ancients, with an account of their Mystic Initiations and the History of Spiritism. Translated from the French by WILLARD L. FELT. Roy. 8vo, pp. 275, cloth gilt. 12s. net.

Jastrow (M.).—A Dictionary of the Targumim, the Talmud Babli and Yerushalmi, and the Midrashic Literature. With an Index of Scriptural Quotations. 2 vols. 4to, pp. 1736, half-morocco. £4 10s. net.

"This is the only Talmudic Dictionary in English, and all students should subscribe to it. The merits of this work are now too well known to need repetition." *Jewish Chronicle.*

Jayakar (Lieut.-Col. A. S. G.). See **Ad Damîrî.**

Jinalankara, or "Embellishments of Buddha." By BUDDHA-RAKKHITA. Edited with Introduction, Notes, and Translation, by JAMES GRAY. Two parts in one. 8vo, cloth. 6s.

Johnson (E.).—The Altar in the Wilderness. An attempt to interpret Man's Seven Spiritual Ages. Small 8vo, pp. 117. 1s. 6d. net.

—— The same, cloth. 2s. 6d. net.

Johnston (C.).—Useful Sanskrit Nouns and Verbs. In English letters. Compiled by C. JOHNSTON, Bengal Civil Service, Dublin University Sanskrit Prizeman, etc. Small 4to, pp. 30, cloth. 2s. 6d.

Johnston (C.).—The Memory of Past Births. 4to, pp. 55, paper covers. 1s. 6d. net.

—— The same, cloth. 2s. 6d. net.

Johnston (C.).—The Awakening to the Self. Translated from the Sanskrit of Shankara the Master. Oblong 8vo, pp. 31. 2s. net.

Journal of the Anthropological Society of Bombay. Vol. VII in progress. Price 5s. each number.

Journal of the Buddhist Text and Research Society. Vol. VII now in progress. Published irregularly. Subscription price, 8s. net.

Journal of the Siam Society. Vol. I, Nos. 1 and 2. Subscription price, 25s. net.

Judge (W. G.).—The Ocean of Theosophy. Thirteenth Edition. 8vo, pp. 154. Paper covers, 1s. 6d.; cloth, 2s. 6d. net.

Judge (W. G.).—The Culture of Concentration of Occult Powers and their Acquirement. Reprint. Small 8vo, pp. 29, paper covers. 6d.

Judson's Burmese-English Dictionary, revised and enlarged by R. C. STEVENSON, Burma Commission. Roy. 8vo, pp. xiv, 1188, 6. 25s. net.

—— The same, half-bound. 30s. net.

Judson (A.). — English-Burmese Dictionary. Fourth Edition. Roy. 8vo, pp. 930, half-bound. 25s. net.

King (Leonard W.). — Babylonian Magic and Sorcery. Being "The Prayers of the Lifting of the Hand." The Cuneiform Texts of a Group of Babylonian and Assyrian Incantations and Magical Formulæ, edited with Transliterations. Translations, and full Vocabulary from Tablets of the Kuyunjik Collection preserved in the British Museum. By LEONARD W. KING, M.A., Assistant in the Department of Egyptian and Assyrian Antiquities, British Museum. Roy. 8vo, cloth. 18s. net.

" We cannot pretend to form an adequate judgment of the merits of Mr. King's work, but it is manifestly conceived and executed in a very scholarly spirit."—*Times*.

" Mr. King's book will, we believe, be of great use to all students of Mesopotamian religions, and it marks an era in Assyriological studies in England. . . . A word of special praise is due to Mr. King for the excellence of his autograph plates of text." —*Athenæum*.

King (Leonard W.).—The Letters and Inscriptions of Hammurabi, King of Babylon about B.C. 2200, to which are added a Series of Letters of other Kings of the First Dynasty of Babylon. The Original Babylonian Texts, edited from Tablets in the British Museum, with English Translations, Summaries of Contents, etc. By L. W. KING, M.A., F.S.A., Assistant in the Department of Egyptian and Assyrian Antiquities, British Museum. In three volumes. Vol. I: Introduction and Babylonian Texts. Vol. II: Babylonian Texts (continued). Vol. III: Transliterations, English Translations, Vocabularies, Indices, etc. Roy. 8vo, cloth. Vol. I, 21s. net; Vol. II, 18s. net; Vol. III, 18s. net. [Luzac's Semitic Text and Translation Series, Vols. II, III, and VIII.]

" The concluding volumes of this important book are out at last. Mr. King supplies an excellent vocabulary for both the Sumerian and Semitic words used in these texts, and although his translation differs somewhat from that adopted by German Cuneiform scholars, he has kept most commendably clear from philological discussion. . . . Altogether, both he and the Museum are to be congratulated on the completion of a difficult task."—*Athenæum*.

" Mr. King may be congratulated on his copies of the Cuneiform texts, and still more on his translations and notes. . . . The notes contain very full references to the dates found in the legal documents of the period, by means of which several of the mutilated passages in the annals can be restored. . . . The value of these annals can scarcely be over-estimated."—(Prof. Sayce) *Expository Times*.

King (Leonard W.).—**The Seven Tablets of Creation,** or the Babylonian and Assyrian Legends concerning the Creation of the World and of Mankind. Edited by L. W. KING, M.A., F.S.A., Assistant in the Department of Egyptian and Assyrian Antiquities, British Museum. In two volumes. Vol. I: English Translation, Transliteration, Glossary, Introduction, etc. Vol. II: Supplementary (Assyrian and Babylonian) Texts. Roy. 8vo, cloth. Vol. I, 18s. net; Vol. II, 15s. net. [Luzac's Semitic Text and Translation Series, Vols. XII and XIII.]

" Students of religion and mythology will find this book a mine of wealth. For the world of Orientalists this is undoubtedly the book of the season."—*Globe.*

' This important work gives, with the aid of the most recent material, a critical text and full exposition of the Babylon epic of the creation of the world and of mankind."—*Times.*

" To all students of comparative religion, to those who are interested in the dualism of the Zend Avesta and cognate subjects, we can commend this remarkable archaic literature, possibly the very oldest the world possesses."—*Scotsman.*

King (Leonard W.). See **Studies.**

King (Major J. S.).—**History of the Bahmanî Dynasty.** Founded on the Burbân-I Ma, Asir. 8vo, pp. 157, with Map, cloth. 7s. 6d. net.

Kittel (Rev. F.). — **A Kannada-English Dictionary.** Roy. 8vo, pp. l, 1752, half-bound. £1 12s. net.

Klenzo (Camillo von).—**The Treatment of Nature in the Works of Nikolaus Lenau.** An Essay in Interpretation. Reprint. 4to, pp. 83, paper covers. 6s. net.

Koran in Arabic. A photo-zincographed reproduction so as to avoid the objections to printing or lithographing the sacred text of the Manuscript of the Koran of Hafiz Osman written in 1094 A.H. and famous for its correctness. The frontispiece is splendidly illuminated. 8vo, cloth gilt, Oriental binding with flap. 5s. net. The same can be had unbound, but stitched ready for binding, 4s. net.

A testimonial as to the accuracy of the reproduction, signed by leading Muhammadan Divines, is photographed at the end of the work.

Koran. See **Hirschfeld.**

Korea Review. Edited by H. B. Hulbert. Published monthly. Vol. V now in progress. Annual subscription, post free, 8s. 6d. net.

Kosegarten.—Hudsailitarum Carmina. Arabic Text. Edited by J. G. L. KOSEGARTEN. Sumptu Societatis Anglicæ quæ Oriental Fund nuncupatur. Vol. I. (All published.) London, 1854. 30s. net.

Kosegarten.—Taberistanensis Annales Regum atque Legatorum Dei. Edited (in Arabic and Latin) by J. G. L. KOSEGARTEN. Greifswald, 1843. Vol. III. 8s. net.

To students of Arabic literature it is likely to be of great interest to hear that of the two works indicated above, both edited by Kosegarten, and long looked upon as being out of print, there have been found, after the death of the printer, some copies which we are able to sell at a very reduced price. Whereas the second work, forming a certain part of the great historical work of al-Tabari, has to some extent been superseded by the complete edition of this monumental work under the editorship of Prof. de Goeje, in Leiden, it is particularly gratifying that the famous collection of the Poems of the Hudsailites, made by the renowned philologian al-Sukkari, about 275 A.H., which has, for the first time, been edited by Kosegarten, and afterwards continued by Wellhausen, has been preserved in some copies. We are glad to be thus enabled to put this work, which has been sold of late for £3 and £4, on sale at the *greatly reduced price* of £1 10s.

Land (J. P. N.).—The Principles of Hebrew Grammar. By J. P. N. LAND, Professor of Logic and Metaphysics in the University of Leyden. Translated from the Dutch by REGINALD LANE POOLE, Balliol College, Oxford. Demy 8vo, pp. xx, 219, cloth. (Published 7s. 6d.) Reduced price 5s. net.

Levertoff (P.).—The Son of Man. A survey of the Life and Deeds of Jesus Christ. In Hebrew. Roy. 8vo, pp. 113, paper cover. 2s. 6d. net.

Loewe (L.).—A Dictionary of the Circassian Language. In two parts: English-Circassian-Turkish and Circassian-English-Turkish. 8vo, cloth. (Published 21s.) Reduced price 6s. net.

Loewe (L.).—Efes Damim. See **Efes**.

Light on the Path. A Treatise written for the Personal Use of those who are ignorant of the Eastern Wisdom, and who desire to enter within its influence. Written down by M. C. With Notes and Comments. Small 8vo, pp. 92, cloth. 2s. 6d. net.

—— The same, leather. 3s. 6d. net.

Luzac's Oriental List and Book Review.—A Record of Oriental Notes and News and containing a Bibliographical List of all new Oriental works, published in England, on the Continent, in the East, and in America. Published every two months. Annual subscription, 3s. Vols. I to IV are entirely out of print. Vols. V to XV are still to be had at 5s. each vol.

'It deserves the support of Oriental students. Besides the catalogue of new books published in England, on the Continent, in the East, and in America, it gives, under the heading of "Notes and News," details about important Oriental works, which are both more full and more careful than anything of the sort to be found elsewhere."—*Academy.*

"A bibliographical monthly publication which should be better known."—*The Record.*

Luzac's Oriental Grammars Series. See **Aston, Crow, Rosen, Wynkoop.**

Luzac's Oriental Religions Series. See **De Boer, Fausböll.**

Luzac's Semitic Text and Translation Series. See **Budge, King, Scott-Moncrieff, Thompson.**

Macnaghten (Sir W. Hay).—Principle of Hindu and Mohammedan Law. Republished from the Principles and Precedences of the same. Edited by the late H. H. WILSON. 8vo, pp. 240, cloth. 6s. net.

Majumdar (Purna Ch.).—The Musnud of Murshidabad (1704–1904). Being a Synopsis of the History of Murshidabad for the last two Centuries. To which are appended Notes of Places and Objects of Interest at Murshidabad. With many Illustrations. 8vo, pp. 322, xxiv, cloth. 7s. 6d. net.

Margoliouth (D. S.).—Chrestomathia Baidawiana. The Commentary of El-Baidâwi on Sura III. Translated and explained for the use of Students of Arabic. By D. S. MARGOLIOUTH, M.A., Laudian Professor of Arabic in the University of Oxford, etc., etc. Post 8vo, cloth. 12s. net.

"The book is as scholarly as it is useful. Of particular importance are the numerous grammatical annotations which give the beginner an insight into the method of the Arabic national grammarians, and which form an excellent preparatory study for the perusal of these works in the original. . . . The introduction, and the remarks in particular, show how well Mr. Margoliouth has mastered the immense literatures of Moslim Tradition, Grammar, and Kalaim. . . . The perusal of the book affords pleasure from beginning to end."—*Journal Royal Asiatic Society.*

Mead (George H.).—The Definition of the Psychical. Reprint. 4to, pp. 38, paper covers. 2s. net.

Michell (R. L. N.).—An Egyptian Calendar for the Koptic Year 1617 (1900–1901 A.D.). Corresponding with the Years 1318–1319 of the Mohammedan Era. By ROLAND L. N. MICHELL. Demy 8vo, 130 pp. Cloth, 3s. ; paper covers, 2s. 6d. net.

Some Notices of an Egyptian Calendar for the year 1395 A.H. (1878 A.D.), published by Mr. Michell in Egypt in 1877 :—

' One of the strangest pieces of reading probably ever offered under the name of contemporary literature. . . . There is no fear that anyone who uses this little book for consultation during a visit to Egypt will fail to see any particular celebration for want of exact information as to its probable date."—*Saturday Review.*

"This quaint and entertaining pamphlet may claim a foremost place among curiosities of modern literature. . . . Never was information so new, so old, so varied, so fantastic, or packed in so small a compass. . . . The Glossary may be described as a local gazetteer, a brief biographical dictionary of holy and historical personages, an epitome of popular customs and superstitions, and a handbook of the agricultural and natural phenomena of the Nile Valley."—*Academy.*

Minayeff (J.).—Pali Grammar. A Phonetic and Morphological Sketch of the Pali Language. With an Introductory Essay on its Form and Character. Translated and rearranged with some modifications and additions for the use of English Students. By C. G. ADAMS. 4to, pp. xliii, 95. 5s. net.

Mirkhond.—The Rauzat-us-Safa ; or, Garden of Purity. Translated from the Original Persian by E. REHATSEK ; edited by F. F. ARBUTHNOT. Vols. I to V. 8vo, cloth. 10s. each vol. net.

Vols. I and II contain : The Histories of Prophets, Kings, and Khalifs.
Vols. III and IV contain : The Life of Muhammad the Apostle of Allah.
Vol. V contains : The Lives of Abú Bakr, O'mar, O'thmân, and Alí, the four immediate successors of Muhammad the Apostle.

Modern Philology. A Quarterly Journal devoted to Research in Modern Languages and Literatures. Vol. III now in progress. Annual subscription, post free, 15s. net.

Monier-Williams (Sir Monier).—Indian Wisdom; or, Examples of the religious, philosophical, and ethical Doctrines of the Hindus, with a brief History of the chief Departments of Sanskrit Literature, and some account of the past and present Condition of India, moral and intellectual. By Sir MONIER MONIER-WILLIAMS, K.C.I.E., M.A., Hon. D.C.L. Oxford. Fourth Edition, enlarged and improved. Post 8vo, pp. 575, cloth. 21s.

" His book . . . still remains indispensable for the growing public, which seeks to learn the outline of Indian literature and thought in a simple and readable form. We are glad to welcome the fourth edition of this eminently readable book."—*Daily Chronicle.*

" It is a fine volume and contains valuable additions by the author . . this edition will be more than ever prized by students of Indian lore."—*Scotsman.*

Moorat (Mrs. M. A. C.).—Elementary Bengali Grammar in English. Small 8vo, pp. vi, 135. 3s. net.

Moorat (Mrs. M. A. C.).—Pahari and Santali Music. Containing two Pahari and five Santali airs with words. Folio, pp. 10. 3s. net.

—— The same can be supplied with English translation in MS. Price 5s. net.

Moore (A. W.).—Existence, Meaning, and Reality in Locke's Essay and in present Epistemology. Reprint. 4to, pp. 25, paper covers. 1s. 6d. net.

Mostras (C.).—Dictionnaire Géographique de l'Empire Ottoman. 8vo, pp. xii, 241. 3s. 6d. net.

Muallakat.—The Seven Poems suspended in the Temple at Mecca.
Translated from the Arabic. By Capt. F. E. JOHNSON. With an Introduction by Shaikh Faizullabhai. 8vo, pp. xxiv, 238. 7s. 6d. net.

Müller (F. Max).—Selections from Buddha. 4to, pp. 52, cloth. 3s. 6d. net.

Müller (F. Max). Address delivered at the Opening of the Ninth International Congress of Orientalists, held in London, September 5th, 1892. 8vo, pp. 66. 1s. 6d. net.

Müller (Wilhelm), Diary and Letters of. In German. Edited by P. S. ALLEN and J. T. HATFIELD. With Explanatory Notes and a Biographical Index in English. With Portrait. 8vo, pp. 200, cloth. 6s. net.

Niemand (J.).—Letters that have helped me. Compiled by JASPER NIEMAND. Reprinted from *The Path*. Fifth Edition. 8vo, pp. 90, cloth. 2s. 6d. net.

Nitiprakāsika. In Sanskrit. Edited with Introductory Remarks by GUSTAV OPPERT. 8vo, pp. 83. 3s. 6d. net.

Noer (Frederick Augustus).—The Emperor Akbar, a Contribution towards the History of India in the 16th Century. Translated and in part Revised by A. S. BEVERIDGE. 2 vols. 8vo, cloth. 8s. net.

Oltramare (P.). — **Le Role du Yajamana dans le sacrifice Brahmanique.** Mémoire présenté au xiiie Congrès des Orientalistes, à Hambourg. Reprint. Roy. 8vo, pp. 34. 2s. net.

Oppert (G.).—On the Weapons, Army Organization, and Political Maxims of the Ancient Hindus, with Special Reference to Gunpowder and Firearms. 8vo, pp. vi, 162. 6s. net.

" A very interesting and instructive work, throwing great light on the early use of explosives in warfare."

Oppert (G.).—Contributions to the History of Southern India.
Part I: Inscriptions. 8vo, pp. 73, with Plate. 2s. net.

Oppert (G.).—On the Classification of Languages. A Contribution to Comparative Philology. 8vo, pp. 146. 6s. net.

Oppert (G.).—On the Classification of Languages in Conformity with Ethnology. Reprint. 8vo, pp. 20. 1s. net.

Oppert (G.).—On the Ancient Commerce of India. A Lecture delivered in Madras. 8vo, pp. 50. 2s. net.

Osborn (L. D.).—The Recovery and Restatement of the Gospel.
8vo, pp. 253, cloth. 6s. 6d. net.

Oudemans Jzn. (A. C.).—The Great Sea-Serpent. An historical and critical Treatise. With the Reports of 187 Appearances (including those of the Appendix), the Suppositions and Suggestions of Scientific and Non-Scientific Persons, and the Author's Conclusions. With 82 Illustrations. Roy. 8vo, pp. xv, 592, cloth. 25s. net.

The volume is extremely interesting."—*Athenæum.*

Oung (Tha Do).—A Grammar of the Pali Language. (After KACCĀYANA.) In 4 vols. Roy. 8vo, pp. 380. 21s. net.

Vols. I and II contain the whole of the Pali Grammar (I. Sandhi Nāma and Kāraka, and Samâsa; II. Taddhita, Kita, Unâdi Akhyâta, Upasagga, and Nipâta particles), 6s. 6d. each. Vol. III, Dictionary of Pali Word-Roots, 6s. 6d. Vol. IV, Chandam, etc., 3s.

Paracelsus.—The Life and Doctrines of Philippus Theophrastus, Bombast of Hohenheim, known by the name of Paracelsus. Extracted and Translated from his Rare and Extensive Works and from some Unpublished Manuscripts by F. HARTMANN, M.D. With Portrait. 8vo, pp. 367, cloth. 9s. net.

Parker (E. H.).—The Taoist Religion. Reprint. 8vo, pp. 35. 1s. 6d. net.

Parker (E. H.). See **Tao-Têh King.**

Persian Historical Series. Edited by EDWARD G. BROWNE, M.A., M.B. See '**Awfi—Dawlatsháh—Faridu'ddin 'Attar.**

Pfungst (Arthur). — A German Buddhist. (Oberpräsidialrat T. SCHULZE.) Translated from the Second German Edition by L. F. DE WILDE. 8vo, pp. 79, cloth. 2s. net.

Picart (Bernard).—Scènes de la vie Juive, dessinées d'après Nature par BERNARD PICART, 1663-1733. Sixteen Plates (Reproduction en heliogravure Dujardin). Together in a beautiful Cloth Cover, richly ornamented with Gold and Colours. Folio. (Frs. 50.) 12s. 6d. net.

Picton (N.).—The Panorama of Sleep, or Soul and Symbol. With Illustrations by R. W. LANE. 8vo, pp. 160, cloth. 4s. 6d. net.

Pischel (Richard).—The Home of the Puppet-Play. An Address delivered by RICHARD PISCHEL on assuming the office of Rector of the Königliche Vereinigte Friedrichs-Universitat, Halle-Wittenberg, on the 12th July, 1900. Translated (with the Author's permission) by MILDRED C. TAWNEY (Mrs. R. N. Vyvyan). Small 8vo, pp. 32, cloth. 2s. net.

Poletti (P.).—Chinese and English Dictionary. Arranged according to Radicals and Sub-Radicals. New and Enlarged Edition. Roy. 8vo. pp. cvii, 307, half-bound. 15s. net.

Poletti (P.).—Explanation of the use of the Sub-Radical. 8vo, pp. 17. 1s. net.

Pryse (J. M.).—Reincarnation in the New Testament. 8vo, pp. 92, paper covers. 1s. 6d. net.

—— The same, cloth. 3s. net.

Pryse (J. M.).—The Sermon on the Mount, and other Extracts from the New Testament. A Verbatim Translation from the Greek, with Notes on the Mystical or Arcane Sense. 8vo, pp. 80, paper covers. 1s. 6d. net.

—— The same, cloth. 3s. net.

Radloff (W.).—Das Kudatku Bilik des Jusuf Chass-Hadschih aus Bálasagun. Theil I: Der Text in Transcription herausgegeben. 4to. pp. xciii, 252. 13s. 6d. net.

Radloff (W.).—Kudatku Bilik. Facsimile der uigurischen Handschrift der k.k. Hof-Bibliothek in Wien. Folio, pp. xiii, 200. £2 10s. net.

Ray (Prithwis Chandra).—The Map of India. From the Buddhist to the British Period. An open Letter to Lord Curzon. 4to, pp. 36, with 6 Maps. Calcutta, 1904. 1s. 6d. net.

Records of the Reign of Tukulti-Ninib I. See **Studies in Eastern History.**

Redcliffe.—The Life of Lord Stratford de Redcliffe, K.G. By STANLEY LANE-POOLE. Popular Edition. With 3 Portraits. 8vo, pp. 377, 2s. 6d. net.

Reis (Sidi Ali).—The Travels and Adventures of the Turkish Admiral Sidi Ali Reis in India, Afghanistan, Central Asia, and Persia, during the years 1553-1556. Translated from the Turkish with Notes by A. VAMBERY. 8vo, pp. xviii, 123, cloth. 5s.

Reuben (Paul).—Critical Remarks upon some Passages of the Old Testament. By PAUL REUBEN, Ph.D. 4to, pp. ii, 24, 14, cloth. 3s. 6d. ; paper covers, 2s. 6d.

" It may suffice to congratulate ourselves that a scholar of vigorous mind and accurate philological training is devoting his leisure to a subject worthy of attention. . . . . Very many of the notes are in a high degree stimulating and suggestive. The get-up of the book is excellent."—*Academy.*

" Dr. Reuben shows much originality, a wide knowledge of authorities, and a true grasp of critical principles."—*Jewish Chronicle.*

Rhys Davids (Mrs. C. A. F.). See **Dhamma-Sangani.**

Rockhill (Hon. W. W.).—China's Intercourse with Korea from the Fifteenth Century to 1895. Illustrated. 8vo, pp. 60. 3s. 6d. net.

Rogers (R. W.).—A History of Babylonia and Assyria. By ROBERT WILLIAM ROGERS, Ph.D. (Leipzig), D.O., LL.D., F.R.G.S., Professor in Drew Theological Seminary, Madison, New Jersey. Third Edition. Two vols. Roy. 8vo, pp. xx, 430, and xv, 418, cloth. 20s. net.

' The first volume of one of the most useful works yet published on Assyriology has just appeared. It is not only a history of Babylonia and Assyria brought up to date, it is also a history of Assyrian and Babylonian excavation and of cuneiform decipherment. For the first time the reader has placed before him a full and interesting account of one of the romances of historical science—the discovery and decipherment of the cuneiform inscriptions."—*Expository Times.*

" I consider Rogers's ' History of Babylonia and Assyria ' a really useful book, the best of its kind so far written in English. The fairness with which the author endeavours to represent different views so frequently held with regard to the earlier dynasties and events makes his work especially desirable for the student in the class-room."—H. V. Hilprecht, Ph.D., D.D., LL.D., Professor in the University of Pennsylvania, Scientific Director of Babylonian Exploration Fund.

Rosen (Dr. F.).—Modern Persian Colloquial Grammar. Containing a short Grammar, Dialogues, and Extracts from Nasir Eddin Shah's Diaries, Tales, etc., and a Vocabulary. 8vo, pp. xiv, 400, cloth. 10s. 6d. [Luzac's Oriental Grammars Series, Vol. III.]

" Dr. Rosen's learned work will be useful to all who have occasion to go to Persia, Baluchistan, and Afghanistan. The Vocabulary will be a boon to students, especially as it is in the same volume with the grammar and the dialogues."—*Publ. Circular.*

" Very useful to students."—*Westminster Review.*

" Model Grammar. Excellent Guide to the acquisition of Persian."—*Asiatic Quarterly Review.*

Rosen (Baron von).—Notices sommaires des manuscrits arabes du Musée Asiatique. 1er livr. 8vo, pp. ii, 256. 3s. 6d. net.

Rosthorn (A. de).—On the Tea Cultivation in Western Ssuch'uan and the Tea Trade with Tibet via Tachienlu. With Sketch-Map. 8vo, pp. 40. 2s. net.

Samālochak.—A Literary Review. In Hindi. Vol. II. 8 parts. August, 1903—July, 1904. 7s. 6d. net.

Sankaranarayana (P.).—English-Telugu Dictionary. By P. Sankaranarayana, M.A., M.R.A.S., Tutor to their Highnesses the Princes of Cochin. 8vo, pp. 61, 756, 2, cloth. 10s. 6d. net.

Sarkar (Kishori Lal).—The Hindu System of Self-Culture, or the Patanjala Yoga Shastra. Small 8vo, pp. iii, 160, cloth. 2s. 6d. net.

Sarkar (Kishori Lal).—The Hindu System of Moral Science. A few words on the Sattwa, Raja, and Tama Gunas. Second Edition. Small 8vo, pp. iv, 156, cloth. 2s. 6d. net.

Sarkar (Kishori Lal).—A Synopsis of Lectures on the subject of the Rules of Interpretation in Hindu Law, with special reference to the Mimânsâ Aphorisms as applied to Hindu Law. 8vo, pp. 91. 2s. net.

Sarnalata, or a Picture of Hindu Domestic Life. Translated from the Bengali by DAKSHINA CHARAN ROY. 8vo, pp. 280, cloth. 4s. net.

Sastramukthavali.—A collection of Vedanta Mimansa and Nyaya Works. Edited by P. B. ANANTHACHARIAR.

Sastri (Pandit S. M. Natesa).—Tales of Tennalirama, the famous Court Jester of Southern India. 8vo, in boards. 1s. net.

Satvotpatti Vinischaya and Nirvana Vibhaga. An Enquiry into the Origin of Beings and Discussions about Nirvana. Translated by H. M. GUNASEKARA and Revised by JOSETTA SINHA. With an Introduction in German by A. BASTIAN. 8vo, pp. 66, xli, 8. 5s. net.

Sauerwein (G.).—A Pocket Dictionary of the English and Turkish Languages. Small 8vo, pp. 298, limp cloth. 3s. 6d. net.

Sayce (A. H.).—Address to the Assyrian Section of the Ninth International Congress of Orientalists. 8vo, pp. 32. 1s. net.

Schmidt (I. J.).—Grammatik der Mongolischen Sprache. Mit 1 Tafel in Steindruck. 4to, pp. xii, 179. 5s. 6d. net.

Schmidt (I. J.).— Grammatik der Tibetischen Sprache. 4to, pp. xv, 320. 11s. 6d. net.

Schmidt (I. J.).—Mongolisch-deutsch-russisches Worterbuch, nebst einem deutschen und einem russischen Wortregister. 4to, pp. viii, 613. 9s. net.

Scholia on Passages of the Old Testament. By MAX JACOB, Bishop of Edessa. Now first edited in the original Syriac, with an English Translation and Notes by G. PHILLIP, D.D. 8vo, paper covers. 5s. net.

Seth (Mesrovb J.).—History of the Armenians in India. From the Earliest Times to the Present Day. 8vo, pp. xxiv, 199, cloth. 7s. 6d. net.

Shorey (Paul).—The Unity of Plato's Thought. Reprint. 4to, pp. 88, paper covers. 6s. net.

"Sinnatamby."—Letchimey. A Tale of Old Ceylon. Small 4to, pp. iii, 54, cloth. With Photograph Plates and Illustrations. 2s. 6d.

"It is an interesting and characteristic tale of old times, prettily illustrated and bound, and will be read with pleasure both by young and old."—*Indian Magazine.*

Srauta-Sūtra of Drahyayana (The). With Dhanvin's Commentary. In Sanskrit. Edited by J. N. REUTER. Part I, containing Patalas 1-10. 4to, pp. 216. London, 1904. 10s. 6d. net.

The work will be completed in three parts, each 10s. 6d.

Sreemut Vidyaranya Swami.—Panchadasi. A Handbook of Hindu Pantheism. Translated with copious Annotations by NANDALAL DHOLE. Second Edition. Two vols. in one. 8vo, pp. 333, cloth. 8s. net.

Sri Brahma Dhàrà.—"Shower from the Highest." Through the favour of the Mahatma SRI AGAMYA GURU PARAMAHAMSA. With Portrait. 8vo, pp. vii, 87, cloth. 3s. 6d. net.

This book of teachings is the work of one of the most distinguished leaders of Indian thought.

Stein (Dr. M. A.).—Catalogue of the Sanskrit MSS. in the Raghunata Temple Library of His Highness the Maharaya of Jammu and Kashmir. 4to, pp. 423, cloth. 12s. net.

Strong (D. M.).—The Doctrine of the Perfect One; or, The Law of Piety. Compiled by Major-General D. M. STRONG, C.B. Small 8vo, pp. 19. 6d. net.

Strong. See **Udana.**

Studies in Eastern History.—Records of the Reign of Tukulti-Ninib I, King of Assyria, about B C. 1275. Edited and translated from a Memorial Tablet in the British Museum, by L. W. KING, M.A., F.S.A. Vol. I. 8vo; pp. 204, with 10 half-tone Plates; cloth gilt top. 6s. net. Vol. II. **Chronicles concerning early Babylonian Kings,** now in the Press.

"The records furnish us with a wholly new and deeply interesting chapter in the history of the Kings of Assyria. Mr. King's book contains not only the translation of the tablet, but also portraits of the tablet itself, its text, and notes. And he has added to it other text and translations which throw light upon Tukulti-Ninib's place in history. Few will require to be told that Mr. King's work reaches the highest mark of scholarship and insight."—*Expository Times.*

"Mr. King explains certain discrepancies in the different Babylonian Chronicles, and gives a new reading of some lines on a seal of the Assyrian King, whence it appears that the seal was originally the property of Bibeashu's father, and was altered by Tukulti-Ninib more than three thousand years before it found its way to the British Museum. Mr. King is to be congratulated not only upon this excellent piece of work, but also upon having materially enriched our national collection."—*Athenæum.*

Subhāsita-Samgraha.—An Anthology of Extracts from Buddhist Works compiled by an unknown author, to illustrate the Doctrines of Scholastic and of Mystic (Tāntrik) Buddhism. In the Roman character. Edited by C. BENDALL. Extract. Roy. 8vo, pp. 100. 3s. net.

Suhrilleka (The); or "Friendly Letter," written by LUNG SHU (Nāgārjuna) and addressed to King Sadvaha. Translated from the Chinese Edition of I-Tsing, by the late Rev. S. BEAL. With the Chinese Text. 8vo, pp. 51, xiii. 5s. net.

Talcherkar (H. A.).—Lord Curzon in Indian Caricature. Roy. 8vo, pp. 48, boards. 2s. 6d. net.

This work consists of a collection of cleverly executed cartoons illustrating the career of Lord Curzon in India, selected from the illustrated comic journals of that country and arranged in chronological order, with an explanatory narrative of the events dealt with.

Tao-Têh King.—A Translation of the Chinese Classic. By E. H. PARKER. Reprint. 8vo, pp. 40. 1s. 6d. net.

Tarbell (F. B.).—A Greek Hand-Mirror in the Art Institute of Chicago and a Cantharus from the Factory of Brygos in the Boston Museum of Fine Arts. With 3 Plates. Reprint. 4to, pp. 4, 4, paper covers. 2s. net.

Tattvārthadīpa of Vallabhāchārya. In Sanskrit. Edited by Nandakisora Ramesa Sastri. Roy. 8vo, bound in red silk cover. 6s. net.

Taw Sein Ko.—Suggested Reforms for China. Second Edition. Reprint. Roy. 8vo, pp. 32. 1s. net.

Tawney (C. H.).—The Kathakoça, or Treasury of Stories. Translated from Sanskrit Manuscripts. With Appendix, containing Notes, by Professor ERNEST LEUMANN. 8vo, pp. xxiii, 260, cloth. 10s. net.

Temple (G.).—A Glossary of Indian Terms relating to Religion, Customs, Government, Land, and other Terms and Words in Common Use. To which is added a Glossary of Terms used in District Work in the N.W. Provinces and Oudh, and also of those applied to Labourers. With an Appendix, giving Computation of Time and Money, and Weights and Measures, in British India, and Forms of Address. Roy. 8vo, pp. iv, 332, cloth. 7s. 6d.

"The book is handy, well printed, and well got up, and no student of Indian subjects should be without it."—*Asiatic Quarterly Review.*

Temple (Col. R. C.).—Notes on Antiquities in Ramannadesa. (The Talaing Country of Burma.) 4to, pp. 40, with 24 Plates and a Map. 18s. net.

Thomas (F. W.).—Deux Collections Sanscrites et Tibétaines de Sādhanas. Extract. Roy. 8vo, pp. 42. 2s. net.

Thomas (F. W.). See **Bāna's Harsa Carita.**

Thompson (R. Campbell).—The Reports of the Magicians and Astrologers of Nineveh and Babylon. In the British Museum. The Original Text, printed in Cuneiform Characters, edited with Translations, Notes, Vocabulary, Index, and an Introduction. By R. CAMPBELL THOMPSON, B.A. (Cantab.), Assistant in the Department of Egyptian and Assyrian Antiquities, British Museum. In two vols. Vol. I: The Cuneiform Texts. Vol. II: English Translations, Vocabulary, etc. Roy. 8vo, cloth. 12s. 6d. net each. [Luzac's Semitic Text and Translation Series, Vols. VI and VII.]

"Mr. Thompson gives us the cuneiform text of what is, practically, the complete series of the Astrological Reports of the Royal Library at Nineveh—that is to say, copies of about 280 tablets and transliterations of about 220 duplicates, without reckoning the transliterations of the texts of the original series. In addition, we find a translation of the tablets in English, and a vocabulary, with references, and a subject index. The work in each of these sections has been carefully done."—*Nature.*

"The value of the book is enhanced by its excellent indices. Those who wish to know what the astrological lore of Babylonia was like cannot do better than study it."—*Expository Times.*

Thompson (R. Campbell).—The Devils and Evil Spirits of Babylonia, being Babylonian and Assyrian Incantations against the Demons, Ghouls, Vampires, Hobgoblins, Ghosts, and kindred Evil Spirits which attack Mankind. Translated from the Original Cuneiform Texts with Transliterations, Vocabulary, Notes, etc. By R. CAMPBELL THOMPSON, M.A., Assistant in the Department of Egyptian and Assyrian Antiquities, British Museum. In two vols. Vol. I: Evil Spirits. Vol. II: "Fever Sickness" and Headache, etc. Vol. I, 15s. net; Vol. II, 12s. 6d. net. [Luzac's Semitic Text and Translation Series, Vols. XIV and XV.]

"To the commentator and theologian, whether Christian or Jewish, these volumes of Mr. Thompson's will be of decided advantage, bringing to light, as they do, much of the more occult philosophy of ancient Babylon. . . . The labour involved in the production of these volumes must have been immense, incalculable; and the result is a work which will render abiding service to the cause of Biblical antiquities and theological learning."—*Asiatic Quarterly Review.*

"Mr. Thompson's work will be found a mine of wealth to all students of the weird and occult . . . The valuable introduction with which Mr. Thompson prefaces his first volume shows that the Jews were not the only students who drank from this fountain of mysticism, for much Chaldean magic survives in the charms and incantations in use among the Syrian Christians. . . . The most important point which Mr. Thompson clearly demonstrates is the immense vitality of this magical literature."—*Times.*

Thompson (R. Campbell).—On Traces of an Indefinite Article in Assyrian. 8vo, pp. 31, boards. 2s. net.

Tiele (C. P.).—Western Asia, according to the most Recent Discoveries. Rectorial Address on the occasion of the 318th Anniversary of the Leyden University, 8th February, 1893. Translated by ELIZABETH J. TAYLOR. Small 8vo, pp. 36, cloth. 1s. 6d. net.

"An authoritative summary of the results of recent Oriental research and discovery."—*The Times.*

"The address presents a graphic picture of the political situation in Western Asia in the fifteenth and fourteenth centuries B C."—*Morning Post.*

Tilbe (H. H.).—Pali Grammar. 8vo, pp. 115, cloth. 6s. net.
Students' Pali Series.

Tilbe (H. H.).—Pali First Lessons. 8vo, pp. 124, cloth. 6s. net.
Students' Pali Series.

Tilbe (H. H.).—Pali Buddhism. 8vo, pp. viii, 55, boards. 1s. 6d. net.

Tolman (A. H.).—What has become of Shakespeare's play "Love's Labour Won"? Reprint. 4to, pp. 34, paper covers. 2s. 6d. net.

T'oung Pao.—Archives pour servir à l'étude de l'histoire, des langues, de la géographie, et de l'ethnographie de l'Asie orientale. (Chine, Japon, Corée, Indo-Chine, Asie Centrale, et Malaise.) Rédigées par MM. G. SCHLEGEL et H. CORDIER. Annual subscription, 20s. net.

Transactions of the Ninth International Congress of Orientalists.— London, 5th to 12th September, 1892. Edited by E. DELMAR MORGAN. 2 vols. Roy. 8vo, cloth. 21s. net.
Vol. I contains: Indian and Aryan Sections. 10s. 6d.
Vol. II contains: Semitic, Egypt and Africa, Geographical, Archaic Greece and the East, Persia and Turkey, China, Central Asia and the Far East, Australasia, Anthropology, and Mythology Sections. 10s. 6d.

Tropical Agriculturist (The). Published Monthly. New Series. Vol. XXIV now in progress. Annual subscription, 26s. net.

Tyler (T.).—The Hittite Seal from Bor. Reprint. 8vo, pp. 7. 6*d*.

Udana (The), or the Solemn Utterances of the Buddha. Translated from the Pali, by Major-General D. M. STRONG, C.B. Roy. 8vo, pp. viii, 129, cloth. 6*s*. net.

Uhlenbeck (C. C.).—A Manual of Sanskrit Phonetics. In Comparison with the Indogermanic Mother-Language, for Students of Germanic and Classical Philology. 8vo, pp. xii, 115, cloth. 6*s*.

It is a lucid, handy, and comprehensive review of the subject, so arranged as to form an admirable textbook for the study of Aryan Comparative Philology."—*Asiatic Quarterly Review*.

"Un excellent résumé de phonétique sanscrite: rigeureusement exact."—*Revue critique*.

Vallée Poussin (L. de la).—Bouddhisme—Etudes et Matériaux. Vol. I : Adikarmapradīpa, Bodhicaryāvatāratīkā. 4to, pp. iv, 417. 10*s*. 6*d*. net.

"It only remains to express admiration for the very wide and varied learning which this book shows, and for the brilliance with which it is written."—*Journal Royal Asiatic Society*.

Valmiki.—The Ramayan of Valmiki. Translated into English Verse, by R. T. H. GRIFFITH, M.A., C.I.E. Complete in one volume. 8vo, pp. ix, 576, cloth. 10*s*. 6*d*. net.

Vambery (A.). See **Reis (Sidi Ali).**

Vivekânanda (Swâmi). — Jnâna Yoga. 12mo, pp. 356, cloth. 6*s*. 6*d*. net.

"One of the great thought challengers of the day is this work by the Swâmi Vivekânanda. The book goes deep and treats of startling things, but when analyzed and viewed from the author's standpoint, they are found to be links in the great chain of truth. He alone will deny who is out of sympathy or limited in vision."—*Transcript*, Boston, Sept. 24th, 1902.

"Students of religion will find much of interest in it ; those who care for India in any way will be glad to receive an indication of high Hindu thought in one of the most striking religious movements of the day ; while the orthodox Christian will derive some information from the work regarding the attitude of cultured Hindus toward Christianity and its Founder. After reading the book one is inexcusable if his ideas concerning Vedanta are hazy."—*New York Saturday Review of Books*, July 12th, 1902.

Vivekânanda (Swâmi).—Râja Yoga. Portrait of Author, frontispiece. pp. 376, cloth. 6*s*. 6*d*. net.

Besides lectures on Râja Yoga the book contains Patanjali's Yoga Aphorisms with Commentary, a copious Sanskrit Glossary, a lecture on Immortality, and the Swâmi's lectures on Bhakti Yoga.

Vivekânanda (Swâmi).—My Master. 12mo, pp. 90, cloth. 2*s*. 6*d*. net.

"This little book gives an account of the character and career of the remarkable man known in India as Paramahamsa Srimat Râmakrishna, who is regarded by a great number of his countrymen as a divine incarnation. It is not more remarkable for the story it tells of a holy man than for the clear English in which it is told, and the expressions of elevated thought in its pages."—*Journal*, Indianapolis, May 13th, 1901.

"The book, besides telling the life of Sri Râmakrishna, gives an insight into some of the religious ideas of the Hindus and sets forth the more important ideals that vitally influence India's teeming millions. If we are willing to sympathetically study the religious views of our Aryan brethren of the Orient, we shall find them governed by spiritual concepts in no way inferior to the highest known to ourselves, concepts which were thought out and practically applied by those ancient philosophers in ages so remote as to antedate history."—*Post*, Washington, May 13th, 1901.

Vivekânanda (Swâmi).—The Vedanta Philosophy. An Address before the Graduate Philosophical Society of Harvard College, with Introduction by Prof. C. C. EVERETT. Price 9d. net.

Vivekânanda (Swâmi), Pamphlets by. Price 6d. each net.
>The Ideal of a Universal Religion.
>The Cosmos.
>The Atman.
>The Real and Apparent Man.
>Bhakti Yoga.
>World's Fair Addresses.

Vizianagram Sanskrit Series. Under the Superintendence of ARTHUR VENIS, M.A. Oxon.; Principal, Sanskrit College, Benares. Various prices.

Vopadeva.—Mugdhabodha. Herausgegeben und erklärt von OTTO BÖHTLINGK. 8vo, pp. xiii, 465. 9s. net.

Waddell (L. Austine).—The Buddhism of Tibet or Lamaism, with its Mystic Cults, Symbolism, and Mythology, and in its relation to Indian Buddhism. By L. AUSTINE WADDELL, M.B., F.L.S., F.R.G.S. Roy. 8vo, pp. xix, 593, cloth. With numerous Plates and Illustrations. 25s.
"This is a book which considerably extends the domain of human knowledge. He is the first European who, equipped with the resources of modern scholarship, has penetrated the exoteric Buddhism of Tibet. . . . . Every page of his closely-printed volume contains new material; many of his chapters are entirely new, and the whole forms an enduring memorial of laborious original research."—*Times.*

Walker (E. D.).—Reincarnation. A Study of Forgotten Truth. 8vo, pp. 350, cloth. 7s.; paper covers, 5s. 6d. net.

Wassiljew (W.).—Der Buddhismus, seine Dogmen, Geschichte, und Litteratur. Aus dem Russischen übersetzt. Erster Theil. 8vo, pp. xv, 380. 5s. net.

Watters (T.).—On Yuan Chwang's Travels in India, 629-645 A.D. Edited after his death by T. W. RHYS DAVIDS, F.B.A., and S. W. BUSHELL, M.D., C.M.G. 8vo, pp. 401, cloth. 10s. net.

Werner (A.).—Zulu Exercises. 8vo, pp. 51. 1s. net.

West (Sir Raymond).—Higher Education in India, its Position and Claims. 8vo, pp. 61. 1s. net.

Wildeboer (G.).—The Origin of the Canon of the Old Testament. An Historico-Critical Enquiry. Translated by WISNER BACON. Edited with Preface by Prof. GEORGE F. MOORE. Roy. 8vo, pp. xii, 182, cloth. 7s. 6d.
"We will only add that we cordially echo the Professor's hope that his book may not only be read by professed students, but that it may come also into the hands of such as have already left the University."—*Guardian.*

Wilkinson (J. R.).—A Johannine Document in the First Chapter of St. Luke's Gospel. Roy. 8vo, pp. 38, cloth. 2s.; paper covers, 1s. 6d. net.

Winckler (H.). — The Tell-El-Amarna Letters. Transliteration, English Translation, Vocabulary, etc. Roy. 8vo; pp. xlii, 416, and 50 pages Indices; cloth. 21s. net.

—— The same, in paper covers. 20s.

"The present work does not aim to give the final exposition of the Tell-el-Amarna Letters, but only the beginning of such exposition. The author has solved many difficulties."

"The purpose of the vocabularies and catalogue of proper names is to make easy the penetration and independent investigation of our subject. Especially in case of the first, it was important to hit upon a selection from the innumerable repetitions. A full citation of all the places would make their examination almost impossible."

Winternitz (Dr. M.).—Catalogue of Sanskrit MSS. in the Royal Asiatic Society's Library, with an Appendix by F. W. THOMAS. 8vo, pp. xvi, 340. 5s. net.

Word (The). A Monthly Magazine devoted to Philosophy, Science, Religion, Eastern Thought, Occultism, Theosophy, and the Brotherhood of Humanity. Vol. I. Roy. 8vo. Annual subscription, 9s. net.

Wright (W.).—The Book of Jonah in four Semitic versions— Chaldee, Syriac, Æthiopic, and Arabic. With corresponding Glossaries. 8vo, pp. 148, cloth. 4s. net.

Wu-Wei. See **Borel.**

Wynkoop (J. D.).—Manual of Hebrew Grammar. Translated from the Dutch by C. VAN DEN BIESEN. 8vo, cloth. 2s. 6d. net. [Luzac's Oriental Grammars Series, Vol. II.]

"We have nothing but praise for the Rev. Wynkoop's Manual of Hebrew Grammar. It is clear and concise; the rules are very intelligible, and the examples are telling. . . . We heartily recommend this book, and congratulate Messrs. Luzac on the style of its production."—*Asiatic Quarterly Review.*

Wynkoop (J. D.).—Manual of Hebrew Syntax. Translated from the Dutch by C. VAN DEN BIESEN. 8vo; pp. xxii, 152, and Index; cloth. 2s. 6d. net. [Luzac's Oriental Grammars Series, Vol. I.]

"It is a book which every Hebrew student should possess . . . we recommend it for general usefulness, and thank Dr. van den Biesen for giving it to the English reader."—*Jewish World.*

"It is one of those books which will become indispensable to the English student who will desire to become acquainted with the construction of Hebrew syntax . . . this takes a high rank and will undoubtedly become a general textbook on the subject in many colleges and universities."—*American Hebrew News.*

Yatawara (J. B.).—The Ummaga Yataka. (The Story of the Tunnel.) Translated from the Sinhalese by J. B. YATAWARA, M.C.B.R.A.S., Ratemahatmaya. Roy. 8vo, pp. vii, 242, cloth. 10s. 6d. net.

Made in the USA
Columbia, SC
17 September 2024